The Cinema of Adolescence

for Gail and Kent
with my love and gratitude

DAVID M. CONSIDINE

The Cinema
of Adolescence

Jefferson & London : McFarland 1985

Library of Congress Cataloging in Publication Data

Considine, David M., 1950–
 The cinema of adolescence.

 Bibliography: p.
 Includes index.
 1. Youth in moving-pictures. 2. Moving-pictures and
youth. 3. Social problems in motion pictures. I. Title.
PN1995.9.Y6C66 1985   791.43'09'09352054   84-42604

ISBN 0-89950-123-0

Printed in the United States of America

McFarland & Company Inc., Publishers
 Box 611, Jefferson, North Carolina 28640

Preface

Scattered here and there among the childhood memories that survive, I find myself with the indelible images of my earliest motion picture experiences: the sound of the axe in the opening of *River of No Return*; the snow-covered New England landscape of *Peyton Place*; Anna's swirling ball gown in *The King and I*. The first film I ever saw, or so I am told, was *The Third Man*. Ever the critic, I vociferously disapproved, causing an irate father to carry me crying from the theater. It would be twenty years before he had the opportunity to see the film in its entirety. In the meantime I had survived my first encounter and taken the medium to heart.

Yet I was no film buff. Football far more than movies dominated my adolescent years. When I liked a film I embraced it passionately and, in the case of *Cleopatra* and *Camelot*, went time and time again until I knew the dialogue verbatim.

Almost a decade later, teaching another generation of adolescents, I began, almost by accident, to toy with motion pictures in the classroom. What I discovered then in an old Australian red brick high school by the sea, more than anything else, started me on this book. Jim Stark's struggle with his parents in 1955's *Rebel Without a Cause* seemed as relevant to these young people as it had been twenty years earlier. Humphrey Bogart and the Dead End Kids were capable of spellbinding a group of underachievers. Tough teenage girls, locked into the dictates of the peer group, could be reduced to tears while watching a screen animal suffer. Lebanese students who spoke almost no English were delighted by the Marx Brothers' antics in *Duck Soup*.

More than anything else however, these teenagers seemed to enjoy looking at images of themselves. What, I wondered, did they see on the screen that so captivated them? When they looked at these screen characters, what did they learn about life and what was the relationship between the lives they led and the life Hollywood depicted? These questions led me halfway around the world where, after hundreds of hours of viewing films in major museums and archives, I began at last to formulate answers.

The Cinema of Adolescence would not have been possible without the support, encouragement and good wishes of individuals and institutions in the United States, England and Australia. First and foremost among these were the James Deans, Billy Halops, Matt Dillons, Timothy Huttons, Sandra Dees, Judy Garlands Jodie Fosters and the countless other actors and actresses who, in their performances, provided the raw material that is the primary source of this study. I would like too to acknowledge the inspiration and insight given to me by the hundreds of youngsters who have spoken to me about their film experiences, particularly the students of Williamstown High School in Melbourne, Australia.

I have been fortunate to have had the advice and direction of Professor Russell Merritt of the Communication Arts Department at the University of Wisconsin–Madison; Russell provided enthusiasm, optimism and the comfort of a friend and mentor throughout the writing of this book.

My friend and typist, Nancy Graham, served above and beyond the call of duty, helping a struggling graduate student to turn a dream into a reality. Without her, this book would be little more than scribbled notes on countless pages of scrap paper.

I am in debt to Professor Jefferey Lukowsky; to the staff of the film division of the State Historical Society in Madison, Wisconsin; the Museum of Modern Art; the Library of Congress; the British Film Institute; and the U.C.L.A. film archive, all of which contributed to bringing this work to completion. Last, I would like to think my parents, who first took me to the movies, especially my mother who still dreams of *Mr. Lucky* and romantic encounters at *Waterloo Bridge*.

Table of Contents

1. The Cinema of Adolescence

*"The average movie-goer's intelligence is that
of a fourteen-year-old child"* — Adolph Zukor.

Following the attempted assassination of President Reagan in March 1981, the world learned of the accused assassin's infatuation with teenage actress Jodie Foster. The young star had achieved notoriety in Martin Scorcese's *Taxi Driver* (1976), in which she played the role of a young hooker. In a curious coincidence, the character she played obsessed a young man who stalked a politician, intent on shooting him.

The night after the Reagan shooting, Timothy Hutton became the first teenager in the history of motion pictures to win an Academy Award. Hutton's first role as the tormented teenager of *Ordinary People* (1980) was a sensitive and moving performance that earned him the best supporting actor award. Among his competition was Michael O'Keefe, who was nominated for his role of the adolescent son of *The Great Santini* (1980).

In July of the same year, teenage temptress Brooke Shields (*Pretty Baby*, 1977; *The Blue Lagoon*, 1980; and *Endless Love*, 1981) testified before the United States Congress. Shields, whose sixteen-year-old face had graced the cover of *Time* magazine, was rejected by her government as a suitable role model for American youth. The anti-smoking campaign she had been working on was officially abandoned.

Three seemingly unrelated events, yet each one testifies in its own way to the pervasiveness of the teen screen.

When teenagers are not actually present on the screen, it is still apparent that the industry is actively catering to the adolescent market. *Star Wars* (1977), *Close Encounters of the Third Kind* (1977), *Superman* (1978), *Flash Gordon* (1980), and *Raiders of the Lost Ark* (1981) all operate on the level of fantasy and, while no doubt also appealing to adults, they fulfill the same function for the young that comic books did for an earlier generation. Equally prominent at the box office in recent years has been the spate of teen terrifiers, each of which seems intent upon outdoing its predecessor in gore and senseless violence. *Carrie* (1977), *Halloween* (1979), *Prom Night* (1980), and a seemingly inexhaustible list of others continue to provide entertain-

1

tainment for an audience that seems eager to watch the mutilation and murder of young people. And yet, despite the high visibility of young people on our motion picture screens, there has been little research into the impact of film upon youth or of youth upon the film industry.

In recognizing the cinema of adolescence, this work acknowledges the relationship between the film industry, the image-making process, and the impact of that image-making on audience members, particularly young audience members. While Shields, Foster, Hutton, and others may currently attract attention, the cinema of adolescence has long roots that stretch back before the introduction of the talkies. Mary Pickford, for example, was barely sixteen at the time she was placed under contract to D.W. Griffith.

While biographies and autobiographies have illuminated the personal and public lives of juvenile performers like Mickey Rooney, Judy Garland, Jackie Cooper and others, we remain largely uninformed about the types of roles they played or the impact of these images upon the adolescents who made up such a large proportion of film audiences.

From its inception, the cinema has attracted the attention of individuals and groups who believed that it exerted an undesirable influence upon the young. Today, both in the United States and throughout the world, the existence of motion picture censorship and ratings systems in one form or another serves as testimony to the belief that motion pictures are capable of exerting a negative influence on some members of the audience. In the case of the American film industry, concern about the influence of the cinema on the young was one factor that led to the establishment of the Hays Office (1922) and self-regulation by the industry. Will Hays believed that:

> This industry must have towards that sacred thing, the mind of a child, towards that clean virgin thing, the unmarred slate, the same responsibility, that same care about the impressions made upon it that the best clergyman or most inspired teacher would have.[1]

Throughout the 1930's, evidence of this concern can be found in works like the Payne studies, which investigated the relationship between youth and the cinema. Films' impact on morals, juvenile delinquency, patterns of courtship, sleep, and a range of other factors was considered. The Second World War and, in particular, Nazi Germany's successful application of film propaganda encouraged the development of film research in the United States. It was during this period that Paul Lazarsfeld noted the film industry's youth orientation. "They are," he observed, "patterned to the tastes of younger people."[2]

In Britain, Wall and Simson reported that the motion picture played an important part in the life of the young, filling a knowledge vacuum and serving in many cases as the adolescent's only source of information in regard to such matters as social intercourse and human relationships. "The emotional and social education of the growing youth," they concluded, "is left to the vivid realism of the screen."[3]

While box office receipts continue to testify to the high concentration of young people in film audiences, and cinema courses in colleges and campuses across the nation continue to attract the attention of the young, there has been no corresponding interest in research geared to the relationship between film and youth. While studies dealing with television and children or television and youth proliferate, the relationship between this special audience and the film industry, which so obviously caters to it, remains largely unexamined, uncharted and unrecorded.

By its very nature, the adolescent film audience is a special and unique group responding to the cinema in a way markedly different from the way in which either children or adults respond. This phenomenon exists partially because of the young person's strength at the box office, where he functions as a powerful force operating on the cinematic product he consumes. In part, also, while his economic affluence enables him to influence the industry, his very immaturity renders him susceptible to its influence and manipulation. Unlike the adult, the adolescent is still in a stage of identity development, still formulating basic values and attitudes. Thus film must be regarded as one in a range of forces potentially capable of shaping either positively or negatively the young person's visions of himself and his society. The relationship between the young person and the film industry is thus a dichotomy—while the young viewer is capable of exerting an influence upon the product he consumes, it in turn is equally capable of exerting an influence on him. While the search for self renders the adolescent susceptible to suggestion, there is evidence that at the same time, the young person is more perceptive and aware of film than at any other time.

If not as vulnerable as the young, the film industry remains nonetheless susceptible to the powerful influence American youth have long asserted at the box office. Nowhere, perhaps, is this more dramatically indicated than in the headline that dominated *Variety* on January 7, 1970. "BO Dictatorship by Youth," the paper declared in its analysis of box office receipts for the 1960's. The following year a UNESCO report made the point more obvious still:

> The American motion picture industry now caters primarily to the under-twenty-fives, the boys and girls who leave their parents to watch old films on television at home ... and take in their movie at the drive-in. What they see on the screen, what the industry now tries to put on the screen, is what it thinks reflects the attitudes of this new generation.[4]

For more than forty years, American youngsters both on and off screen have exerted a powerful influence upon the film industry.

With the decade of the 1930's coming to a close, the top box office draws across the country were juveniles. "Rooney a Juve Draw in Omaha"[5]; "Rooney 38 B.O. Champ"[6]; "Miss Garland Drawing Plenty of Kids"[7];

> Heavy Run of Kid Films. Moppets Prove B.O. Naturals ... give us this day another Rooney ... Durbin or a Temple is the entreaty of studio chieftains as they cast eyes on b.o. returns rolled up so far this year by pictures starring kid personalities.[8]

On January 3, 1940, while *Variety* announced that Rooney had tied with adult star James Stewart as the top star of 1939, they admitted that, holding strictly within the limitations of films released during a twelve-month period, Rooney had once again topped the male star list at the box office. Not only did Rooney contribute to the success of MGM, but his personal appearances with Judy Garland managed to benefit the industry.

> Mickey Rooney and Judy Garland personally on the Capitol stage are booming not only that house but helping the other nearby Broadway theaters. Screen juveniles opening with *Wizard of Oz* are pushing the house to nearly 65,000, tremendous for this theater, especially at this time of year. It smashes the Capitol's record since the stage policy was abandoned a number of years ago and it is believed that actual attendance will exceed any previous week in house's history.[9]

Rooney proved to be more popular than two of the screen's leading males, Robert Taylor and Clark Gable. But his success represented only the surface of a decade that had seen juvenile performers coming to screen prominence. In 1939, Jackie Cooper's salary was $3,500 for six days' work and his contract guaranteed him plenty of that, providing for four roles annually for Universal, four for Paramount, and at least two for Monogram.

In 1937, Frankie Darro, aged nineteen, signed a contract for ten pictures with no more than fourteen days' work on each, and a salary ranging from $1,750 to $2,250 per picture. Bonita Granville, who had begun work at $300 per week, had advanced by 1937 to $2,000 per week and a seven-year contract. Freddie Bartholomew, who had starred opposite Greta Garbo and Spencer Tracy, earned $1,100 per week and was given a monthly allowance of $800.

The Mauch twins, who had featured in the Penrod series and in *The Prince and the Pauper*, had commenced at $250 per week, and advanced to $1,500 plus 50 percent of any of the radio work that came their way. When Deanna Durbin starred at the age of fourteen in *Three Smart Girls* (1937), *Variety* suggested, "It is not going to be easy to find stories for this girl because of her youth and the fact that she is being starred."[10] Later that year, after the success of her next film, *One Hundred Men and a Girl*, the paper was forced to revise its opinion:

She is a cinch for a starry career of major money importance to film theaters ... this one is a socko. It augers well for Miss Durbin's future. She's arrived.[11]

To the stable of young stars established in the thirties, the forties added a new list of names and faces. Child stars Shirley Temple and Dickie Moore grew into juvenile performers, while newcomers included Joyce Reynolds, Ann Blyth, Jeannie Crain, Jane Powell, and Elizabeth Taylor. With the exception perhaps of Elizabeth Taylor, few of these youngsters succeeded at the box office in the manner of young performers of the thirties. In the war years adult material and adult themes dominated the motion picture industry. At the same time, however, young audiences were recognized by the industry as being of vital importance to their financial success.

TEENAGERS AS ROAD TO BO MOST FAITHFUL THEATER GOERS ... surveys have consistently shown that the teenagers are the most frequent and faithful theater goers and that, as a matter of fact, the nineteen-year-old group leads all others in attendance.... The second Gallup point, one of which has made something of a preachment is that profits do not lie in a producer's knocking himself out trying to get into the theater that portion of the public which infrequently buys tickets or that doesn't naturally take to this type of pic. Producers can do much better, ARI claims, in spending the coin and extra steam on pitching to the natural easy-to-get group.[12]

The findings of Audience Research, Inc., reported to the industry at the end of the 1940's, might explain in part the increase in juvenile performers throughout the 1950's and the increasing evidence of screen conflict between older and younger generation. Since adults were tending to stay at home it may be that motion picture producers decided to pitch their films increasingly towards the young. Such a theory explains, at least in part, the sympathetic treatment afforded youth and the negative image given to parents in films such as *East of Eden* (1954), *Peyton Place* (1957), *The Restless Years* (1958), and *The Young Stranger* (1957).

Under the studio system, movie moguls like Louis B. Mayer had been able to guide and groom juvenile performers, so that their on-screen persona became a reflection of the views and values of their owners. With the decline of the studios it was not possible for such control to be exerted. Rooney had grown up around cameras. The theater was his life and he understood its codes. James Dean, on the other hand, was a product of the fifties. Raised in Indiana, he experienced minor success on the New York stage and came to Hollywood as an outsider who would not willingly conform to what the industry wanted him to be. The decline of the studios, therefore, was one factor in the changing image of the adolescent throughout the 1950's. At the same time it must be acknowledged that other factors were at work. In particular, the challenge from television required more adult material in motion pictures and this in turn had been made possible by relaxed censorship conditions after the Miracle case. Rock and roll also served to foster a separate youth culture and create a climate in which young people could be seen as more than appendages of the family, the school, and other institutions created by adults.

Whatever the reasons, the industry remained extremely conscious throughout the 1950's that they needed to appeal to youthful audiences. "THEATERS MUST GO AFTER KIDS REARED IN VIDEO INFANCY."[13] Ted Schlanger, Philadelphia zone manager for Stanley Warner theaters, told a meeting of theater managers that they needed to do the odd and unusual to attract youngsters. The posthumous success of James Dean, who became something of an overnight cult figure with the young, served to dramatize for the industry the strength and dedication of the teenager market.

> H'WOOD AGE OF TEENS. NEEDS STARS WITH COKE SET DRAW. In its desperate effort to maintain and build audiences via the development of new star personalities, the film industry has become teenage conscious.... The influence of the teenagers from the bobby-soxers of the Frank Sinatra era to the blue jean worshippers of the late James Dean has been a social phenomenon of the last fifteen years.... The mysterious aura of adoration that still exists for James Dean and the wild cultist attraction that surrounds Elvis Presley among the teenage set have played important roles in awakening the film industry.[14]

Among stars signed in the wake of Dean's death and the industry's recognition of the need for new young stars were John Saxon, who joined Universal, and James MacArthur, who signed with RKO. The sixties added Warren Beatty, the now-adolescent Natalie Wood, Sue Lyon, and beach movie stars Frankie Avalon and Annette Funicello. In March, 1968, *Variety* reported that being young and single was the overriding demographic precondition for being a frequent and enthusiastic movie-goer. The youth group, considered to be those in the 16 to 24 age bracket, made up 48 percent of the current box office admissions. The same group, which represented only 18 percent of the public, made up 76 percent of the motion picture audience.

For more than thirty years adolescents, whether on screen or off, had played a powerful role in the American motion picture industry. Yet as the sixties came to an end, a decade that had seen the most articulate, aware, and self-conscious generation of youngsters ever produced, the industry seemed singularly unable to reach out and relate to them. On November 13, 1968, a National Association of Theater Owners meeting in Los Angeles declared, "There is almost unbounded confidence that this time the film business is attuned to the desires of this vital young audience."[15] Yet within a year it was apparent that the industry had no such understanding. At the next annual meeting of the Association, confusion was evident:

> The fact that the limits of youth as the ally of theater survival were being recognized after about five years of exaltation of the young crowd as core, jury and key to everything, cannot be dismissed. Emerging from the obvious confusion in the film trade as old values and indeed old established trade marks falter and collapse is a realization that the industry cannot afford to put all its eggs in one youth basket. The idea was enunciated that youth itself is unpredictable, swings wildly in taste and is subject to the attrition of its own maturation.[16]

The following week the top film grosses included *Easy Rider*, *Alice's Restaurant*, *Last Summer*, *Wild in the Streets*, and *Monterey Pop*. The next year, despite its Jury Prize at the Cannes Film Festival, *The Strawberry Statement* did less than anticipated business and prompted MGM to re-write some of their planned projects in an attempt to gear them for a wider market. By November of 1971, *Variety* was reporting on the failure of such 1971 films as *The Last Movie*, *The Hired Hand*, *Dusty and Sweets McGee*, and *Joe Hill*, all aimed at the youth market. What seemed evident was that while the industry realized the potential of the youth market, they seemed incapable of presenting that audience with consistent images and themes that won their approval. The result, as *Variety* noted, was that studios were left wondering "what to do when youth films bore the young."[17]

None of this, however, is to imply total domination of Hollywood or the movie industry by the young. In the 1950's, despite the enormous publicity given the young, despite the high visibility of the youth culture and icons like Elvis and James Dean, the film industry still depended to a large extent upon adult members of the audience. In 1951, for example, the top movies had nothing to do with teenagers or crazy, mixed-up kids. *David and Bathsheba*, *Showboat*, *The Great Caruso*, *An American in Paris*, *A Streetcar Named Desire*, and *Born Yesterday* were the year's top films. Not a teenager among their characters! One has to go to the twelfth highest grossing film of the year to find a youngster, and then it's a delightfully pleasing child in Kipling's classic, *Kim*. The top stars of the year were similarly devoid of youth, though perhaps not youth appeal. Gregory Peck, Howard Keel, Martin and Lewis made up the male listings; on the distaff side were Susan Hayward, Virginia Mayo, and Ann Blyth.

In 1956, after the emergence of both Presley and Dean and after *Blackboard Jungle* had burst upon the scene, little had changed. The top films of that year were *Guys and Dolls*, *The King and I*, *Trapeze*, *High Society*, and *I'll Cry Tomorrow*. Inroads, however, were being made. The twelfth largest grossing film of the year, bringing in four and one-half million dollars, was the James Dean vehicle, *Rebel Without a Cause*.

We cannot, however, judge the adolescent impact on the industry in terms of box office alone. As we have seen, the industry, while it followed the box office lead, was often slow to spot the connections. Dean would be dead before Hollywood fully understood his strength, not simply in the revenue he generated but in the image he projected. Having perceived that, they would not be slow in repeating it. Indeed, it is this emphasis upon formula, format and repetition that constitutes so much of Hollywood history in its depiction of the young.

In looking at this history one finds that, despite its obvious dependence on the young, the American film industry has been spectacularly unsuccessful in realistically depicting adolescence. Whether within the family unit, the school, or the peer group; whether in their relationships with their parents, their teachers, or themselves; the young people Hollywood has presented to us over more than half a century have seldom been representative of American youth as a whole.

In the 1930's the most visible and successful young performers were Judy Garland, Mickey Rooney, and Deanna Durbin, most noticeable perhaps in light optimistic fare that offered them every opportunity to sing and dance their way into the hearts of millions. At a time when American adults and adolescents alike confronted the Depression, Hollywood ignored the issue, depicting young people in gangs (*Boys of the Streets*, 1937; *Angels With Dirty Faces*, 1938) or in the make-believe middle America of Andy Hardy's Carvel, Idaho.

Rooney, largely through the Hardy series, remained very visible throughout the next decade which, while producing no singular actor or actress to rival those of the thirties, was noticeable for its insistent portrayal of the bobby-soxer. While juvenile delinquency was becoming a major social problem and other young people were selflessly working for the war effort, Hollywood seemed to envisage adolescence as one endless prom night.

By the 1950's, the clean-cut middle-class youngsters that had occupied the screen for more than a decade were replaced by a more sinister and bitter image as the juvenile delinquency genre took hold, heavily influenced by the James Dean image. The bobby-soxer set of the forties was quickly engulfed by a wave of new screenagers preoccupied with flick knives and an answer to the urgent question of "will she or won't she?" Through the agency of television and tabloids, those that lived through the 1960's witnessed the most articulate, aware and outspoken generation of young people in the history of the nation. From Watts to Woodstock, from the campus at Columbia to the streets of Chicago, American young people were coming together to make their voices heard in a way that had previously not

Opposite: The Andy Hardy series (1937–1946) moved film families from Skid Row to Middletown, creating an idealized image of father and son relationships which found its way to television in following decades.

been done. Yet when one turns to movies of the time to encounter this generation, one finds them startlingly absent. The young people who occupied the screens throughout much of the 1960's were strikingly lacking in altruism. Lost in an almost mystical search for self or intent to ride the wild surf, they seemed caught up in the hedonistic pursuit of surf, sand and sex in an endless torso opera on Muscle Beach.

While the sensitive portrayals of Robby Benson and Glynnis O'Connor in a number of movies throughout the 1970's marked them as the dominant screen adolescents of the time, they were surrounded by anguished adolescents, addicted, possessed, and tormented by a host of afflictions.

Such a summary, however superficial and generalized, serves to dismiss some long held misconceptions about the depiction of adolescents in the motion picture. Writing in "The Adolescent and the Screen," H. Keith Evans had, for example, claimed:

> It is possible from dozens of different portraits to build up an identity picture of the screen teenager. He is a brooding young man who wears clothing of a close but uncomfortable fit. His demeanor is often rude, his introversion broken only in the company of his peer group. He has a motorcycle, a transistor radio, powerful loyalties and strong views; a loving, bewildered mother and father who has been to him a vague shadowy figure forever saying (ineffectually) "Don't." He lives according to his own lights, hypersensitive to hypocrisy. Rejecting adults, middle-class bureaucratized society, he sees in his clear uncompromising way that his elders have made a bargain with life, agreeing to live only a little in order not to die a great deal.[18]

One need only examine the films of the Dead End Kids, Mickey Rooney, Elizabeth Taylor, or Sandra Dee to realize that this vision of the depiction of adolescents is narrow, negative and unrepresentative.

In the cinema of adolescence, one of the crucial determinants is not simply what we see but what we choose not to see. Evans describes a screen-ager that did indeed exist and in some ways still survives. But the suggestion remains implicit in his description that this is the ultimate, overriding, and dominant image. It is an observation that, among other things, totally ignores the presence of the female adolescent in motion pictures, and one which indicates the necessity for a thorough and exhaustive analysis of the depiction of adolescence in the cinema.

In the process, while we may discover much about youth and the way the film industry has depicted young people, it is possible that we may discover much more. In looking at the relationship between motion pictures and the audience that views them, film scholars have frequently employed the mirror metaphor. Kracauer, for one, refers to "the world they mirror,"[19] and Rosen suggests that films have been "a mirror held up to the porous face of society."[20] Whether this mirror provides an accurate reflection or distorts the image it reveals must of necessity be one of the chief concerns of this study, for in looking at images of adolescence we are looking at much more than the way one particular medium chose to reflect one social group at a given moment in time. By looking at young people we are afforded a means by which we may view ourselves and our major social institutions.

> The quality and nature of the treatment of youth is an incisive commentary on a society in its entirety — on the family, the schools, the economy, the government, the culture, the beliefs of the people, their standard of conduct toward one another. In its youth, society can see itself in a huge but distorted mirror — as in a fun palace.[21]

As we begin to gaze into the mirror of youth it is necessary to keep in mind that the images we see, the plots we encounter, the recurring themes and motifs that unfold, reflect not simply the views and values of the audience, not only the attitudes and ideas of the film creators, and not just the social conditions of the day, but an intricate and interwoven association of all these factors. Which one of them was dominant in any particular movie or at any particular period of time can, as of yet, remain only a mystery. Before we can answer why, we must yet know what.

2. From Skid Row to Middletown 1930–1949

"We taught you how to think, your mother and I, and if you make a mistake, it's our mistake too"— Judge Hardy: The Andy Hardy series, 1937–1946.

"Mom, where's my screwdriver?" With these four forgettable words, American audiences were thus introduced to Andy Hardy. The year was 1937, the film, MGM's *A Family Affair*. Released in April, it was a low-budget motion picture based on the 1928 Broadway success, *Skidding*, by Aurania Rouverol. Between 1937 and 1946 the studio churned out sixteen more Hardy family stories, bringing them $25 million and becoming what *Variety* called "the biggest money makers in relation to investment in plant's [*sic*] entire history."[1]

The family pattern established in the Hardy series extended beyond the ten-year production period and beyond the medium itself. Watching Jim Anderson talking to his son Bud in the 1950's television series *Father Knows Best*, we are simply watching the Hardys transplanted from Carvel, Idaho to Springfield, Illinois—from the big screen to the small screen. The fact that the Hardys could still be located on American Saturday morning television in the late 1970's, and that *Father Knows Best* was enjoying re-runs at the same time testifies to the durability of the lifestyle and values they espoused. Yet both families were peculiarly out of place.

The adventures of Jim and Margaret Anderson and their brood, while standard fare in the television world of the Nelsons, Cleavers, and Stones, were miles away from the family image occupying the nation's big screen in the 1950's. Anguished adolescents in fractured middle-class families, typified by the Starks in *Rebel Without a Cause*, were in sharp contrast to the essentially tranquil domestic existence of the Andersons and those they represented. So too the Hardys came to prominence as a happy and harmonious family when the screens exuded images of families fractured by the ravages of depression, disillusionment, and divorce.

13

The Hardys were no accident. Their success, although initially surprising to studio and critic alike, was the outcome of what had gone before. On their coattails followed the rise to screen prominence of the middle-class family of the 1940's. But behind the Hardys is where the real story began. The 1930's was the last decade of American filmmaking to seriously address itself to working-class existence. For all that we may remember of Andy's boyish enthusiasm and the domestic bliss of life in Carvel, it was not the Hardys or families like them who dominated the screens of the 1930's, but the numerous, nameless, unremembered, and largely unrecorded families of the working class and lower middle class who have remained so unnoted in film studies of the period. As Andy is the key to the MGM series, so too it is the adolescent offspring of these families who provide such a valuable and unique insight into family life as represented in that pre-Hardy period.

The decade opened with the war movie, *All Quiet on the Western Front*. Adolescent Paul, like many of his friends, is swept up into a wave of patriotic fever, propelling him from the classroom to the battlefield. At the start of the film the camera moves us from the private sphere—the domestic life of the common people—out into the public sphere, the streets where the troops gather and the future of the nation is being shaped. As the audience is directed from the private to the public domain, so Paul, like thousands of others his age, moves from domestic simplicity to the Spartan existence of life at the front. In so doing he is removed both physically and psychologically from his family. When he returns home he feels himself a stranger, alienated from this once familiar environment. His mother continues to look upon him as a boy, to be provided with clean underwear and warned against the dangers of the wrong type of woman. Paul, however, can no longer relate to his mother or to the bedroom of his boyhood. There is for him now only the world of war and the camaraderie of the ranks. The army has become his substitute family.

The peer group at the front is a major theme in the cinema of adolescence as it emerges in the 1930's, and this is in part a reflection of wider concerns of the period represented in Berkeley's "Forgotten Man" sequence, songs such as "Brother, Can You Spare a Dime?" and the plight of James Allen in Warner's *I Am a Fugitive from a Chain Gang* (1932). More significantly, the military theme was seized upon by FDR in his inaugural address, which abounded with such imagery. For adolescents and adults alike, many of the conditions of wartime were repeated as the battleground moved from a foreign shore to the slums of the inner cities. What appeared time and again in films of the period were images of essentially masculine groups, marching feet, a constant sense of movement, and the ever-present threat of danger and conflict. J.M. Mogey has noted that "wandering about the countryside by bands of adolescents has always accompanied war and revolution."[2] When the boys of these gangs and street armies were not wandering the city streets in search of kicks, they were wandering the nation seeking survival in the battle against the common enemies of depression and the pervasive poverty so evident in these films.

Another example of the fractured family and military imagery is evident in the surprisingly high number of children and adolescents who are ill, injured, mutilated, or killed in motion pictures made during the 1930's. Johnny Stone dies from ill treatment in *Mayor of Hell* (1933); Tommy Gordon has a leg amputated in *Wild Boys of the Road* (1933); Snapper Sinclair is badly injured in a fall from a horse while trying to help his surrogate mother in *Down the Stretch* (1936); Burley is burned to death in a forest fire he fights in the 1937 Monogram and CCC project, *Blazing Barriers*; Sheila Bromley is killed in a shootout in *Girls on Probation* (1938). In *Barefoot Boy* (1938), Billy Whittaker is shot while trying to reunite Kenneth with his own family; Sally Ward lingers at death's door in the screen adaptation of Lloyd C. Douglas' novel *White Banners* (1938); Micky Falloon is mistaken for his brother and shot by police in *Off the Record* (1938); Frankie is brutally whipped in *Crime School* (1938); Sleepy is burned to death in *Angels With Dirty Faces* (1938); Eddie is whipped in *Boys Reformatory* (1939), and Joey dies from mistreatment in the reformatory in *Hell's Kitchen* (1939). While many of these films are examined in Part IV on crime and delinquency, the link between behavior and home life is so strong that it must be acknowledged here.

Almost without exception the injuries, illnesses and deaths occur because the youngsters are not part of a normal family life. As the army serves as a surrogate family for Paul, the street gangs, cliques, and adolescent groups function as families for these screen youngsters. They serve not only the function of peer group, establishing an alternative to parental values, but as a substitute for and a replacement of parental authority, which is either alienating by its excesses or totally absent.

This absence of parental authority is, of course, hardly a characteristic peculiar to the 1930's. Frederick Massyat, for example, writing in the nineteenth century, observed:

> Anyone who has been in the United States must have perceived that there is little or no parental control ... beyond the period of infancy there is no endearment between parents and children; none of that sweet affection between brother and sister; none of the links which unite one family; of that mutual confidence, that rejoicing in each other's successes.[3]

Such an extreme view would normally be discounted, but when one looks to motion pictures from the 1930's it is easy to believe that Massyat's earlier observations were based on a reality that, if it did not exist then, had in fact come to exist, at least in the minds of the motion picture industry.

The evidence of parental absence or impotence on the screen is so overwhelming that it cannot be ignored. Over and over one witnesses youthful figures, devoid of parental guidance, left to their own devices. In part this can be seen as a reflection of real conditions in Depression-afflicted America. The Lynds, in their 1937 study of *Middletown in Transition* had, for example, noticed "the relaxation of discipline and lessened contact with their children by harried working class parents."[4]

What one encounters on the screen, however, is much more than relaxation of discipline and lessened contact between parent and child. Time and time again one encounters images of parental abdication of authority, parental neglect and parental abuse. So dislocated is the typical screen adolescent's family that in many cases the courtroom replaces the kitchen or living room as the center of family contact. In *Mayor of Hell*, Jimmy Smith appears only once with his parents, and that encounter takes place in a courtroom. The brief time we see the boy with his father is sufficient to establish the hostility of their relationship. Like many of the fathers of Depression films, Mr. Smith is either unwilling or unable to find work. The boy's mother, meanwhile, functions lovingly but ineffectively as she attempts to keep the household on an even keel and adjudicate quarrels between father and child. Jimmy's plight, rather than depicted as unique, is regarded as typical. The courtroom is full of boys with similar problems. The stereotyped Jewish father seems more concerned with his business than his son's problems. One father sleeps while the court decides his son's future. "Take him if you want. I'm sick of supporting him anyway," another declares, totally abandoning his parental responsibility. In such films, the judge comes to serve as the social architect of an essentially invisible family.

When parents are not negatively depicted, they are often mysteriously absent. In *Dead End*, teenager Tommy Gordon, played by Billy Halop, is brought up by his sister, who functions as a surrogate mother. It was a role which Halop repeated in *Crime School*, and a relationship that pervades many of the screen families of the period.

Boy of the Streets, a 1937 offering, presented the familiar faces and drab environment of tenement life. At the start of the film, Chuck, Brennan (Jackie Cooper) and his street pals have stolen the door from the butcher shop as a Halloween prank. In a rare image of an understanding policeman, an officer comments, "Sometimes I think we had better times than kids have nowadays. We had the woods to tramp in, the fields to play in, a decent home to live in. Poor little devils, born without a chance. They're all trying to be hard and tough because they figure that's the best way to get along in the world."

Chuck has quit school, but rather than look for a job he spends his time roaming the street with his gang and generally getting into trouble. Like Jimmy Smith, Tommy Gordon and the others, he is a basically decent boy who, in the absence of any real parental direction or guidance, is left to his own devices. But it is more than simple parental abdication. Chuck's father not only establishes no control, but sets a bad example. "Only saps work, you told me that yourself," Chuck tells his father. While the boy thinks his father is a big shot downtown, the truth is that he is a drinker, a loafer, and a man who daydreams his life away with wild schemes of tunneling under the Atlantic. "You've wasted 365 days every year since I knew you," his wife complains.

As so often happens in these film families, it is left to her to take up the burden of supporting the family both financially and morally. Some indication of the basis of this image in real life is given in a July, 1934, account in "The Family," in which Marjorie Boggs, describing one effect of the Depression, wrote:

> The father, robbed of his status as provider and protector, became the blustering, overbearing taskmaster in the home or found solace for his loss in the symptoms of physical illness. The wife reacted to the deprivation by blaming the husband, increasing his feelings of helplessness, hence his tendency to fight or retreat. Children rebelled, sometimes ran away. They were not to blame. They should have had what they were entitled to.[5]

Chuck Brennan's environment is recognizable. The family consists of the peer group united in opposition to other neighborhood gangs and the blood ties to the old countries that define these gangs and their membership. One of the most moving scenes in the film comes as adolescent Nora, watching her mother die, stands by the tenement window and sings, "Did Your Mother Come from Ireland?" An eerie silence falls upon the streets below as faces strained and lined with worry appear at doorways and windows, summoned by the call of the emerald isle from which they and their parents had fled in the hope of finding a better home.

In his analysis of Depression films, Bergman has suggested that "the neighborhood was a cheery conglomerate of nationalities."[6] But there is little to offer cheer in the environment of these neighborhoods. Blood ties, like crimson threads of kinship, bind them together, but they are locked into their own cultures and divisions exist among old and young alike. By the final reel, Chuck is saved from a life of crime and returned to the bosom of his family, where both he and his father come to a better understanding of each other. Yet despite this concession to a happy ending, it is the image of the fractured family that remains strongest.

The failure of these film families often exists inexplicably, with little or no attempt to explain parental absence, neglect or excess. William Wellman's 1933 production, *Wild Boys of the Road*, however, is an exception which clearly relates the family and its failure within a comprehensible social environment. Early in the film adolescent Eddie returns home from a school dance to encounter his mother, her eyes red from crying, as she and her husband struggle with the family budget. This is not the inner city slum life we are familiar with, but respectable and comfortable middle-class life. Eddie has his own car and has recently been able to order a new suit. The

effects of the Depression, however, have started to be felt and his family is feeling the pinch. "You're old enough to realize the seriousness of this," his father tells him, taking him into his confidence.

From this point on a transition takes place and Eddie gradually assumes the traditional role of adult and provider. He gives up his new suit and the next day sacrifices his beloved "sweet little bus" in order to provide his father with much needed cash. The traditional role of the father as provider has been reversed. "No matter what you ever do, Edward, you'll never make me feel as proud of you as you have this minute," his father tells him. With tears in his eyes, Eddie looks at him and then, fearing he'll crack completely, retreats to that peculiar form of fondness allowed males and trades punches until, no longer able to hold back his emotions, he runs from the house. For Eddie and thousands like him, home can never be the same again. He hops a freight with his friend Tommy and they encounter Sally, a teenager who, like them, is leaving home in order to save her parents the burden of supporting her. "We got a big family. With me gone, it's just one less mouth to feed," she tells them.

Eddie Smith's parents are intended to be taken as typical and decent parents, average men and women who, like Lillum's parents in *Harold Teen* (1935), find that economic circumstances threaten their home, their lives and the future they have dreamed of and planned for their children. Yet images of parents like them are rare. More often than not we see parents not as victims but as victimizers, as liabilities rather than assets, who operate in the lives of their children as negative rather than positive influences. So low is the image of the parent that in 1935's *Tomorrow's Youth* we see a child taken into court and asked to determine which parent he wishes to live with. This is no adolescent with some degree of rational thought but a child barely old enough to be at school. Youngster Dickie Moore fixes the judge squarely in the eye and tells him, "Gee whiz, that ain't a fair thing to ask a fella." In the absence of parents prepared to function as adults, the child is asked to take on their responsibility. As a newspaper covering the case comments, "If you ask us, the serious question is what will happen to the young unsuspecting offspring.... We pity any child compelled by law to change his mode of living just to satisfy the selfish whim of a parent." It may be a reflection of more enlightened times and parents that, faced with the prospect of dragging his son into court in *Kramer vs. Kramer* (1979), Dustin Hoffman, as the boy's father, refuses to subject his son to such an ordeal.

But the parents of adolescents in films of the thirties are far from enlightened and intentionally or not, they often become the bane of their children's lives. In *Down the Stretch* (1936), orphaned Snapper Sinclair finds that, rather than being free to grow and to establish his own identity, he must constantly answer for the sins of his father. "If the kid's anything like

Opposite: In *Wild Boys of the Road* the death and mutilation of adolescents served as a metaphor of the fractured family in films of the thirties.

his old man you can buy him for a quart of Scotch," one worker comments. In the parlance of the stable where he works, Snapper finds it's a matter of "like sire, like colt." In *Hoosier Schoolboy* (1937), Charkie Carter's life is made miserable by his father's reputation as the town drunk. Set in Ainsley, Indiana, it is a refreshing break from the dominant image of the metropolis and provides an interesting image of small town life as seen in the Hardy, Aldrich and Penrod series. Only the death of Charkie's father liberates the boy to establish a life of his own, in which he can be judged for what he is himself and not forever held accountable for his father's actions.

Connie Heath (*Girls on Probation*: 1938) similarly finds her life plagued by her father, who is so domineering and repressive that the girl is ultimately driven from the family home. Wrongfully accused of a crime, Connie settles for jail rather than give her father the satisfaction of believing "that he was right, that I was bad all along." And in a musical, *Babes in Arms* (1939), the decade drew to an end with yet another image of a parent serving as a negative force in the life of his child. Mickey Moran, like Charkie and Snapper (all, incidentally, played by Mickey Rooney), finds that his father is more of a hindrance than a help. When he determines on a life in the theater, the boy is dismayed to find that his father, a failed vaudevillian, rejects the plan outright. "If I ever hear show business, song writing, or vaudeville mentioned again, I'll kick the tar out of you." Angrily, his son turns on him. "It makes me sick to hear you talk like that!" When his father hits him, the boy leaves home to make a life for himself. Not only does he succeed in spite of his father, but ultimately, in a role reversal that harks back to *Wild Boys of the Road*, he assumes the function of provider by getting a job for his father.

While these films essentially deal with working-class or lower middle-class families, the type of families we would most expect to be affected by economic difficulties which might fracture family harmony, their behavior is seldom justified in terms of economic hardship. The fact that money does not solve the problems of the family is nowhere more evident than in the Bonita Granville vehicle, *Beloved Brat* (1938). Despite the wealth and opulence of the Morgan household, teenage daughter Roberta encounters only a paucity of spirit and understanding. Lost in the whirlwind of their business and social activities, her parents fail to realize that charity indeed begins at home. "I have all I can do without shouldering the discipline of a child; that's your job," Roberta's father tells her mother, but she cannot find time to fit the girl into her schedule. Unloved, alienated, and increasingly rebellious, the girl is finally committed to a home when she becomes responsible for the death of a man. As the judge observes, "My opinion of a reform school is that it should be for parents and not for children."

Writing in 1939, Winona Morgan observed that few serious studies had attempted to look at the average American family. While she was not addressing family life as presented on the screen, her comments seem particularly applicable. There have been, she suggested,

very few studies of normal family life. So little has been heard about the
ordinary American family which, despite numerous setbacks and
misfortunes, may still be classed as happy, that the general reader may be
pardoned for doubting whether such families actually exist. [7]

Such doubts might well plague the viewer of films from the period. The
constant repetition of these negative images demands either surrender and
capitulation to their existence as an authentic record of the time, or a
questioning of their relevance as social documents. Kracauer has suggested
that films reflect and reveal the inner life of the nation that makes them. We
might deduce from that, that during the thirties particularly in the wake of
the Depression, the fear of the fractured family, whether it existed in reality
or not, came to exist as a concern that was manifested in motion pictures.
This seems a far more viable proposition than believing that family condition s as represented in these films were an accurate reflection of American
family life at the time. While the films concentrate on New York City and
the day-to-day struggles of the working class, the America that existed
beyond Manhattan was seldom considered — at least until the emergence of
the Hardys, the Schofields, and the Aldriches. Yet while films were showing
the problems of family life in the great cities, studies of rural and small
town America tended to suggest that, despite some hardships and adjustments, the Depression was nowhere near as devastating as indicated by the
subject matter of the films, or as implied by their imagery and themes. The
Lynds in their study, for example, commented that in Middletown there was
a "feeling that the Depression has, in a vague general way, been good for
family life."[8] And Morgan reported:

> Only nine percent of the mothers felt that the effects of the depression
> had been entirely unfavorable for their family life, while nearly 40%
> said that the depression had brought their family closer together. In only
> fourteen families in 1933 were the husband and wife distinctly less close
> together than they had been in 1927, and only three of these represented
> divorces or separations. [9]

Family life, it would seem, not only went on during the decade, but
in many cases it actually improved. In the film families, the Hardys became
the light at the end of the tunnel. Somewhere between their appearance and
the start of the decade exists the thin line of films that represent the movement towards this positive image. Warner's *Merry Frinks* (1934), while
played essentially for laughs, presents an image of an overworked, under-
rewarded mother and her parasitic brood. In the Frink household the
mother is the long suffering victim of selfish children, a lazy husband prone
to hit the bottle, and a collection of cantankerous and eccentric relatives
intent on extending both the family and mother's patience to the limit.
Teenage daughter Lucille dreams of becoming a singer. Her brother

Stella Dallas (1936): **Self-sacrifice and mother love, thirties' style.**

Norman cuts school in favor of assuming a career in boxing. Emmet, the oldest child, moves his law office and communist clients into the family living quarters, firm in the belief that the revolution is on the way. Grandmother Frink berates every member of the family and surreptitiously drinks her days away. In the midst of all this, Mrs. Frink is left to adjudicate squabbles, maintain the peace, and try to keep the family going. She excuses

Norman's truancy as "spring and all," but will not indulge him and draws the line when it comes to boxing. When on Mother's Day not one member of the family acknowledges the occasion she is pushed to the breaking point. "I'm through," she announces. "You're heartless and selfish and ungrateful." Only when she leaves them does the family come to its senses and understand just how much they have depended upon her. When she returns, it is to a family that has come to respect and value her.

Despite the fact that the *New York Times* felt inclined to comment, in 1937, "We cannot accept Stella. She is a caricature all the way,"[10] the opening of *Stella Dallas* at the Music Hall was accompanied by the shedding of a communal tear, the clearing of a communal throat, and the resounding clamor of cash in the register — the ultimate barometer of public approval. Barbara Stanwyck played a mother who, unfit to bring up her daughter, realized the situation and sacrificed her own needs so that her daughter could have a better life. Marjorie Rosen has condemned the film as a "grotesque hyperbole of mother love," suggesting that "the depression, smelling of anti-feminism, gave Hollywood a perfect excuse for such ludicrous allegories of sacrifice, tears and female humiliation."[11] Yet Stella, when taken with Mrs. Frink, Dreena Gordon, Mary Colbrook and others, suggests an image of parenthood that is peculiarly positive in a period of such negativism. While feminists may find the image of motherhood and the emphasis on sacrifice, selflessness and service distasteful, the simple truth of the matter is that alongside the indolent, aggressive and alcohol-sodden image of the father so often present in these films, mothers emerge much more sympathetically.

Mary Colbrook, for example, a recently widowed woman, struggles to satisfy the middle-class tastes of her sons and daughters in the 1938 Warners production of *My Bill*. Set in Colbrook, Massachusetts, the film concerns a rather well-to-do family who fall upon hard times following the death of their father. As the family money begins to run out, Mary discovers that teenagers Gwen, Muriel and Reggie are far more concerned with their individual whims and needs than the welfare of the family as a whole. They are in part the Frinks gone middleclass. Only the youngest child, Bill, played by Dickie Moore, has any real sense of the situation, and only he defends his mother and her efforts on their behalf. "What does mother know? She's always getting into some sort of mess," the others complain. When these thankless adolescents see a chance to improve their position, they decide to move in with their wealthy aunt, leaving their mother and Bill to fend for themselves. The children's aunt, however, rules with a rod of iron and, quickly realizing that all that glitters is not gold, they contritely and humbly return to the fold, much more appreciative of mother and Bill.

The struggling and self-sacrificing mother is once again present in *White Banners* (1938). Set in Middale, Indiana, in 1916, it is part of the developing film formula that suggests, if not states, that real family life can only exist beyond the metropolis. As Stella has made a better life possible for Laurel, so in this film we see Hannah give up her child, played by Jackie Cooper, in order that he may turn out better than his father. Unaware of her real identity, Peter thus comes under her influence and care, and when she is sure that he has grown into the decent boy she had hoped he would become, she steps anonymously back into the snowstorm from which she has entered.

With the rare exception of films such as *Beloved Brat* and *Little Tough Guy* (1938), mothers are depicted as the emotional, moral and economic strength and backbone of family life. The father, as has been suggested, is negatively depicted. The family in which both mother and father are presented in a harmonious situation with shared control of the family is a rare exception throughout the decade, and makes its strongest appearance after 1937, when three family series come to the screen. The paucity of such images may in fact have some basis in reality. Writing in *Parents Magazine* in February 1939, Paul Popenoe, for example, said:

> The modern family is supposed to be a community enterprise directed by a partnership of two persons, husband and wife, who have equal rights, equal privileges, equal responsibilities, equal duties and equal obligations. How often does it obtain this ideal? Even a casual survey of your own acquaintances will convince you that many of them have not reached a fifty–fifty basis. [12]

Popenoe went on to suggest that, in a survey of more than one thousand American families, 28 percent were dominated by the wife, 35 percent by the husband, and 37 percent were marriages in which duties and responsibilities were shared.

The Schofields, Aldriches and Hardys were all film families depicting at least some degree of shared parental responsibility. The Schofield home, in the Penrod series, presents an interesting example. Mr. Schofield, whether played by Mat Moore or Frank Craven, is presented as the stern but loving father with a somewhat misguided sense of justice. In each film his son Penrod clashes with him and in each film it is the father who is ultimately revealed as being in the wrong. This pattern is also quite prevalent in the Henry Aldrich story and in images of middle-class families during the forties.

In almost all the Penrod stories the boy is forced into an untenable position by his father and subsequently emerges as the moral victor. This pattern exists in the first Penrod feature in 1931 and also in the later films. In 1931, we see Mr. Schofield take his son to the woodshed and punish him for an act we know the boy did not commit. In the re-make some years later, Rodney, the town bully and wise-acre, becomes involved in a street fight with Penrod. Young Schofield in fact has gone to the aid of a small black boy whom Rodney has been picking on unfairly. "I don't care what the provocation was, I'll not have you disgracing your mother and I by street fighting," his father condemns him. At this point, Mrs. Schofield (Spring Byington) intervenes, pointing out that she understands boys better. As she comes to her son's defense, the lad's eyes light up, knowing that in his mother he will receive the benefit of the fair hearing his father has denied him. "You told him yourself it was his duty to protect the weak at all times," the woman insists. Faced with the contradiction between his precepts to the boy and the punishment he feels he cannot back down from, Mr. Schofield sends the boy to his room, depriving him of his supper. Realizing the unfairness of the punishment, Mrs. Schofield sends food to the boy, thus undermining the authority of her husband.

This is perhaps not quite the shared responsibility Popenoe had in mind, but it may be exactly what Helen Ellwanger Hanford meant when she wrote in 1939:

> All of us would subscribe wholeheartedly to the theory that parents are a sort of firm appointed to manage a child's interests until such a time as he is capable of taking care of them himself; and then with fine inconsistency we proceed to act as no member of a firm would dare to do. In fact, the amount of sabotage that goes on in some families would send a business firm into bankruptcy.[13]

In the same film in which Mr. Schofield has abused his son for street fighting, he himself becomes involved in a fight, thus reversing the traditional role model, as father assumes the behavior of child. When the black boy is orphaned, this is extended further. Penrod insists that his family take the boy in, but his father advises, "You'll have to stop carrying the world on your shoulders." That night, as Penrod goes to bed, he refuses to kiss his father goodnight. Stung by the boy's rejection, Mr. Schofield ultimately comes round to the boy's point of view and Vernon is taken into the family.

In *Penrod and His Twin Brother* (1938), circumstances conspire to have the boy's dog wrongfully accused of attacking neighbors. Although the boy proclaims its innocence long and loudly, his father believes him guilty, and a rift grows between them as he determines to get rid of the dog. "If you send Duke away," his son tells him, "I'll never speak to you again as long as I live." "You remember that," his father challenges him, "and don't ever speak to me again until you're ready to say you're sorry."

In *Penrod's Double Trouble* (1938), a similar clash finds the youngster being punished as he insists, "I can't help it, a fella's gotta have some self-respect," and so refusing to give in once more to his father's misguided sense of justice, the boy once again marches to his room for punishment. In every instance the boy is proved right, his father wrong, and mother, the fount of understanding, remains firmly in between to soften the father's hand and to explain the boy and his motives to her husband.

While the family is never totally harmonious, its upsets are tempests in teacups that cannot disguise the love and unity of the household. In the boy's words, no matter what happens, they are still "a swell mother and father." Even today, one comes away from these films with a sense of warmth and understanding, and a sense of having shared something special. The values they represent, while being part of the late 1930's movement towards an idealized screen family, are not that far removed from family fare of the 1970's, particularly in the television world of the Ingalls and the Waltons.

If Mr. Schofield learns from Penrod, then clearly Andy Hardy learns from his father the judge. If Schofield's justice is misguided, then Judge Hardy's is scrupulously fair. If Mrs. Schofield in part undermines her husband's authority, Mrs. Hardy complements her husband. The image has been perfected. In the middle America of Carvel, Idaho, the world we see is the idealized image that has in part grown out of the negative images that have preceded it. It is "the world not as it was but as it ought to have been; with virtues intact, pieties unfeigned, commandments unbroken, good rewarded, evil foiled. There were problems and crises, but none that could not be tidily solved, usually by the generous application of good sense and fatherly advice."[14]

When the Hardys first came to the screen, their name was not even in the title. *A Family Affair* was greeted with little excitement by the public or the press. *Variety* commented that the film would "probably seek the bulk of coin in double bill spots,"[15] whilst acknowledging that it would probably attract followers in the family homes. It did well enough at the box office for a follow-up to eventuate in the form of *You're Only Young Once*; but it was not until Andy's name was actually put into the title and Judy Garland given a supporting role that the real success became apparent. Recognizing that they had a winning formula, MGM began to churn out the series. They had found an image of family life that, however valid, touched a sensitive nerve in the American audience. Margaret Thorpe, in her 1939 study, *America at the Movies*, suggested that this image, rather than being a casual accident, once discovered was preserved, researched, and meticulously maintained:

> The Hardy pictures are based on research as intelligent and thorough as that which goes into the making of the most elaborate historical ... the things that happen to the Hardys are the sort of things that might happen to almost anyone, and their responses to the various situations are both entertaining and accurate. Because they are so genuine an American norm, families in the various brackets, far above or below them see themselves mirrored in the Hardys.[16]

Thorpe proclaimed the Hardys an American norm in the very year that Morgan lamented the lack of serious research into family life in the United States.

If one feels tempted to believe in life as the Hardys lived it, we should keep in mind that above all else the Hardy series, like all motion pictures, was the product of an industry that expected a profit. As such, the maximum efforts were made to ensure that nothing appeared that might offend. Mickey Rooney has made it quite clear that "there was no connection between what you saw of Andy Hardy on the screen and what was the reality of Mickey Rooney off-camera."[17] The same source has suggested that the overseer of the series, Louis B. Mayer, privately "refused to assume the role of monk, but in his pictures he stood four-square behind purity, virtue, and virginity."[18]

Andy Hardy existed in an extended family that consisted of his mother and father, his sisters Marion and Joan, and his aunt Millie. In each movie, Andy both causes and confronts problems that become obstacles in his path to manhood, which is defined as being like his father. Taken in all, these films provide us with an image of the transition from boyhood to manhood, and all the while he is protected, guided, steered and advised by his parents who share his life. "We taught you how to think, your mother and I, and if you make a mistake then it's our mistake too," his father tells him.

The Hardy household, unlike those before it, functions harmoniously with a shared responsibility, obligation, and involvement. In the opening of *A Family Affair*, we find ourselves in the town of Carvel, population, 25,000. The judge is established as a fair and just man who will not be intimidated or pressured into acting in a way he does not believe to be right. Whether played by Lionel Barrymore as in this instance, or in the more familiar form of Lewis Stone, the character of the judge remains essentially as established in this first feature. World-wise, he runs his family as he runs his courtroom, with patience, understanding, and justice. He is as capable of disciplining a community as he is of administering punishment to his children. He can save his daughter's marriage and the jobs of local citizens with equal skill, sensitivity, and dedication, for he knows and understands that the stability and happiness of the community is founded in the happiness and stability of the home. He knows the ways of the world and understands life through which he comes to deal with old and young alike, knowing that despite the outward differences, a common thread of human values binds the generations together. "Everyone says today young folks live in a different world; well, they're doing the same thing," he comments as he watches his youngest daughter kissing her boyfriend.

But the judge's rule is not altogether absolute. He knows his place in the home as well as in the courtroom, and if he gives way to his wife, it is only in her domain, which is clearly the kitchen. Here she can function as the supreme court and reverse his decisions, but generally she will embark upon nothing more radical than asking him to carve the roast. Her justice and judgment are largely of the tea and sympathy variety. When one daughter feels her marriage is on the rocks, Mrs. Hardy is there to dispense hot cocoa and tucks the oldest of her brood into bed. It is Mrs. Hardy who sets Andy on the road to his amorous adventures by arranging for him to attend Polly Benedict's party, and it is mother again who makes him attractive to the world. In the boy's words, "If it wasn't for you, I'd go around looking like something to bury."

In *Andy Hardy's Double Life* (1942), the boy, preparing to head off to college, is mortified to discover that his father intends to accompany him and show him around his old alma mater. Struggling with his adolescent desire to assert himself and find his way in a new world, Andy finds himself unable to hurt his father by telling him he wants to go alone. Here it is Mrs. Hardy who plays the pivotal role in bringing father and son to a better understanding not only of each other but of themselves. "You're going to start college," she tells Andy. "That means you're a man. Well, your father's only a man. Now if there's anything between you, you go right up and talk to him." For Andy, so often the recipient of the father and son monologues in the study, the electric chair seems a more pleasant prospect. But when he does climb the stairs, we are presented with a moment that, taken with his mother's advice, so clearly crowns this series as cinema's most enduring image of the harmonious home. "I've got to straighten something out with you, Dad.... You're always thinking of yourself, you're never thinking of me." And so, standing face to face with his father for the first time, Andy finds the inner strength to be able to explain that he must live his own life and cannot go on tied to his father's shirttails.

Many setbacks will follow on the road to adulthood, but when Andy sets out for Wainright he has made the biggest step, a step which he would be the first to acknowledge would not have been possible without the positive influence and encouragement of both his mother and father. It is an image of family life that stands singularly alone in the American cinema of the 1930's, and one which would be repeated in the decade ahead. Reviewing *Love Finds Andy Hardy*, the *New York Times* touched upon part of the Hardys' appeal and its link in the mainstream of American literature:

> The best of it is that not only does love find Andy Hardy but finds him being played by Mickey Rooney, who ranks second to Walt Disney's Dopey as our favorite movie hero of the year. Watching Mickey's Andy on the screen is practically as good as reading Mark Twain and Booth Tarkington; he's the perfect composite of everyone's big brother.[19]

But behind this image lay the darkness that dominated the decade. The image of the family in film throughout the 1930's emerges as a peculiar distortion of reality that both confirms and denies, heeds and ignores the changing nature of the American family. That the family was a major concern of the filmmakers cannot be denied. That these films found success at the box office is equally apparent. Yet between the start of the decade and the end, the family as Hollywood depicted it underwent a major transformation. *Motion Pictures and Standards of Morality*, published in 1933, said that in regard to parental behavior in real life and as depicted in films:

We have found that motion pictures diverge from the mores upward more than downward in the matter of treatment of children by parents; they set patterns that call up admiration more often than patterns that elicit condemnation and they stand prevailingly above current practice.[20]

Yet as we have seen, the dominant image of the parent, particularly the parent of the adolescent, was a negative one. One study reported:

In a total of some 45 families seen in 40 films, there are only twelve families intact and half of these are strife-ridden. Alongside that, we find 33 images in which the family is fractured, fragmented and in ferment emotionally or physically.[21]

In contrast, the Cavan and Ranek study of Depression-time Chicago reported that, in the 100 families they examined:

The parental make-up varied. In 84 families the two biological parents were present; in three homes the father was dead and there was a mother and a stepfather; in five homes the mother was dead and there was a father and a stepmother; in six homes, the natural parents were divorced, the parents consisting of a mother and a stepfather in three cases, and of the father and a stepmother in three cases; in two homes there were adoptive parents.[22]

Clearly, at least in terms of family unity, motion pictures presented a much bleaker picture than existed in reality.

The 1930's, particularly the period marked by the Depression, had a major impact upon society and by implication the family. That this impact had an influence on young people is obvious from reports of the time:

We cannot too much emphasize that the disappearance of these various activities and strivings marks the passing of a way of life. To marry, have children, acquire property, gain a position of respect and dignity in the community, share in the common body of beliefs and affirmations about the universe and man's place therein—these made up a way of life ... the patterns for this older way of life remain but the social economic situation to which they are addressed has altered. Young men and women face either frustration in their efforts to conform to the older patterns or confusion and anxiety as they explore for new patterns of conduct.[23]

Yet rather than seeing adolescents faced with these problems, the economic issues and their impact upon old and young alike are more or less ignored, with the result that fractured families are located against obscure backgrounds that suggest social and economic problems are

somehow the result of corrupt officials or lazy individuals. While *Dead End*, *Mayor of Hell*, *Boy Slaves*, and a host of other films may appear to depict adolescents as victims of the harsh economic times, they exist in reality as pleas for urban renewal and human kindness more than as any attempt to seriously confront the economic climate of the day. Conservative as ever, the industry that boomed while the market bombed, more or less ignored the Depression as a subject for film comment. Yet while we cannot see it on the surface of these films, its impact is ever present.

The fractured families of these films are less a reflection of actual family life than a reflection of the shattering of the old traditional values and roles the Depression brought with it. When Wall Street crashed, it is hardly surprising that the reverberations were felt along the sensitive, golden umbilical cord that connected it to Hollywood and the studios. Unable or unwilling to confront the Depression head on as a source for movie material, the industry translated its fears and hostility through the fractured family. But the family as they showed it often had little relation to those encountered by the Lynds or Morgan. When parental excesses and failures did not drive children from home, parents were often mysteriously absent, leaving their young alone to cope as best they could.

Given the repetition of such images throughout much of the decade, it is hardly surprising that the Hardys were so warmly embraced. For parents, it meant an opportunity to see children who respected authority and traditional values. More importantly perhaps, it showed them an image of themselves with which they could identify, and an image of family life that promised that love and hard work would be rewarded. For adolescents, it was a rare opportunity to see themselves as part of society. *Boys Town*, *The Devil Is a Sissy*, *Crime School*, and a host of other films throughout the thirties continually depicted young people as some sort of cinematic orphans, outcast from society. As the decade drew to a close, they were at last coming in out of the cold.

Such a trend is particularly apparent in *Babes in Arms*, which in many ways sums up the changing image of screen youngsters. "It's not for you youngsters to be carrying the grown-up burden," Mickey Rooney and his team of juvenile entertainers are told. For too long, the young people that appeared on American screens had been obliged to fend for themselves. In *Babes in Arms*, Mickey, Judy and the others are obliged not only to stand on their own feet, but to help their parents as well. The show they put on not only asserts their independence, but provides work and inspiration for their parents, whose spirits have succumbed to the Depression. Their success is clearly intended as a lesson. The show, we are told, is "for the millions of kids who never had a chance; for the millions for kids who had a wise-acre tell them there's no such thing as the American Dream." Fact and

Opposite: In *The Devil Is a Sissy* working-class family life was depicted as a constant battle between adolescents and their parents.

fantasy blur. Mickey and Judy appear as the Roosevelts and sing "God's Country." In their on-screen characters and in the reality of their own lives, Rooney and Garland came to represent a faith, a belief, and a hope of youthful promise that had been denied their predecessors.

The slums of New York gave way to Andy Hardy's Carvel, Henry Aldrich's Centerville, and Penrod's Midvale. The fractured family became whole. Snow White, with her extended family of loving little men and animals, won the hearts of audiences and became one of the decade's biggest grossing films. Judy Garland, retreating from the fractured family of her own life, found momentary happiness with the good fairy of Oz and a farm in middle America. Like many victims of the Depression, Dorothy longed for happier days somewhere over the rainbow. Like Penrod, Andy, and other screen youngsters, she came to realize "there's no place like home."

If the fractured families of the thirties had painted too bleak a picture, the idealized image of the Hardy family was equally guilty of inaccuracy. Indeed, the very notion of a typical family was still in the process of being defined. In 1934, the White House Conference on Child Health and Protection asserted that "to describe a typical American home at the present time is impossible."[24] By the start of the forties, the family was undergoing closer scrutiny than at any time in its history. While the film industry was unable to accurately reflect the American family, the extremes it presented serve as some indication of the major changes taking place within it.

Writing in *The Journal of Marriage and Family Living* in the winter of 1940, Sidney E. Goldstein asserted that, "The simple patterns of the past have been shattered, and the family is utterly confounded in the presence of a social order that is in a state of cultural, economic and political confusion."[25] Loss of self confidence, a corrosion of the human spirit, and a sense of resentment and despair were, according to Goldstein, the result of the economic situation. Ten million men and women permanently out of work; four million families dependent upon public aid; and twenty-two and one half million men and women and children living in a state of destitution: this was the America Goldstein saw.

Wherever one looks in the popular magazines and the serious journals of the day, one encounters a growing concern about the changes taking place in the American family. Lawrence K. Frank commented that "Most of the ideas and beliefs that are taught to the children with respect to these basic organizing concepts of life are obsolete and no longer credible except to those who have dedicated their lives to the perpetuation of the archaic and the anachronistic."[26] In the article, "Democracy and the Family," written in 1940, Una Bernard Sait saw the patriarchal patten of family life in a state of dissolution, and family life as unstable. Jean Walker MacFarlane looked at American parents in 1941 and found them to be insecure and uncertain of their roles:

Parents in the present American scene, made uneasy by mental hygiene, parent education propaganda, and by their own sincere eagerness to do a good job, have let themselves be run into a defensive corner by such professional parent substitutes as psychiatrists, psychologists, pediatricians, school teachers, and counselors. No one is to blame. In the shift of philosophy from the sanctity of parental authority to the sanctity of the child, it was inevitable that parents became insecure and increasingly sought authoritative advice.[27]

This shift toward the sanctity of the child is apparent throughout the forties, and evident in the number of film families where life seemed to center around the exploits of the young. If Andy, Henry, and Penrod had emerged as Hollywood's favorite sons, then *Margie* (1946), *Janie* (1944), *Cynthia* (1948), and a long list of others came to the screen as America's favorite daughters. Whereas the youngsters of the 1930's were depicted as youths, that is to say, as young people accorded with no unique nature or needs, the young people who populated the screen throughout the 1940's were increasingly depicted as a subculture, with their own concerns, interests, attitudes, and mannerisms.

Between 1940 and 1949, one can trace the emergence of adolescence as a fact and phase recognized by the motion picture industry. When Jackie Cooper appeared in *Seventeen* in 1940, he was praised for "his ability to play the typical American boy of high school years." Cooper played a love-struck youngster intent on convincing his parents he was growing up. "You call me baby names. You don't seem to realized I'm not a child," he complains. One review for the film greeted it as "a story of adolescent youth and problems in the realms of finance and romance."[28]

While the term "adolescent" had not yet entered the American consciousness, the movies were serving to bring it out in the open. A 1942 review for *Miss Annie Rooney*, prepared for the Library of Congress, described it as "basically adolescent with their jitterbugging, first dates, romances and heartbreaks."[29] *Parents Magazine* began to move away from the word "youth" and in 1945 ran an article entitled, "Adolescence: What Is It?" If American parents were beginning to wonder about this new stage of life, Hollywood saturated them with its impression of the rites and rituals associated with it, striving to sell them as representative.

Jackie Moran starred in *Barefoot Boy* (1938) and *Tomboy* (1940). Studio publicity suggested that he and his brother "are great pals and both are typical American boys. Jackie has the same interests and hobbies that any youth his age would have." Elaborate publicity campaigns were designed, not simply to promote his films, but to assert their representativeness. Competitions were held to find the local tomboy. Kids were given apples at special screenings, and twelve million Dixie vortex ice cream cups were printed, featuring the faces of Moran and fifteen-year-old co-star, Marcia Mae Jones.

Tomboy: **Elaborate publicity campaigns attempted to convince movie audiences that the adolescent stars were typical American kids.**

The very structure and style of the films themselves deliberately attempted to convey the impression that the Hollywood image was reality. Mention has already been made of the towns where the characters lived. There is little doubt that they served to symbolize what the industry wished to be seen as the typical American town. Indeed, in more than one film we are introduced to these towns and characters as though taking a guided tour. *A Date with Judy* (1949) starred Jane Powell as adolescent Judy Foster. The film opens with a voice-over narration introducing us to the town and the folks who live there. In Santa Barbara, "the people here are the same as everywhere—there's always something going on, especially when Judy Foster and her friends are around." This is mythical America, where life centers not around industry and business, not around commerce or education, and not around politics, but around the interests and activities of the bobby-soxer set.

Narration also introduced us to Hortonville in 1944's *Janie*. It is, we are told, "an average homey little town like yours or mine, calm, quiet,

Janie: The emergence of the bobby-soxer obscured the impact of war on adolescents and the rise in juvenile crime.

Junior Miss: **In the wake of the Hardy's came the middle-class families that dominated screens of the forties.**

where nothing much happens." Janie (Joyce Reynolds) is introduced like some species in a display case. She is, the narrator continues, "sixteen and vice-president of the senior class; a girl who frequents the drugstore where she buys her malts, magazines, and breaks a heart on the average of twice a week." Her father publishes the town newspaper and spends the rest of his life complaining about "the horrible music" that Janie and her "platterbug friends" seem to play relentlessly. She takes on all the cliches and mannerisms of the Hollywood adolescent. Constantly on the phone, she is the quintessential bobby-soxer, a forerunner of *Bye Bye Birdie's* telephone song.

Much to her father's chagrin, she and her gang invent a new language, designed in part to prevent their parents from knowing what they are talking about. "It is English, Dad, we're just modernizing it," she explains in a moment that is reminiscent of Patty Duke's encounters with her father in the sixties' television series. To her hapless father, Janie appears as a foreigner. While his wife does her best to cope with any situation, he can only denounce "the way the children of today dance and the records they play." Unable to really communicate, he looks upon his daughter as an alien; she speaks differently, acts differently, and seems to live in world with customs and codes totally unknown to him. This, Hollywood claimed, was the typical American home.

Throughout the 1940's the American family was defined by the Hollywood adolescent. If Jackie Cooper found his parents unwilling to allow him to grow up, Jane Withers was no happier with her screen parents. In *Her First Beau* (1941), she played fifteen-year-old Penny Woods, a girl who complains, "You and mother won't try to understand me." *Kiss and Tell* (1945) featured Shirley Temple as Corliss Archer, "the teenaged brat who does more than her share to upset several households." In *I'll Be Seeing You* (1945), Temple played seventeen-year-old Barbara Marshal, who is "spoiled and pretty." Her father finds her music "awful stuff for a man to wake to first thing in the morning." Barbara complains that her parents "treat me like a child," but is forced to realize that she is not yet in control of her emotions, and can inadvertently hurt people.

In the same year Fox released *Junior Miss*, which *Life* reviewed as Film of the Week, giving their cover story to thirteen-year-old star Peggy Ann Garner. Based on Max Gordon's stage production, it was "a rollicking comedy of juve effects upon family life," with "animated young maniacs that made life at times miserable but never uninteresting for their parents."[30] Set in New York City, the movie follows the escapades of Judy Graves and her friend Buffy Adams, who create havoc for their families, particularly Judy's father. In the course of the film Judy manages to suspect her father of having an affair, causes him to lose his job, and ultimately gets it back for him. Like Janie, she has so much energy, good humor, imagination, and genuine concern that she leaves her perplexed but proud papa proclaiming her to be "one of the outstanding personalities of our time and very likely to be the first woman president of the United States."

Mingled against the tapestry of juvenile high jinks, *Junior Miss* furthured the screen depiction of adolescence. As Christmas Day approaches, Judy experiences all the ambivalence and uncertainty of the age. Proudly sporting her first pair of high heeled shoes, she feels that she is at last becoming a woman. Sitting beneath the Christmas tree, wearing the shoes and sucking on a peppermint stick, she is a perfect image of the adolescent caught somewhere between childhood and adulthood.

Although neither *Margie* (1946) nor *Adventures in Baltimore* (1949) were set in America of the 1940's, both films drew parallels between family life past and present. *Margie* is set in the 1920's, where we watch the painful adolescence of Margie McDuff, a young girl whose dominant emotion seems to be embarrassment. Her father is a mortician, an occupation that plainly plagues her. "I'd give anything on earth if he was just a plumber or something." The girl's grandmother, a strident feminist, proudly displays the chain with which she locked herself to the White House fence. When she constantly suggests that Margie might become the first woman president, the girl pleads with her to stop telling people that. The twenties, with its adolescent escapades of flagpole sitting and golfish eating, is seen to be not so far removed from America of the forties.

This fact is clearly addressed in *Adventures in Baltimore*. As the film opens the narrator asks, "What could be more symbolic of America than the modern American school girl; intelligent, refined, dignified, and..." The image, however, gives lie to the soundtrack, as we see a young bobby-soxer sprawled on the stairway, radio blasting, telephone in hand. The scene dissolves to 1905, where we encounter Shirley Temple as Dina Sheldon. Although she may not resemble the bobby-soxer in appearance, Dina is every bit as vocal and vociferous as the star-struck youngsters who screamed for Frankie. Expelled from school because of her unconventional behavior, she leads her family a merry dance, taking them from one disaster to another in the manner of Judy, Janie, and other screenagers of the day. In the same year, Temple featured in Sydney Sheldon's Academy Award-winning script of *The Bachelor and the Bobby Soxer*.

It was also in the same year that the word "adolescence" finally found its way to the screen. In *Father Was a Fullback*, a hapless Fred MacMurray played George Cooper, a man clearly at a loss to understand what is happening to his daughter Connie (Betty Lyn). Awkward and shy, the girl is terrified by the prospect of never getting a date and becoming an old maid. Girls like Connie, we are told, "think like Madame Pompadour, feel like Lana Turner, and look like Connie Cooper." Her father arranges for one of the neighborhood boys to ask her for a date. Unfortunately, the scheme gets out of hand, and the house is suddenly full of boys, all wanting to date the girl. Mortified by her father's act, the girl flees to her room. "Her psyche will be scarred from this for the rest of her life," her mother explains to a somewhat bewildered MacMurray. The daughter he has known and loved for so long is suddenly a stranger. Like screen fathers throughout much of the decade, he finds that he needs his wife to translate the situation for him. "It's just adolescence, dear, she'll live through it."

Through all of these films, it becomes apparent that in the 1940's American films turned their back on the working class. While the film families of the thirties had dwelt upon life in the inner city and the social conditions in which these people lived, the forties retreated from the tenements to apartment life and to small town middle America. The search for working-class images reveals few films that touched upon the once familiar image. Of those the forties did produce, the most visible are *A Tree Grows in Brooklyn* (1945) and *I Remember Mama* (1949).

Based on Betty Smith's best-selling novel of the same name, *A Tree Grows in Brooklyn* dealt with the struggle of Katie Nolan (Dorothy McGuire) to bring up her children, Neely (Ted Donaldson) and Francie (Peggy Ann Garner). Like many of the images of mothers in films of the 1930's, Katie struggles to make ends meet, hindered rather than helped by her drinking and daydreaming husband (James Dunn). She has brought the children up on a combination of the Bible and Shakespeare in the hope that "it may get you somewhere and maybe a job." It is her hope, like that of all parents, that her children will be able to have a better life than she has managed. As their grandmother observes, America's greatness lies in the fact that children can in fact grow up to be better than their parents. In the old world she well remembers, children's futures were determined for them by the station in life into which they were born. Yet Grandmother is not pleased with Katie. In striving to help the children get through life, Katie has, she believes, hardened her heart and lost touch with her own emotions. Life for Katie has been a disappointment. When she first married Johnny they worked as janitors at a local school and fantasized about life in Europe as they looked at the classroom maps. Instead of the Alps, they had to settle for the tenements rising out of the slums of New York. Disillusioned and unable to settle for this reality, Johnny has sought his escape in a bottle. He is neither a vicious nor violent drunk; he simply finds the warm comfort which alcohol offers more assuring than the painful reality of everyday life.

While he constantly vows to get off the bottle, Katie will not allow herself the luxury of such an illusion. "You ain't got a chance.... It's the truth and I can't change it." For Francie Nolan, a girl on the edge of adolescence, her father is a romantic figure. In the austere world of her mother, the girl finds little warmth and loving. Her father, on the other hand, with his dreams and schemes and tall stories, opens a doorway to another world. The dreams he has had to forego still exist for Francie as a reality she can share with him in each telling of a story. Apart from the time she spends with him, the highlight of the girl's life is school. While the teacher views the poetry of John Keats as a matter of meter, for Francie it is an insight into her father's struggle for truth, beauty and goodness. When she tells her father she wants to go to a bigger and better school, he indulges her in the fantasy that it might be possible, telling her they might be able to move to a new house and a new school when their ship comes in.

In the meantime, however, they see a house and pretend it's theirs, thus enabling Francie to arrange transfer papers. Mrs. Nolan is furious at the deceit. "It's dishonest, that's what it is. You're setting the child a bad example. You're making her live a lie!" But Francie's lie becomes reality and her father has made her dreams come true. By daring to dream, he has been able to transcend the reality over which he himself could never leap.

When her mother becomes pregnant, the strain upon the family's income is too much to bear. With each and every day, life seems to close in on them, squeezing the hope and energy from them. But it is really only Katie who must shoulder the brunt of the awesome burden. Johnny, eternally optimistic, never fully comes to terms with their situation. Neely is too young to understand, and Francie, content in the world of her new school, cannot see what her mother does. Feeling they can no longer afford the luxury of having two children at school, Katie tells her husband that Francie should quit. "You gotta quit gettin' her so all excited about schoolin'. Maybe it'll do her good to get out into the world, to learn something, to learn how to take care of herself, learn something practical while she's young." But Johnny would rather have his daughter stay in school. He knows only too well the disappointment and disillusionment life holds when one grows up and "you get to see things like they really are."

Trying to get work in order to keep her in school, he catches pneumonia and dies. With her father gone, Francie feels singularly alone and unloved. The romance, fantasy and cheer have gone from her life. Her mother's world is too harsh for her, but it is a world into which the girl now finds herself plunged for the first time in her life—plunged with a purpose. Since they cannot afford a hospital or a midwife, Francie will have to help with the birth. Throughout the long period of the pregnancy, mother and daughter discover a new understanding of each other. "I didn't want for you to grow up so soon," Katie tells her, but in the slums one always grows quickly.

A Tree Grows in Brooklyn portrays a somber but hopeful world in which real people struggle with real problems and somehow survive. It is a world not unlike the Depression experiences revealed in studies of the 1930's society. Betty Smith said that many readers had related her characters' experiences to their own childhoods. The difference between life as depicted in this film and those that dealt with similar subject matter in the previous decade is best expressed in a review of the book that appeared in the *New Yorker* in August, 1943:

> The author sees the misery, squalor and cruelty of slum life but sees them with understanding, pity, and sometimes with hilarious humor. A welcome relief from the latter-day fashion of writing about slum folk as if they were all brutalized morons.[31]

In this sense, at least, the film has made a literal translation of the original. It was an image of a section of American life almost totally ignored in the 1940's.

One other film that did, however, touch upon similar subject matter was RKO's *I Remember Mama*. Based on John van Druten's play and directed by George Stevens, it starred Irene Dunne as a mother attempting to bring up her Norwegian family in San Francisco. In contrast to the flighty and scatterbrained domestic life of middle-class America seen in so many films of the period, *I Remember Mama* retreats to an earlier time in which each member of the household complemented rather than conflicted with each other. Rather than a world in which children seem to make the decisions, it is a world in which children ask advice, and in which parents involve themselves in the interests and activities of their young. With no blaring record players to limit conversations, the family is free to sit around the kitchen table and share a good book together. When Niles wishes to go on to high school, it is a concern for the whole family, each of whom pitch in to make it possible. The father agrees to give up tobacco, his son will take on a job after school, the girls will babysit, and mother will once again give up her dream of a warm coat for the winter.

In the Hanson family, adolescence comes as a natural part of life. At the time in their daughter's life when they feel she is old enough, Mr. and Mrs. Hanson offer Katrine a cup of coffee. It is a ritual that symbolizes to her that, in her parents' eyes, she has come of age. Similarly, when their son decides to take to smoking a pipe, he is met not with indignant rage but by his father who hands him a match. In another unusual image of parental perception, Mrs. Hanson takes the girl to visit her dying uncle, explaining, "I'd like you to know what death looks like, then you're not frightened of it ever."

Francie Nolan and Katrine Hanson grow up in the warm fold of their families, experiencing life and death firsthand, as the natural experiences they are. Far from brutalizing them or plunging them too suddenly into life, one suspects the experiences leave them all the better as human beings. They are exposed to life to the extent that their parents feel they can deal with it and benefit from it. Mrs. Hanson constantly reviews the family's financial state, always deciding that it will not be necessary for them to go to the bank. Only when they are old enough do the children learn that there never was a bank account. Their parents had invented it to keep them from worrying. As their mother explains, "It's not good for little ones to be afraid, to feel insecure."

Alongside the values and lifestyles of the Nolans and the Hansons, the film families that dominated American screens throughout the forties seem singularly empty and shallow. The decade had marked a major departure in the image of the family. With few exceptions, what we are presented with are images of middle-class American families. Penrod's father is a banker, Mr. Aldrich is a lawyer, a profession shared by Billy's dad in *Father's Son* and Harry Graves in *Junior Miss*. Andy Hardy's father is a judge, and Susan's sister occupied a similar role in a rare image of a working mother (surrogate) in *The Bachelor and the Bobby Soxer*. The middle-class nature of the home is further reinforced by the presence of a maid, servant, or cook in films such as *The Decision of Christopher Blake*, *Always in My Heart, Janie, Father Was a Fullback, Margie*, and *A Date With Judy*. There is no question that such families existed in reality. In the 1949 study, *Elmstown's Youth*, Hollingshead described just such conditions in the homes of middle-class Americans:

> Prestige appears to depend as much upon civic leadership as upon economic success ... the family's income is earned largely by the male head through active daily participation in the practice of a large independent profession (law, medicine, engineering, dentistry...). Wives as homemakers, mothers and social secretaries run the home with the help of one general servant, usually part time, or the hourly services of one scrubwoman.[32]

In movies of the 1930's there was no such creature as an adolescent. There were adults, children, and youth or young people. In the films of the forties, however, we see what amounts to almost an obsession with adolescence, treated as a separate stage of life replete with its own views, values, and tribal customs. Again, there was some basis in reality for such a situation. With the war on, adolescence remained one of the few areas of society left intact. The drain of adult men into the theater of war, and the absorption of adult women into the war industry on the home front left these youngsters to their own devices. In the absence of the adults, they became a much more visible section of the population than before. Rosen suggests that "Hollywood movies exploited adolescent girls as if eager to fill the vacuum of female docility adult women had temporarily escaped."[33]

While this is true in part, there is much more to it. Clearly, adolescence as a stage of development was becoming a culturally accepted notion throughout the decade. Havighurst outlined his stages of adolescent developmental tasks in 1949, and in the same year Hollingshead wrote that:

> Elmstown's culture did not provide any community-wide procedures to help the adolescent define himself as an adolescent in the transition from child to adult. Of course, there are no rites and ceremonies such as are found among many preliterate people to signify the end of childhood and the beginning of adulthood. But what is more important, the culture has developed very few substitutes; so neither adults nor adolescents have group-wide conventions to guide them in their definitions of what to expect from either youth or adult. Moreover, the culture has few definitions either relative to the borders or divisions within the period called adolescence. Consequently, both age groups function in an ill-defined no-man's land that lies between the protected dependency of childhood where the parent is dominant and the independent world of the adult.[34]

But while it was right in recognizing the emergence of adolescence as a separate stage of development, Hollywood's depiction of it was somewhat one-sided. Rosen complains that more girls than ever attended college in the period before the outbreak of the war, yet rather than dealing with such realities, the industry chose instead to dwell upon the superficial and highly visible extremes of the bobby-soxer cult. More puzzling, perhaps, is what appears to have been the industry's reluctance or inability to deal with the war and the serious implications it held for the young.

While newspapers of the day abound with stories of war-fractured families and growing delinquency in the wake of parental absence, the industry, with the exception of rare examples such as *Youth Runs Wild* (1944), totally ignored what was clearly a national concern. When the war does become a concern of the young, more often than not it is trivialized. Thus we hear Miss Annie Rooney complaining that, "It's so difficult to get a proper gown, what with the war and all." In March 1945, when *Parents Magazine* was drawing attention to the involvement of the young in working for war bonds, infantile paralysis and Red Cross drives, Hollywood seemed more preoccupied with the pranks of the younger set. Given their failure to address the role of youth in the CCC and other organizations during the thirties, it is hardly surprising that the movie makers paid little attention to the response of young people to the war.

In looking more closely at film families of the forties one encounters, beneath the celluloid surface, evidence that changes were taking place. Despite Hollywood's preoccupation with the middle class, with bobby-soxers and with comedy, it is still possible to uncover images that can now be seen as forewarnings of a less humorous future. Between 1939 and 1949, despite the dominance of Andy Hardy, Janie, and those they represented, there existed a faint but discernible subterranean rumble that was to erupt in the years ahead.

In 1939, in an attempt to counter the Hardy series, Paramount introduced film audiences to Henry Aldrich in *What a Life*. Based on George Abbott's stage success, the screenplay was written by Charles Brackett and Billy Wilder, and featured Jackie Cooper as adolescent Henry. The series which emerged after the initial success in no way rivaled the quality of the Hardy films, although in some ways they closely followed the MGM series. Henry's initials were a reversal of Andy's. Andy's father was a judge while Henry's was a lawyer. Andy lived in the middle America of Carvel; Henry lived in Centerville. Both boys had live-in aunts, making for a kind of extended family.

The similarities tend to end there, however. While we have seen indications that critics and audiences alike saw in the Hardys a mirror of their own lives and dreams, the Aldrich series were often way off base. When *Variety* reviewed *Henry Aldrich, Editor* in 1942, they touched upon this very aspect:

It is possible that there is a high school and a community in this country today as shown in this opus. If so, it is an exception. Certainly parents aren't as stupid as portrayed in this latest Aldrich flight of the imagination.[35]

By the time this film was made, Jackie Cooper was too old for the role and had been replaced by Jimmy Lydon. As Henry, he is the perennial scapegoat and probably the most put-upon, down-and-out screen character of the day. Whether played by Cooper or Lydon, the character remains consistent. "Gee whiz, ever since I was a kid everybody discouraged everything I wanted to do," he complains. In contrast to the support Andy Hardy gets from his Aunt Millie, Henry's Aunt Harriet tells him, "When you start setting type for that paper, I'll stop reading it." In one film Henry sets about winning a competition that will take him to Alaska. Rather than find support or encouragement from his family, he finds himself rebuffed. His father dismisses the scheme as an idiotic idea, telling him, "You've got just one job and that's to prepare yourself to enter Princeton."

Throughout the series, whether accused of arson, of rigging school elections, or forced to do battle with his father in a courtroom, Henry proves to be a headache and a heartache for his parents, his principal and his friends. When he succeeds, it is not because of support and encouragement from home but from his own initiative and drive. When he runs for school president, his father does not want his election campaign cluttering up the house, and his sister is plainly embarrassed by him. In just about every film he winds up in trouble, usually through no fault of his own, and in the end, even when he has cleared his name and been embraced once more by his family, he remains in essence the misunderstood kid.

In this sense, he is a forerunner of a character who will become increasingly familiar in the next decade and in a distinctly more serious context. While Andy Hardy is part of his parents and they of him, Henry Aldrich stands apart, separated in speech, dress and manner from the lifestyle of his parents and, in particular, his father. Like so many screen parents of the 1950's, the Aldrich parents, as amusing and harmless as they may seem, stand too ready to condemn, too quick to blame, and too unwilling to believe in their own child. In the 1940's this could still exist as a source of mirth, but the next decade would quickly transform it to misery.

The films of the forties quite clearly establish the beginning rumbles of the youthquake that would explode on the screens in the following decade. The issues they deal with and the problems they raise all appear in one form or another in the fifties' cinema. While it may be Andy Hardy that we call to mind when we think of film families of the late thirties and early forties, if we scratch the surface long and hard enough, one can find evidence that there was more going on in the American family than life at the Hardy household might suggest.

In Warner's 1942 production of *Always in My Heart*, the problems of adolescence in a broken family were dealt with. Marty (Frankie Thomas) and Vicki (Gloria Warren) have been without a father for years. What they do not know is that their father is in prison in Chicago for a crime he did not commit. Their mother, whom they call Marge, begins dating businessman Philip Aimes who assures her, "What they need is a little masculine authority." The kids themselves are divided in their response to the prospective father. Marty accepts him because "he's got all his own teeth and a wad of dough," but Vicki rejects him because he talks down to the servants and "doesn't fit in." While Marty succumbs to the materialistic lure, accepting Philip's offer of new clothes, access to his boat, a new car, and ready cash, Vicki stands her ground, refusing to accept an offer to an expensive music school. She will not consider leaving her mother.

Parolled from prison, their father determines to observe how they are doing without them knowing who he is. When his daughter discovers his identity she asks bitterly, "Why has everyone been lying to me?" His response that "There are some things that you're not quite old enough to understand" seems destined to both infuriate and isolate a confused adolescent. Caught between her confused response to her discovery and a sense of betrayal at home where Philip has booked her into the music school, she runs away, only to be rescued from a dangerous sea by her father. Safe on shore, she and the family are united, the truth told, and a new life opened for them. While such a story could have dwelt on the relationship between Philip, Marge, and her husband, in the new consciousness of the early forties it is seen through the eyes of the children.

My Reputation (1946) examined the effect of a father's death upon his widow and children. Based on the Claire Jayner novel, it was directed for the screen by Curtis Bernhardt and starred Barbara Stanwyck as widowed Jess Drummond. Set in Lake Forest, Chicago, in 1942, the film opens after the death of her husband. In a letter he has left, her husband has advised her to "bring up the boys to stand alone," and she sets about fulfilling his wishes. Twelve-year-old Kim (Scotty Beckett) and fourteen-year-old Keith (Bobby Cooper) are anxious to see the Cubs and Dodgers game. Even though it follows so soon upon their father's death, Jess feels the boys should be out of the house. "Ball games don't happen every day in the week," she says understandingly, suggesting they tell her all about it afterwards, "the way you did with Dad." It is the first obvious attempt on her part to fulfill the role of both father and mother for the youngsters. Her action, however, shocks and infuriates her mother who favors a more formal period of mourning. Jess will not be dissuaded and defends her action: "Kim and Keith are too young to have their lives changed by their father's death."

But like it or not, her own life has been unalterably changed. Whereas the boys had been part of her life before, now she has to make them all of it. Alone and lonely, she needs them more than she ever has. But boys, as she discovers, will be boys. She plans an elaborate farewell to send them back to school only to discover that their budding interest in the opposite sex takes priority. Miserable, depressed and lonely in their absence, she has to brace herself and hide her feelings from them. "Of course I'll write, Mom, but gee whiz, a fella has a lot to do," one of them tells her as she feels the pang every parent must endure when realizing they are no longer the primary force in their children's lives. While the boys lose themselves in their school activities, Jess finds life without them increasingly difficult. "The house is closing down on me, everything is closing down on me."

Into her life comes Major Scot Landis, and what began as just a friendship blossoms into a romance. When her mother complains that the relationship is creating a bad reputation, Jess determines to "give the old biddies something to gossip about." The gossip reaches the ears of the children, home on Christmas leave. Upset, they confront their mother, demanding, "Mom, did you go to the fights with Mr. Landis? You came home on the train from Chicago at four o'clock in the morning." While they hope she will deny the stories and call them lies, Jess assures them she has done nothing wrong, that they have nothing to be ashamed of, and that she intends to continue seeing Landis.

When he tells her he is to be posted overseas and asks her to see him off, she is forced to decide between her own happiness and her obligation to the boys. If she goes with Landis she will be unable to be with them for their holidays and will not even be able to see them back off to school. For Kim and Keith, it is impossible to put themselves in their mother's position. All that they understand is that she has rejected them and betrayed their father. At this stage of their development, their egos are strong enough to lead their own lives without worrying about her needs and loneliness, while at the same time they are fragile enough to feel threatened by any rival for her affection. They run away to their grandmother's. When a distraught Jess follows them, they tell her, "You lied to us. We don't know what to believe. Don't you remember Dad at all? You belong to Dad. It doesn't make any difference whether he's dead or not." In tears she tells them of her loneliness. "Someday when you're older you'll understand that one can give one's heart to more than one person and still remain sincere and loyal."

Difficult as it is for them to understand, the boys know that they want and need their mother. She, in nearly losing them, realizes that at least for the time being, they are the most important people in her life. She cannot go to New York with Landis. "If I go now, it'll never be the same between them and me." Like so many of the mothers we have seen, Jess Drummond sacrifices her own happiness for her children.

The Decision of Christopher Blake (1948) continued the image of the troubled family. As the film opens, twelve-year-old Christopher (Ted Donaldson) returns from camp and is met by his mother at the station. Observing his father's absence the boy comments, "Guess now that I'm getting old he's getting tired of me." What he does not know but we come to rapidly suspect is that his parents have separated. Watching her son, Evie Blake (Alexis Smith) struggles to break the news to him. "Don't depend too much on anything, Chris, or people. I mean, everyone likes things to be just right, but it doesn't always work out that way. I know you think your father and I are pretty close to being perfect. We're not, Chris. Remember I told you that." In the end, however, she cannot bring herself to tell him. Once again back home, the boy happily occupies himself in the garage thinking of the atom bomb, practicing to be a radio announcer, and preparing to eat twelve more boxes of cereal in order to get his brand-new imitation tommy-gun. This boyhood world of fantasy and imagination will provide Chris a Billy Fisher-like escape from the problems his parents impose on him.

On the day of his thirteenth birthday, the news of his parents' separation hangs over him like a cloud. For Christopher, the coming of his teens has brought only misery. Neither his new bike, his chemistry set, nor the train can hold his attention, and he spends a miserable birthday with his equally unhappy mother. Uncertain as to how he is meant to feel, he tells her he still likes his dad. His outlet for his problems has always been his imagination. "When I close my eyes I can see what I'm thinking, just like a movie," he has said earlier.

Faced with the greatest problem of his life, it is hardly surprising that he escapes into flights of fantasy. But the dreams and imaginings all have a familiar theme, and in sleep or daydream he finds himself plagued by the issue of his parents' separation and pending divorce. "I wish I'd never been born," he cries in anguish as he feels drawn to them both and unable to make a decision. In one dream sequence he is at the White House to be honored for his peace plan. A Lincolnesque president is narrowly saved from assassination when Chris throws himself in the way. Mortally wounded, he dies while a shocked nation listens on the radio, a heavenly choir sings "Swing Low, Sweet Chariot," and the President announces that "now he belongs to the ages." In their common grief at the death of their son, his dream parents are reconciled.

But reality is not as convenient as fantasy, and the boy awakes to find himself faced with the awesome task of testifying at his parents' divorce and choosing which one he wishes to live with. "I want them both, but they don't want me—they don't care," he cries. Alone in the chamber with an understanding judge, the boy works out a plan by which each parent believes he has chosen the other to live with. Though each is hurt, they agree to go along with his decision, thus demonstrating that they care more for him than for themselves. The knowledge brings them together, and as they head home, a united family once again, the judge, in a familiar indication that parents can be children too, advises Christopher to "take 'em home and take care of them."

Indeed, one of the major concerns of the 1940's films might well be who takes care of whom. The 1930's, as we have seen, left children largely alone to struggle through and make their own way. The absentee parent of

that decade had given way to films that seem particularly concerned with the interaction between parent and child, between parent and adolescent. Although played for laughs, *My Reputation* and other films represented a more serious vision of problems confronting American families.

One of the most visible trends, and one that could not go unnoticed in the fifties, was the decline of the patriarch. While Penrod's mother justifiably intervened on the boy's behalf, the screen increasingly depicted fathers as well meaning but inept. With the exception of the Hardy series, few if any of the film families of the forties could be described as patriarchal. While we encounter films in which fathers do appear to make the household decisions, these decisions are often shown to be wrong or misguided. Thus in *Father's Son* (1941), while attorney Bill Emery is eminently qualified in his field, as a father he is a complete disaster, alienating both his son and his wife. In *The Jolson Story* (1946), while Al's father insists, "I think I know what's best for my son," the rest of the action shows quite plainly that he does not. Similarly, when Janie's party ends in the near demolition of her parents' house and the humiliation of her father's editorial policy, she escapes punishment by announcing she was simply doing her patriotic duty in entertaining the troops. In *My Dog Rusty* (1948), set in "the best little town in the world," Hugh Mitchell finds his wife telling him, "Maybe you lost Danny's confidence because you spanked him instead of listening to him."

Nowhere do we encounter a better example of the failure of the father than in 1948's *Cynthia*. Based on Vina Delma's play, *The Rich Full Life*, it introduces us to Louise and Larry Bishop and their teenage child. In their courting days, Louise and Larry had dreamed of studying in Vienna and building a medical clinic. But married life has not lived up to their expectations. They have allowed their failures and fears to dominate their lives and Cynthia's. As a result, their perfectly normal daughter is reduced to a cot case who is never permitted to enjoy the normal activities of girls her own age. She becomes a battleground over which the parents fight. While her mother believes "she's not a child anymore, she's growing up," Larry, ever fearful, clings desperately to the girl, both shielding and suffocating her. Unable to endure his behavior any longer, Louise turns on him. "There's a sickness here worse than Cynthia's. You, Larry. You're sick — sick with fear. Every day of your life you're afraid of saying or doing anything ... like your job, plodding along year after year because you haven't go the courage to demand what's coming to you."

Midway through the decade, *Since You Went Away* had proclaimed itself as "a story of that unconquerable fortress, the American home." By the end of the decade, although the fortress was still standing, there was increasing evidence that the foundations were extremely shaky.

Opposite: In *Cynthia* the accusations begin as cracks appear in the foundations of the family fortress.

3. Movies' Monstrous Moms

"It's all part of your contempt for the family unit. You think mother's a dirty word" —
Annabel Willart, *All Fall Down*, 1962.

In 1979 Christina Crawford shocked the world with *Mommie Dearest*, a startling account of life with her legendary mother, screen star Joan Crawford. Adding fuel to the fire, Faye Dunaway played Crawford in the 1981 film based upon the best seller. Despite the controversy that surrounded both the film and the book, none should be amazed by the bizarre behavior attributed to the star, nor the torment she appears to have visited upon her children. From its earliest days, Hollywood attracted neurotic, star-crazed mothers who used their children to claw their way to the top.

> My mother was so terrible, so sadistic to me, I could only laugh at her. It was the only reaction—laugh or die. She was good only to create chaos ... She'd slap me across the mouth and shout, "Go out there and sing!" She was completely impossible. She called me a whore—I was two years old.... Can you imagine anyone calling a two-year-old baby a whore?[1]

The words belong to Judy Garland. Sadly enough her story has not been that unfamiliar within the families that inhabit the film capital of the world. It is therefore not altogether surprising to discover the negative treatment that motion pictures have increasingly given to mothers.

In 1981 *Ordinary People* won the Academy Award for best picture. In part it was the story of a failed mother (Mary Tyler Moore) who, unable to respond to the needs of either her husband or son, fled the family home. The year before, the best picture was awarded to *Kramer vs. Kramer*, in which Meryl Streep recognized her inability to function as a mother and surrendered her young son to Dustin Hoffman, as though succumbing to the belief that father knows best. Yet rather than representing a recent trend, the negative depiction of mother has long roots and one finds Joan Crawford at the forefront of the movement.

50

Mildred Pierce (1945): **Film noir introduces screen audiences to an image of a twisted and unrepentant murderess.**

Despite the favorable image created by Mrs. Hardy and other screen mothers of the late thirties and forties, there was a faint but nonetheless visible trend throughout the period to depict mothers in anything but a sympathetic light. The most obvious example occurred in 1945's *Mildred Pierce*, for which Crawford won an Oscar. Directed by Michael Curtiz, it was based upon the James M. Cain novel and presented a fascinating image of Stella Dallas gone wrong. Within the more simplistic cinema of the thirties, Stella's daughter was able to survive the fractured family by being safely transplanted to a new home. By the end of the war, society was less simplistic and less innocent. The cinema of adolescence, while essentially played for laughs, was not immune to the influence of Freudian psychology or film noir. In *Mildred Pierce* we find one of the earliest films to acknowledge the darker side of adolescence.

Joan Crawford starred as working-class Mildred who "never knew any other kind of life, just cooking and washing and having children." She works hard at home and sells cakes to make extra money so that her daughters Kay and Veda can have as much as is humanly possible. Her unemployed husband resents her attempt to raise the children beyond their station. As far as he is concerned, rather than helping them she is making them "fresh and stuck up." The trouble is, he warns her, "you're trying to buy love from these kids and it won't work."

As differences grow between Mildred and her husband it becomes apparent that they can no longer remain together as a family. Her obsession with the children leaves little room in her life to share with him. "Those kids come first in this house before either one of us. I'm determined to do the best I can for them. If I can't do it with you, I'll do it without you."

But Mildred finds the going tougher than she expected. Ballet and piano lessons have given her older daughter, Veda (Ann Blyth), a taste for the better things in life. Despite her mother's efforts and endeavors, the girl looks down on her. "I wouldn't be seen dead in this rag. It's horrible. How could she have bought me such a thing." Seemingly unaffected by her parents' separation, Veda condemns her father's lady friend as "distinctly middleclass," and lobbies for her mother to marry money in order for them to get a new house, limousine and a maid. When Mildred looks to her daughter for affection she is told, "I love you, Mother. I really do. But let's not be sticky about it."

Mildred takes a job in a restaurant to bring in money and even works long hours at home baking for the business. When Veda discovers what her mother is doing she lashes out angrily, "Did you have to degrade us?" She has turned into a first-class snob. "You've never spoken of your people, who you came from." Furious, her mother slaps her. It is the opening shot in the battle between parent and child that broke into open warfare in the decades ahead.

The death of the younger daughter turns Mildred more than ever to a single-minded obsession with Veda. She accumulates money and manages to buy a small business that blossoms into a chain of restaurants. In the meantime, Veda has continued to "grow into a young lady with expensive tastes." She borrows money from her mother's employees, takes up smoking, and takes it for granted when presented with a brand new car for her birthday. Now seventeen, she is more headstrong than ever.

Mildred had encouraged her to spend time with her own boyfriend, Monty Berrigan III. Monty, however, is no better than Veda. Realizing that he's a bad influence on the girl, Mildred severs her relationship with him and warns him to leave Veda alone: "Stay away from Veda. She's only seventeen years old and spoiled rotten.... I'm losing her. She's starting to drift away from me.... She hardly speaks to me anymore except to ask for money or poke fun at me in French because I work for a living." How sharper than a serpent's tooth it is to have a thankless child!

Veda is thoroughly twisted and stands alone in American cinema of the 1930's and 1940's as an obnoxious, evil, and unrepentant adolescent. One review greeted her as "the nastiest brat that ever broke a mother's heart."[2] But if Veda is nasty, the source of her twisted character is clearly identified. While the wayward youth of the 1930's were essentially decent, their problems stemming from social conditions, Veda is clearly the product of the home. Her values and lifestyle spring entirely from what she has learned, not from school or society, but from her parents and from her mother in particular.

Not content to ruin her own family, she sets about ruining others. She traps a wealthy boy into marrying her. Claiming she is pregnant, she forces a financial settlement and then has the marriaged dissolved. There is, of course, no child. She has used the child as an excuse to get money. Mildred, on the other hand, had made the mistake of using money in order to try and win her child. Her total failure comes painfully home to her when Veda triumphantly tells her, "With this money I can get away from you and your chickens and your pies and your kitchens." For the first time Mildred is able to utter the words that she has gradually realized as true: "You're cheap and horrible." When Veda tells her, "You'll never be anything but a common frump," Mildred destroys the check and they set about slapping each other. It is a powerful and profoundly disturbing moment in a cinema that had long been given to at least the outward pleasantries of family life.

The tragedy for Mildred Pierce is not that she has lost her daughter, but that she cannot lose her. Like some alcoholic in need of drink, she cannot keep away from the girl. When Veda leaves, Mildred's life becomes empty and meaningless. She takes to drink. Ultimately she convinces the girl to return home, but when Veda returns it is for money, not mommy. Nothing about her mother has changed. Completely unconcerned by the fact that her mother has married Monty, she begins to resume her relationship with him. Mildred finds them together and Veda insists Monty is leaving to marry her. Monty, however, has no intention of marrying "a rotten little tramp like you." The girl's world of illusion is finally shattered and she must see herself as others do. Angry and rejected, she shoots and kills him.

Even this does not turn her mother from her. Mildred tells the police that she killed Monty, but they know the truth. Veda is led away where she must finally answer for her life to authorities who will demand more from her than her mother was ever capable of. As Mildred steps out into the corridor of police headquarters, a new day is beginning. Her former husband is there waiting for her. Together they must weigh well their daughter's words, "It's your fault I'm the way I am."

Mildred is no monster. Indeed, in some ways she is a character with whom we must sympathize. *Commonweal* called Crawford's role "a moving and thoroughly understanding performance as a suffering wife and mother," observing that "no one deserves the kicking around that life gives this courageous, though frequently mistaken, women."[3]

Understanding the importance of *Mildred Pierce* requires a reading of the film style as much as the statement. While the film is told in flashback and ostensibly is a whodunnit, the real issue is not about the killing of one man but about a pervasive threat to all men.

The film is split between the noir sequences in which Mildred is absorbed into the action, carried along by the tide of events that go on beyond her orbit of influence, and the sequences which she narrates, which are more evenly lit and feature less camera angles. In these scenes, Mildred serves to control the narrative. She expounds on life as she lived it—indeed, as she seemed to control it. But her very control is undermined by the intrusion of the noir sequences in which she is cast into shadows, rendering her somehow incomplete.

When Mildred meets Monty the film appears to be turning into a classic woman's movie with the love theme dominant. Such a suggestion is enhanced by several shots from the male point of view, but again Mildred is rendered incomplete. Monty visits her and we see her sitting on top of a ladder, but only her legs are visible in the frame. The sexual implications of the film's style are best realized in the final scenes. Within the police station Mildred has attempted to subvert justice by covering up for her daughter. Mother love is thus shown to be not simply blind but decidedly dangerous. Throughout her attempted confession, Mildred is shown once again in shadow. Only when the truth is revealed by the paternalistic detective is the scene fully lit. It is the detective who restores light and symbolic social order when he opens the venetian blinds. In the hallway Mildred reconciles with her former husband, thus demolishing the matriarchy and restoring her by implication to society and to the safe and ordered lifestyle of the patriarchal order.

Mildred's attempt to be more than a mother has brought chaos. By seeking to move beyond the home and kitchen, she has displaced her husband as the traditional provider, ruined Veda's life, contributed to the death of her younger daughter, and denied herself her proper role as wife and mother. In her restaurant she has continued the role of castrating woman by assigning potato peeler and apron (traditional woman's props) to her male associates. In her splendid analysis of the film, Pam Cook has written that it is

> based on the brutal and enforced repression of female sexuality, and the institutionalization of a social place for both men (as fathers and husbands) and women (as mothers and wives).[4]

To understand the new image of the mother presented by *Mildred Pierce*, one needs to be aware of changes taking place in American society.

The war had had a major impact: with men removed from the home front, women were increasingly called upon to exercise roles traditionally assigned to males. While Rosie the Riveter made a valuable contribution to the war effort, at least unconsciously she must be taken as a sexual threat to the patriarchal order. Throughout the war years, the government had encouraged women to enter the work force, to assume traditional men's jobs. Films such as *Women of Steel* wholeheartedly endorsed this process. Hollywood also played its part. *Since You Went Away* (1945) found Claudette Colbert forsaking the comforts of middle-class life to don a welder's mask and torch. After the war, however, when the men returned home, they needed jobs to go back to. The same government that had encouraged women to be resourceful and independent now employed movie propaganda to suggest that if they would not fulfill their function as wives and mothers, they were only half women. Such a view was evident in Hollywood's happy homemaker syndrome.

Freudian psychology had also begun to creep into the national consciousness. Freud had died in 1939. In the same year he had appeared on the cover of *Time* magazine. The nazi regime in Europe had driven many of his devotees to the United States, where his works became more widespread. *The American Journal of Sociology* devoted an entire issue to him. At the same time, one encounters evidence of several Hollywood producers who subscribed to *The Psychoanalytical Review*. The war also lead to an increasing awareness of mental illness. *Since You Went Away* found a youthful Jennifer Jones quoting psychological theory and exposed to returning soldiers suffering the aftermaths of war. In 1945 the first *Yearbook of Psychoanalysis* appeared. It is therefore not surprising to encounter, particularly within film noir, themes dealing with Oedipal conflict, castration complexes, or mother fixations. In 1949's *White Heat*, for example, James Cagney played a criminal with a twisted mother fixation. As he dies in a ball of flame, he says, "Look, Ma. Finally made it. Top of the world!"

None of this, however, is to suggest a new and dramatic change in the depiction of movie mothers. Mrs. Hardy, Mrs. Aldrich, and most of the mothers we encounter throughout the films of the forties are still almost sacrosanct. Louis B. Mayer in particular was fastidious about the image projected by Mrs. Hardy, and was not loathe to change lines which showed her in a less than favorable light.

While Hollywood pursued this image of the film mother there were those who, while understanding it, were far from appreciative. Writing in *Their Mother's Sons*, Edward A. Strecker suggested that excessive mothering had resulted in immature young men, which had in turn impeded the American war effort. Mom, he suggested, was

> a convenient verbal hook upon which to hang an indictment of the woman who has failed in the elementary function of weaning her offspring, emotionally as well as physically."[5]

In *A Generation of Vipers*, published in 1942, Philip Wylie condemned the American obsession with motherhood:

> Mom is everywhere and everything and damned near everybody, and from her depends all the rest of the U.S. Disguised as good old mom, sweet old mom, your loving mom and so on, she is the bride at every funeral and the corpse at every wedding. Men live for her and die for her, dote upon her and whisper her name as they pass away, and I believe she has now achieved in the hierarchy of miscellaneous articles a spot next to the Bible and the Flag, being reckoned part of both in a way.[6]

In the cinema of adolescence of the 1940's, it is difficult to find an image of mother as negative and vitriolic as these accounts. It would take another decade before mother came in for the sort of sustained negativism that had for so long been part of Hollywood's vision of the father.

While Hollywood had long cherished the image of motherhood, mother love and self sacrifice, which were seen as constant companions, it did not take long for the fifties to bear witness to a change in attitude. *Our Very Own* (1950) featured Ann Blyth as eighteen-year-old Gail Macauley. On the day of her birthday the girl discovers that she has been adopted. Hurt and betrayed, she is obsessed with finding her real mother. When she does, her dreams of a loving reconciliation are shattered. In a shabby, run-down house full of alcohol, cigarettes, and card-playing men, she at last finds her mother. Discovering neither love nor understanding, she finds instead a pitiful and aging woman who made a mistake and had a baby. She herself was "just one of those things." To her mother she has never been anything but a momentary inconvenience. The girl ultimately returns to the family that raised her, but the mother who had no time for her was to become a familiar screen figure, whether in drama or comedy.

Darling How Could You (1951) was a comedy set in the early part of the century. In the characters of Dr. Robert Gray and his wife Alice, we encounter what were to become familiar film figures. Caught up in their own interests and work they have been away for several years while the children have been raised by a grandmother. Fox's 1953 Bette Davis vehicle, *The Star*, presented a similar image of parental neglect. Although actress Margaret Elliott loves her daughter Gretchen, she places her career first, forcing an unhappy youngster to live with her father and step-mother. It's not simply that the star is too busy for her daughter; she simply has no idea what is involved in being a parent. When asked at one point what the girl is like, she can only reply, "Well, how can you tell what a kid's like?"

Although the book had been written years before, and the story was set in America on the eve of her entry into World War I, *East of Eden* (1954)

Opposite: Steinbeck's classic story *East of Eden* (1954) touched a sensitive nerve in young audiences with its story of a clash between a father and his son.

and in particular the character of Cal Trask were firmly rooted in the American consciousness of the mid-fifties. Directed by Elia Kazan, who had brought Brando to the screen, the movie was made by Warners and was based on a small section of John Steinbeck's novel. Steinbeck, however, did not complain, calling the film the best translation of one of his novels he had seen. In the presence of James Dean, Kazan managed to touch a sensitive nerve in American youth that was galvanized into a cult status upon his untimely death.

As the film opens, our first view of Dean is that of a lone figure, isolated from humanity and dwarfed by his environment. We are in the promised land of California. An American flag flies overhead. The camera tilts and below it, like one of the huddled masses, we encounter Cal as he sits on the sidewalk. He hears Kate approaching and slowly, hesitantly watches as she passes by. What we do not yet know and what the boy merely suspects is that Kate is his mother. Dressed all in black, she is on her way to the bank. She is the town madam. With an empty heart and a full bank account, she is cold, calculating, proud, and aloof; and somewhere out there on the streets of America, beneath the stars and stripes, her son, whom she has walked out on, is reaching out for love and understanding. The image of the American mother had undergone a major transformation. Just ten years before, Mildred Pierce had given everything to try to help her children. Kate has given up her children to get everything for herself.

Cal's character is created for us in that moment as his mother passes him by. He is a curious boy, attractive yet shy, questioning yet unable to express these questions in words, independent yet vulnerable. He breaks from the posture of security rocking and follows the woman home. Outside he marches restlessly back and forth, and then defiantly throws rocks at the house. It is a senseless, futile action.

Later, in the bar of the brothel, he asks a young waitress about Kate. "Is there anything nice about her at all?" By implication, he is hoping that if Kate has a redeeming feature, then he himself cannot be all bad. The scene with the girl, although brief, says so much about Cal's appeal. There is, in his pain and vulnerability, a visible need that says, "Trust me and I will be your friend." As he sits at the bar, the girl is both drawn to him and afraid of him. His presence threatens her yet she cannot reject him. "You sure have got a nerve," she tells him, full of both admiration and fear. Yet in the end, though she knows in helping him she may be hurting herself, she leads him upstairs to his mother's room.

How must Dean himself have felt outside his screen mother's door, playing a character in search of love and answers from the past, while all the while he himself, deprived of his own mother as a boy, looked back, if not in anger, then at least in anguish. One friend of Dean's commented:

> Jimmy had a terrible anger for his mother. She died. He was a nine-year-old child saying, 'how can you leave me?' When he talked about her

it wasn't a twenty-one or twenty-two-year-old. It was a child and he was
deserted. He'd loved her desperately and she left him. I think it had a
profound effect on him and he expressed it in terms of his art.[7]

Entering Kate's office, he finds her asleep in the chair. He draws
nearer and kneels. Madonna and child? But this is no sainted woman.
Instead of embracing the boy, she awakens to have him dragged screaming
from the room. Clutching desperately at the door, terrifyingly intent on
ensuring that he is not once more rejected, Cal finds himself physically torn
from his goal. And for what? What is it that the boy demands? What is it
that he seeks that his parents cannot fulfill? What is it he asks, begs, pleads
for? "Talk to me, please," he screams at her.

The following year Dean once again featured as an adolescent
troubled by sexual imbalance in his family. In *East of Eden* he had been
plagued by parents too strong to exist together, too weak to give him the
love he needed. In *Rebel Without a Cause* he played Jim Stark, a teenager
trying to grow up in a family that seemed more like a circus. While he
struggles with his sense of self, trying to find a code of honor with which he
can live, he watches his mother slowly destroy his father. "She eats my
father alive and he takes it," he complains to a juvenile officer. The boy
struggles to talk to his parents but cannot overcome his mother's domination "She doesn't want to hear. She doesn't care," he screams at his
father, running from the house.

In both films Dean appeared as the victim of a family torn apart.
Rather than an aberration, the image he brought to the screen must be considered as representative of the period. While Dean himself as an icon came
to stand for much more than a boy battling with his parents, in that aspect
of the image as in the rest of the legend that grew up around him, he must be
considered as a barometer of the times. Reuel Denney has written that he
"could say more about post-war youth than most young people themselves
or their parents and teachers."[8]

The image of the mother established in *Rebel Without a Cause*
repeated itself in *The Restless Years* (1958). Set in the small town of Liberty,
it featured Sandra Dee and John Saxon as two young people afflicted by
problems imposed upon them by their mothers. As Melinda Grant, Dee
suffers humiliation and guilt because she is illegitimate. Her trauma is a repetition of a theme that appeared the previous year in *Peyton Place*, where
Allison McKenzie suffered from the stigma of illegitimacy. It is, however, in
the character of seventeen-year-old Will Henderson that one can best see the
impact of Dean. "If there was just one day when I wasn't confused," Jim
Stark had told the juvenile officer, and Will Henderson echoes him: "If I
could stay in one place a little longer, maybe I could figure out a few
things." Jim's family is constantly on the move, shifting from town to town
at his mother's insistence, hoping the boy will finally settle down. The
source of Jim's restlessness, however, is his mother and the stranglehold she

The Restless Years (1958): Sandra Dee as the victim of a sexually repressed mother.

has on the family. Similarly, Will's ambitious mother constantly harasses and henpecks her husband. Like Mrs. Stark, Mrs. Henderson obviously wears the pants in the house. She is plainly ashamed of her husband. "I don't want my son to have to tell his friends that his father is the assistant manager of a supermarket."

The continued negative image of the mother was repeated yet again in the same film where one youngster endured an alcoholic mother. The following year, Dee featured once again as an adolescent troubled by her relationship with her mother. Douglas Sirk's re-make of John N. Stahl's 1934 *Imitation of Life* added to the racial theme a contemporary portrait of a troubled middle-class adolescent (Sandra Dee) in conflict with her mother. Dee, who had made a career out of such roles, would turn back in the same year and retreat to the circa-forties family via *Gidget*. In the Sirk vehicle, however, she played adolescent Susan Meredith, the daughter of a wealthy actress (Lana Turner) who could remember poorer times. Raised in this broken but well-supported home, she has been indulged and has arrived upon her adolescence as a thoroughly spoiled but nonetheless engaging young woman. Like Mildred Pierce, Lora Meredith had determined early that her daughter would never want for anything. "No matter what it costs, Suzy's going to have everything that I missed." In the process, however, the work that provides the money to meet Suzy's needs also deprives her of her mother's company. The girl is forced to write notes to herself so that she will remember what she wants to discuss with her mother. More often than not she turns to Annie Johnson, their black cook, for advice. Annie and her own daughter Sarah Jane (Susan Kohner) have lived with the Merediths since both children were small. For both girls, childhood was a happier if poorer experience. Suzy still had her mother and Sarah Jane had not yet become sensitive to her mother's color. Able to pass as white, she has grown to resent her mother and to reject her race. "I want to have a chance in life. I don't want to have to come through back doors or feel lower than other people, or apologize for my mother's color. She can't help her color but I can and I will." When her white boyfriend discovers that her mother is black he beats her, and the girl determines to leave home. Her ailing mother follows her and an angry Sarah Jane pleads with her, "If by accident we should ever pass on the street, please don't recognize me."

The split between Annie and Sarah Jane is mirrored by the growing rift between Suzy and Lora. As Veda had found herself attracted to Mildred's husband, so Suzy now finds herself drawn to Steve Archer, a longtime boyfriend of her mother. With Lora so often away and preoccupied with business, Suzy has spent much of her time with the man. Though Steve has never encouraged her fantasies, her adolescent imaginings get the best of her. When she learns that her mother is to marry Steve, the scene is set for an explosive encounter. "Miss Lora, you've got to be very careful the way you handle Suzy—she's got a real problem," Annie warns. "Problem? Why don't I know about it? Why didn't she come to me?" "Maybe because you weren't around." When mother and daughter meet, the girl's jealousy and felt neglect are given expression. "So Annie told you! Well, that's how you usually find things out about me. Let's face it, Momma, Annie's always been more like a real mother. You never had time for me."

Tired and heart-broken, Annie dies. In one of the most memorable moments the cinema of sob has to offer, the film closes with her stately funeral. Mahalia Jackson sings. A team of white horses draws a flower-covered coffin through the streets and a marching band plays as respectful bystanders watch, hats in hand. Moments before, a hysterical Sarah Jane has burst through a cordon of police and a crowd of spectators to throw herself at her mother's coffin crying, "I killed my mother! I didn't mean it — I'm sorry, Momma!" Helped into a car, she drives away, comforted by the Merediths who, in the Johnson tragedy, discover a chance to save themselves.

It is a fitting image with which to close a decade, for in the death of Annie, Hollywood buried its long cherished image of the American mother. Like *Rebel Without a Cause, East of Eden*, and so many other films of the era, it resorted to the compulsory happy ending, promising redemption and reconciliation. If tradition demanded such endings, then logic rebutted them. In fashioning a new image of the American mother, the industry created a Frankenstein from which it could not escape. The long-preserved image of the mother as the heart and hub of the home, the one who interpreted life to her husband and the children, underwent a major change.

Kate Trask, though considerably watered down from the book, is a complete reversal of Stella Dallas and Mildred Pierce. Faced with a choice of finding happiness for herself or her children, she does not hesitate in putting herself first. Jim Stark's mother and his grandmother dominate both the boy and his father with disastrous results. In *The Goddess* (1958) Kim Stanley is never able to break from the guilt and insecurity her mother has imposed upon her. *A Summer Place* (1959) crowned the new image in the character of Helen Jorgensen. Shrill, vitriolic, materialistic, suspicious, and predatory, she is a thoroughly anti-life character totally lacking in sensitivity and incapable of functioning as a mother. The vision of mother that Wylie and Strecker had condemned in the forties had at last found expression on the screens of the nation.

> The myth of Big Mama is on the upswing. When Philip Wylie crusaded some years back for misogony, a fair sized opposition went into action. But now everybody's in his corner; you couldn't raise a skirmish if you wanted to. It would seem that Wylie's rantings weren't wrong; he was simply a bit prematurely anti-mom. Today, no one would be caught dead saying a kind word for anybody's mother. The image of Big Bad Bold Mama has become part of the American way of life.[9]

Looking at June Allyson, Rosen has suggested that she typified the film wife of the fifties. In this world, Rosen says, "women slipped into masculine shadows and domestic aprons and cleaned house."[10] Yet the cinema of adolescence reveals a distinctly different image of both American mothers and fathers. In the Stark household, it is Jim's father who wears an apron and cleans house, while his wife clearly rules the roost.

Such a dramatic change in the image of the American mother must be seen at least in part as a reflection of changing social conditions. Since the outbreak of the Second World War, women had assumed a greater degree of control in the world of business. In 1940, 450,000 women were classified as managers or supervisors. By 1956, the figure had grown to 932,000. The number of women in the professions had grown during the same period from 1,157,000 to 2,125,000.

Unable to come to terms with this reality, Hollywood responded to this new woman by turning her into the household heavy. When we are not directly presented with momstrous moms, we find ourselves looking at pathetic women, half-human creatures who remain unfulfilled because they have not embraced the traditional role of motherhood. *All About Eve* (1950) presented Margot Channing, a Broadway star capable of pungent lines and stinging dialogue, but a total failure as a woman. *Sunset Boulevard* (1950) repeated the same image in the twisted persona of Norma Desmond. While both films were startlingly successful, the image they presented was hardly new. The wives and mothers that so dislocated the lives of their youngsters throughout films of the fifties are mere extensions of Mildred Pierce. It is their ambition, independence and assertiveness that emasculates their husbands and traumatizes their homes. While Joan Crawford had helped to create the image, she, like the industry, found herself trapped by it. Biographer Bob Thomas has written that:

> from Mildred Pierce on, a show of innocence was impossible. Her portrayals could no longer be complementary to men, they were competitive with men. She sought to destroy them, not to entice them. Crawford detested her own image. She fought against the role of the castrating woman and yet she was drawn inexorably by the image, both off the screen and on. As a woman alone in the world's most competitive business, she was forced to compete as a man, and as an aging star, her only hope for survival was to find roles that stressed her invincibility.[11]

By late in the decade, the monstrous matriarch was seemingly invincible. Tennessee Williams, himself a victim of a domineering mother, filled the stage and screen with clutching, clawing mothers who were unwilling to give their children room to breathe. *The Glass Menagerie* (1950), *Cat On a Hot Tin Roof* (1958), and *Suddenly Last Summer* (1959) continued to add portraits to the rogues' gallery of motherhood. If the neurotic characters of these stories seemed bizarrely out of place, there is ample evidence to suggest they reflected an underlying mood in fifties society.

"Are You an Everyday Neurotic?" *Cosmopolitan* asked in 1952, adding that "This is about you and me and the lady next door."[12] "Does Your Family Have Neurosis?" *Colliers* wondered in February[13] 1953. *Esquire* ran a cover story on "The Crisis in American Masculinity," and *Look* sought to understand the domination of the American male by

American women. To this extent, the cinema of adolescence and in particular its changing image of the American mother can be seen as a mirror of social change. In presenting such changes, however, the industry seemed obsessed with the image and unable to develop the issues that were at their heart. While fifties movies can thus be seen to echo social concerns and problems, they did little to further our understanding of these issues.

In his inaugural speech of 1953, Eisenhower made reference to the swift rush of events which leave us groping to know the full sense and meaning of the times in which we live. With Hollywood as our guide in the case of the family, we came to see only the what, without ever understanding the why.

"You can hate a mountain because it cuts off the sun, but one morning you wake up and find that it's gone and everything's empty without it." The words were spoken by Tony Perkins in 1958's *This Angry Age* as he contemplates the death of his mother. As the new decade opened, Perkins found himself more than ever trapped and terrorized by the stranglehold his mother had on him. In *Psycho* (1960) he played Norman Bates, a young man so obsessed with his mother that he murders her when she takes a lover and then, driven by guilt, exhumes her body and assumes her personality. As the film closes there is no Norman Bates; only his body remains, but for all intents and purposes it is inhabited by his mother.

It is a not insignificant film with which to begin an examination of the adolescent and the family in films of the 1960's. Norman's relationship with his mother represents a new and startling development that, while touched upon in *The Goddess* and more than hinted at in *Suddenly Last Summer*, had its roots in the writings of the forties and was only now coming into its own in the cinema. Years earlier, Wylie had written of Mom that:

> Her boy, having been protected by her love and carefully, even shudderingly, shielded from his logical development through his barbaric period of childhood (so that he has either to become a barbarian as a man or else to spend most of his energy denying the barbarianism that howls in his brain — an autonomous remnant of the youth he was forbidden), is cushioned against any major step in his progress toward maturity. Mom steals from the generation of women behind her (which she has, as a still further defense, also sterilized of integrity and courage) that part of her boy's personality which should have become the love of a female contemporary. Mom transmutes it into sentimentality for herself.[14]

Film after film through the sixties reveals a love/hate relationship between mother and son, between mother and daughter. Paul Morel is more than a little ambivalent in *Sons and Lovers* (1960). Ted struggles with his mother Roberta in *Return to Peyton Place* (1961). The Tyrone family in

Long Days Journey Into Night (1962) is haunted by the spectre of their dope-ridden mother. In *All Fall Down* (1962), Angela Lansbury plays a middle-class mother who emasculates her husband and drives her oldest son from home into a sterile, loveless life. She repeated her role of ballbuster in the same year in another John Frankenheimer film, *The Manchurian Candidate*. So malevolent a mother is she that not only her family but the entire United States and western world is saved from her manipulation only by her assissination. In *The World of Henry Orient* just two years later, she starred as the selfish mother of adolescent Valerie Boyd.

In *The Stripper* (1963), Claire Trevor exerted a hold over her son Kenny (Richard Beymer) that he found difficult to break from. Beymer, who had been mother-dominated in Hemingway's *Adventures of a Young Man* (1962), seemed to be making a career of such roles by the time he played Rosalind Russell's son in 1962's *Five Finger Exercise*. In this play by Peter Schaffer (who would further develop the son as victim in *Equus*), Beymer played a college student, awkward with girls, uncomfortable with his father, dominated by his mother and, although it is never made explicit, quite possibly homosexual.

Movie mothers of the sixties got more than their fair share of the hatchet on both sides of the Atlantic. Deenie's mother in *Splendor in the Grass* (1961) is more than a little responsible for her daughter's mental illness. Jo's mother is treated rather negatively in *A Taste of Honey* (1962), as is Colin Smith's mother in Tony Richardson's *Loneliness of the Long Distance Runner*, made in the same year. Joey Heatherton plays a teenage murderess in 1965's *Where Love Has Gone* and the finger of guilt is pointed quited clearly at both her mother and grandmother. In *Wild in the Streets* (1968), Chris Jones assumed the presidency only to lock his mother and her generation in concentration camps and blow their minds with LSD.

Perhaps the most malicious movie mother of all was Annabel Willart in *All Fall Down*. Based on the novel by James Leo O'Herlihy, scripted by William Inge and brought to the screen by MGM, it introduced movie audiences to a character who called to mind the writings of Strecker. He had written of domineering, grasping mothers exerting a stranglehold on their children. "She treats them," he says, "as possessions rather than individuals who have a right to their own lives."[15] In January, 1961, *American Mercury* had asked, "Lady, Are You the Man of the House?"[16] In the Willart household of *All Fall Down*, we see in Annabel a mother and wife who spectacularly fills both bills.

Set in Cleveland, the film examines in painful detail a family that has gone wildly astray. Dominated by his wife, Ralph Willart (Karl Malden) retreats from her onslaught into a world of bourbon and jigsaw puzzles, as though cushioning the pain with one gesture and searching for an answer in the other. Driven from home by the smothering attention of his mother, Berry-Berry (Warren Beatty) has proved incapable of making anything of his life and drifts from bed to bed with contempt for all women and himself.

At home, younger brother Clinton (Brandon deWilde) inherits his mother's coddling and struggles to suppress his discomfort. Having cut school for months, he seems incapable of organizing his life and already manifests signs of becoming the aimless drifter his brother has become. Neither parent seems capable of exercising any control over him or of being able to help him come to terms with himself. The distance between Clinton and his mother is seen in the fact that he refers to her as Annabel. She is thus reduced to the role of servant rather than mother. By using her Christian name, the boy manages to distance himself from her effusiveness, a process which she resents. "It's all part of your contempt for the family unit. You think mother's a dirty word," she complains. It is a remark that serves as an editorial comment on the vision of family life as presented in motion pictures of the period.

And yet if Ralph and the boys have comtempt for the family unit, Annabel must be seen as a contributing agent to that attitude. Loving neither wisely nor well, she uses her emotions as a web and a weapon with which to ensnare her family. Clinton is in adolescence, but she fusses over him unrestrainedly, calling him "my baby." It is this domination, this desire to possess that has driven Berry-Berry from home and turned him into a misogynist. "I guess you know I hate her guts," he tells Clinton. Yet despite his obvious aversion to his mother he cannot shake free of her. No matter what he does, no matter how irresponsible or malicious he becomes, his mother will not renounce her love for him. Indeed, her love is a sick and poisoned passion that eats at her family like a cancer. When Berry-Berry begins to find himself attracted to a woman, there is no mistaking the jealousy Annabel feels. "It hurts, when the boy you love loves somebody else." In smothering her son with her love she denies her husband the love due him. A brilliant man, he has become a burnt-out hulk, passing his life with puzzles and drink. Unwilling to relinquish the illusion she has of Berry-Berry returning to live with her, she is intent on destroying what few illusions her husband still has.

When he arrives home at Christmas with three drunks, wishing to share season's cheer with strangers, she sets about getting rid of them. In a twisted parody of the Christmas story, she meticulously plots to send the three "wise men" on their way while she awaits the homecoming of Berry-Berry, her "savior." Given the season and particular importance families place on being together at that time, it is hardly surprising that Annabel should not welcome the drunks with open arms. To that extent, she is not unlike many wives faced with a similar situation. The point at which she departs from a reasonable reaction, however, comes when she uses their presence to undermine her husband's authority and belittle him in front of Clinton. Ralph firmly believes that the men want someone to share Christmas with. With a basic faith in the goodness and decency of men he has opened his home to them in the hope that they can share the spirit of Christmas. Annabel more cynically believes that the bums are simply looking for a handout. When Ralph tells her Berry-Berry is not coming home, she turns on him, bitterly intent on reciprocating by shattering his illusion. She offers the men money to leave and they take it and depart.

In destroying each other's illusions, Annabel and Ralph foreshadow the ultimate fractured family presented later that decade in Albee's *Who's Afraid of Virginia Woolf?* Like Annabel, Martha (Washington?) is the smotherer/mother. Like Ralph, George (Washington? father of the nation?) escapes into a bottle. While George and Martha await the coming home of their phantom son, Ralph and Annabel wait for Berry-Berry. In Albee's vision of the American family, the home is reduced to a battle-ground in which phantom parents fight over the life and death of phantom children.

While not all screen parents deteriorated to such behavior, there can be no mistaking the sustained and systematic attack on motherhood. However unrealistic the reconciliations of the fifties may have seemed, they were at least testimony to a faith in the endurance of the family. The film families of the sixties are morally bankrupt, bereft of principles, and unable to offer guidance to the young. Although Daisy loves her mother (*Inside Daisy Clover*; 1966), the woman is incapable of functioning as a positive force in her daughter's life: "My mother says this world's a garbage dump and we're just the flies it attracts." Similarly, when Mick Kelly turns to her mother for advice (*The Heart Is a Lonely Hunter*; 1968), she finds little encouragement. Lost in adolescent daydreams, believing herself to be destined, she finds her mother's view of life startlingly blunt: "If you're lucky you'll meet a fella, you'll get married and you'll have kids. That's what life is." On the other side of the Atlantic, screen mothers had little more to offer their young. "It's your life, ruin it your own way," Helen tells her daughter in *a Taste of Honey*. Even Disney was not immune to the anti-momism that seemed to be rampant. In *The Parent Trap* (1961), Haley Mills finds herself isolated, dominated and ignored by a mother too engrossed in her social world to deal with her, and a grandmother who for too long has been used to giving the orders.

By the end of the decade, the movies had painted a murky mire of matriarchy. In *The Graduate* (1967), the once cherished image of mother-hood was reduced to alcoholic and adulteress in the notorious character of Mrs. Robinson. Mary Tyrone had been addicted; Annabel Willart had been obsessed with her son in a manner that bordered on the incestuous; and so on the list went. At the very time that Albert Ellis was asserting that "there is no such entity as the demasculizing woman,"[17] the film industry was embarking upon a production schedule that would create a psychological land-scape overpopulated with ballbusting wives and mothers.

The image of the mother that dominated the sixties was a logical out-growth of a trend that began in the forties and developed steadily throughout the 1950's. It was an image that seemed to obsess the industry. In the process it served to obscure the issues of the day. While film families throughout the decade are strife-ridden and torn apart, the issues dividing them remain obscure. In looking at these films it is difficult to believe that Watts, Chicago or Woodstock ever occurred. Despite assassinations, the civil rights movement, hippies, yippies, SDS, LSD and Beatlemania; despite being confronted with the most aware, articulate and politically active generation of young people ever raised in the United States, the film industry seemed unable to hit upon the issues that were important to the young and that separated some of them from their parents. What we find instead in these film families is domestic discord based on the possessiveness and aggression of wives and mothers.

While Hollywood seemed incapable of articulating the generation gap, the music industry spoke directly to youth, commenting time and time again on family conflict. Domestic sterility and the meaninglessness of life were addressed by the Beatles in "She's Leaving Home." In "Society's Child," "Younger Generation Blues," and "Janey's Blue," Janis Ian spotlighted the reaction of one section of youth to their parents. The Who's' "My Generation," which proclaimed, "Hope I die before I get old," became an anthem for the young. The Stones saw the hypocrisy of the adult response to drugs and condemned it in "Mother's Little Helper." Even a plastic, manufactured, bubblegum group like The Monkees proved capable of satire and social comment in "Pleasant Valley Sunday" and "Mommy and Daddy." While singles and albums of the era abound with constant references to family life and its perceived failures, films from the same period seem spectacularly lacking in any understanding of the issues of the day. As in the 1950's, the industry was found wanting, capable of dealing in images but not issues.

When John Kennedy assumed office at the start of the decade, he said, "Let both sides explore what problems unite us instead of laboring those problems which divide us." While he was not referring to the older and younger generations, his comments remain remarkably applicable to a period so fragmented by social and family dissension. In the final year of the decade, as Nixon assumed office, he stopped to recall a sign he had seen on the campaign trail: "Bring Us Together" it asked. In its lack of concern for the issues that divided American society in the sixties, Hollywood contributed to the division. In depicting American youth, it concentrated on facile and superficial manifestations of the youth culture. In depicting their homelife, it showed them as victims of emasculated fathers and castrating mothers. The relentless repetition of such an image made it impossible for parents or progeny to understand the common links that still held them together. At a time when, perphaps more than any other, the American family needed a mirror with which to see itself clearly, the industry proved capable once again of only the most superficial rendition of reality.

Since the sixties, Hollywood has moved to a more mature depiction of family life. *Breaking Away* (1979), *Alice Doesn't Live Here Anymore* (1974), and *Ordinary People* (1980) have all contributed richly to the new vision of the American family. Despite this fact, there is little to suggest Hollywood's sudden conversion to a more tolerant, sympathetic or balanced vision of the American mother. In *The Last Picture Show* (1971), Jacy Farrow (Cybill Shepherd) quickly has her adolescent daydreams and romances destroyed by her mother. For Lois Farrow (Ellen Burstyn), "everything is flat and empty." Life is meaningless and without promise. In the tradition of sixties' mothers, she escapes into alcohol and adultery. In the tradition of fifties' mothers, she dominates the home. "I scared your daddy into getting rich," she tells her daughter. In the same year, *Red Sky at Morning* found Josh Arnold (Richard Thomas) assuming the mantle of manhood. With his father away at war, the boy is forced to become the man of the house. Not only does that include experiencing the trauma of moving to a new state, a new school, new friends, and awakening sexuality, for Josh it also involves trying to keep his mother in hand. Lonely and afraid, she retreats into alcohol and pills at the very time in his life when her son most needs her.

The Effect of Gamma Rays on Man-in-the-Moon Marigolds (1972) was based on Paul Zindel's Pulitzer Prize winning play. Produced and directed by Paul Newman, the film starred Joanne Woodward as the mother of two adolescent girls. As the film opens, youngest daughter Matilda (Nell Potts) is seen carefully planting seedlings. In comparison to the meticulous and caring way with which she tends the seeds, her mother Beatrice approaches the task of raising her children in a haphazard and slipshod fashion. Standing in the street outside the schoolground, she screams to Matilda, "Get your sister out of there before she gets pregnant." While she seems totally oblivious to the humiliation and embarrassment she causes her children, Beatrice is particularly sensitive to their embarrassing her. "When they laugh at you, they laugh at me," she admonishes Matilda. Not only are the girls lacking in emotional warmth and support, but they lack the middle-class comforts we so often take for granted in America's film families.

And yet, despite the drab environment of the home which Beatrice openly admits is a pigsty, there is for the audience something refreshingly real, open and honest about the squalor of the environment. It is a house where real people live, argue, love, squabble and dream. Older daughter Ruth (Judith Lowry) only has eyes for her boyfriend. Her sister, somewhat of a recluse, buries herself in the experiments she designs for her science class. Meanwhile, their mother looks back bitterly on the past. "Your father was promises, nothing but promises." For Beatrice, life holds little promise. She dreams of a life that can never be more than a dream and resents men, believing that they all "have only one testicle." If her dreams cannot come true, Beatrice seems unwilling to let her children dream. Caught up in a fantastic world of atoms, molecules and the endless universe mystically held together by a mysterious life force, Matilda finds her science classes and her teacher, Mr. Goodman, to be full of wonderful poetry. Her mother, however, denounces him as a faggot.

Faced with limited income, the family supplement their earnings by taking in a boarder. When Nannie Annie moves in, we realize by the responses of the individual family members that it is Matilda who is most sensitive to the old woman's needs. Ruth, caught up in her own social life and with an adolescent fear of death and old age, is repulsed by the woman. Her insensitivity to Annie is equalled by her lack of understanding of her mother. In a skit at school she wears her mother's clothes and portrays her as scatterbrained and slovenly. The get-rich-quick schemes that Beatrice daydreams of to "get us back on the map" are nothing more than jokes to Ruth. Her mother lives a half-life, caught between a past she resents and a future that eludes her. Unable to have the life she desires, she tells Matilda she hates life. While other parents can take pride and joy in their children and live for them, Beatrice looks at her daughters and admits disheartedly, "They're not exactly triumphs." If the girls are not triumphs, one need look no further than their mother for an explanation. Disillusioned and depressed, she spends most of her life slouching about the house in a tatty bathrobe, chain smoking and drinking beer. Isolated and carrying an abiding sense of fear, loneliness and rejection from her own high school days, she offers little in the way of a positive image for her daughters to aspire to. Yet in her own vulnerability, we encounter a figure with whom we can sympathise if not admire. There is about her some madcap disregard for reality that we find refreshing and entertaining, if not admirable and enviable.

But Beatrice forfeits her right to our compassion when she fails at the one real task she has but refuses to accept. Like it or not, Beatrice's mission is that of mother. One would not deny her her dreams of a chain of tea shops, her bitterness about men, her living in the past. But when these self-indulgences prevent her from dealing with the day-to-day realities of meeting her daughters' needs, she can win no higher feeling from us than pity.

Matilda's science experiment elevates her to the finals of the school competition. As a finalist, she is expected to bring her mother to the prize presentation. That means leaving Ruth at home to mind Annie, and the girl will have none of it. When her mother descends the stairs and prepares to head off for the ceremony, her daughter turns on her viciously. At Warren Harding High School, the same school her mother attended, the girl has overheard teachers refer to Beatrice and the crazy reputation she had as a student. While the school's name is synonymous with normalcy, Ruth has discovered that Beatrice was a bizarre character known as "Betty the Loon." Angered by her mother's order that she stay home, Ruth reveals what she has overheard. "You put us down all the time and we're not crazy, you're the one who's crazy." Shattered, Beatrice consoles herself with alcohol, bracing herself for the return to the school that she plainly dreads. In a drunken state she calls the school and angrily abuses a member of the staff. She kills Matilda's pet rabbit and unsuccessfully tries to unburden herself of Annie.

By the time she arrives at school, Matilda has won first prize for her experiment on the effect of gamma rays on Man-in-the-Moon marigolds. The project her mother had paid scant attention to and had belittled has revealed Matilda as a thoughtful and sensitive youngster, capable of taking on a project and seeing it through to the end. While Beatrice can find only pain and disappointment in life, wishing that she were dead, her daughter looks at the strange mutations life creates and understands that despite their appearance, despite the fact that they may not seem normal, some mutations are still capable of great beauty. It is a lesson she has had to arrive at alone and in spite of her mother. Even as she is bathing in the glow of her first success and public acknowledgement, she finds her moment ruined by her mother. Drunkenly, Beatrice enters the auditorium and sways awkwardly, uncertainly, to the front of the stage where Matilda stands surrounded by parents and peers. Searching for the right words, Beatrice blurts out, "My heart is full." When one of the students giggles, the woman turns to her angrily and screams, "My heart is full!"

Back home at the end of the night, Matilda returns to find that little has changed. In the back yard, her mother chatters animatedly, distractedly, lost in another hair-brained scheme. She dreams of transforming the back yard, putting in a fountain, making it attractive so that the girls can have friends over, but it is Beatrice herself, not the yard, that keeps the girls' friends away. As Beatrice loses herself in her own small talk, Matilda sets about the task of burying her rabbit. But even this petty malicious act of her mother's cannot take from her what the evening has given her. At school, Matilda has found the key to open a door to a world where her mother cannot hurt her.

For Beatrice, life has lost its magic. Each day holds nothing new. Life has become an endless re-run in which she is trapped. Today is like tomorrow, which is just like yesterday. But for Matilda, the experiment has given her the promise of a better tomorrow. "It made me curious about the sun and stars. It made me feel important... No, mama, I don't hate the world." The line harks back to *All Fall Down* and serves to locate the film within the tradition of movie motherhood. Berry-Berry has told Clinton that he hates his mother's guts. By extension he has also confessed that he hates life. As the film progresses and Clinton watches him, he must decide between being like his brother, or finding his own self. To be like Berry-Berry is to accept his life view and to be trapped and twisted forever by his mother's machinations. As Matilda learns to overcome her mother, so Clinton overcomes Annabel. As the film closes, he stands by the brother he loves but no longer admires and tells him, "I like life, Berry-Berry."

In the following year, *Summer Wishes, Winter Dreams* featured Woodward again essaying the role of a somewhat pathetic and destructive mother. Menopausal Rita looks back on her own childhood, remembering a teacher who told her, "Growing up is harder than learning how to fly; one requires truth, the other requires only fairy dust." Having alienated her own

children, she appears to be herself the victim of a neurotic mother she refers to as "the snow queen." Her one happy moment of childhood, she recalls, was spent not with her mother but with her grandmother who, through a combination of homemade jam and poetry was able to transport her to "a town called Don't You Worry on the banks of the river Smile." Yet, though she clearly resents her own upbringing, she seems to have been incapable of learning from it to benefit her children. Her son is a homosexual, a fact we are clearly meant to blame on her. Her daughter Anna has a nervous condition and eats compulsively. If the children are incapable of responding to their mother then she, like Beatrice, feels that they are far from triumphs. "Anna, I may love you, but I do not like you at all."

Carrie (1977) told the story of a teenager girl traumatized by her mother's religious mania. *Bloodbrothers* (1978) featured a battered wife who in turn became a child abuser. *Luna* (1979), although not American-made, featured an American cast and dealt with the incestuous relationship between Jill Clayburgh and her adolescent son. *Foxes* (1980) completely reversed the mother/daughter relationship and had teenage Janie putting her tearful mother to bed with the advice that "You've got to get your prescription checked." Role reversal was equally evident in Neil Simon's *Only When I Laugh* (1981), in which Kristy McNichol played a teenager desperately trying to communicate with a mother recovering from alcoholism. As the film ends, her mother turns to her and says, "When I grow up, I want to be just like you." Disney, of course, had touched upon a similar theme in *Freaky Friday*, in which a young Jodie Foster magically assumed her mother's personality while her mother assumed hers. In *Fame* (1980), mothers still seem to be the prime target singled out for blame in producing homosexual sons.

In *Ordinary People*, Conrad Jarrett (Timothy Hutton) struggles with the death of his brother but finds his mother an obstacle he cannot overcome. "We just don't connect" he tells his psychiatrist, wondering what people have in common with mothers anyway. It is, he suggests, just surface junk like getting good grades and cleaning your teeth. Unable to deal with the death of one son and the attempted suicide of the other, Beth Jarrett maintains the same formal, stiff manner that has got her through life. On the outside she appears all smiles and charm. Inside, however, she is a tense and twisted bundle of emotion. Unable to cry or scream, she is equally unable to communicate with her family when they most need each other. To Conrad she appears at times to be totally uncaring. When he slashed his wrists she did not visit him in the hospital. In his own mind, she was more concerned with what the neighbors would think and with the blood on her walls and rug than with his own health. And yet Beth is not altogether dislikable. While we may feel she is wrong, we can at least sympathise with her.

Opposite: *Ordinary People* (1980): A brief happy moment for a mother who despairs, "I don't know what anyone wants from me anymore."

The boy's psychiatrist advises him, "Don't blame her for not loving you more than she's able."

It we dislike Beth (and there are moments throughout the film in which she forces us to cringe, and moments when we wish to strangle her), we are at least permitted an insight into what forces have shaped her. Fastidious to the point of obsession, she can deal with life only when everything and everyone is in their proper place, neat, ordered and organized. She has fired a maid, we hear, because she couldn't clean the living room properly.

Totally concerned with appearances, she is more worried about the napkin rings she meticulously places in a dresser drawer than she is with the chaos that has intruded upon her son's life. If she is capable of dismising Conrad with the order that he clean his room, she is equally capable of responding to her husband the same way. On the day they buried their eldest son, Beth continued her preoccupation with appearances. "We were going to our son's funeral and you were worried about what I wore on my feet," Calvin tells her incredulously. When Calvin suggests family therapy, Beth dismisses the idea immediately. "This is my family and if we have problems we'll solve them in the privacy of our own home." Again, appearances dominate.

When we encounter Beth's mother, we come a long way toward understanding why she acts the way she does. As the family gather in the living room to take photographs, the mother's main conversation to her own husband seems to be continued orders to "be quiet" and "shut up." If Beth is not as blunt in dealing with Calvin, she is equally as concerned that he keep his mouth shut and remain discreet about their problems. At a party, when Calvin begins to discuss Conrad with a friend, Beth quickly intervenes to terminate the conversation.

There is one other telling insight into Beth's character, which grants her our sympathy and helps to locate her own psyche. After a quarrel with Conrad, she retires with her own mother to the kitchen. In the course of the conversation, her mother reveals her own prejudices about Jews and psychiatrists.

More important, however, as they prepare the meal, they both are shown approaching their tasks with the same neat and fastidious precision which they use in controlling their emotions. But try as she may, Beth cannot disguise the savage disruption that has intruded upon her family. She drops a plate, shattering it. "You know," she says, "I think this can be saved, it's a nice clean break." Unfortunately, the same cannot be said for her family.

Part of the phenomenal success of *Ordinary People* must be attributed to the fact that it touched a sensitive nerve in the American consciousness and laid bare the inner agonies of turmoils of an ostensibly ordinary family. The divisions that racked the Barrett household were echoes of those the nation felt throughout the decade. The 1970 White

Rebel Without a Cause: **Judy, Jim and Plato refugees from failed families of the fifties.**

House Conference on Children, for example, reported that "American families are in trouble so deep and pervasive as to threaten the future of our nation."[18] A host of factors conspired to isolate the American child from the American parent. The fragmentation of the extended family, separation of business and residential areas, occupational mobility, abolition of the apprentice system, the working mother, the delegation of child-care experts, and a plethora of other causes had contributed to decreasing contact between young and old, between adult and adolescent. Parents were not simply separated from their young, they were alienated from them. When *Time* magazine made the middle Americans man and woman of the year in 1970, it spoke to a section of the population, Richard Nixon's silent majority, who were fearful of losing control not only of their young but of their country.

> The American dream they were living was no longer the dream as advertised. They feared they were beginning to lose their grip on the country. Others seemed to be taking over—the liberals, the radicals, the defiant young."[19]

The fractured families that continued to fill the nation's screens throughout the 1970's can be seen as a reflection of the changing nature of the American family. From 1945, when Rosie the Riveter and Mildred Pierce asserted their social and cinematic independence, movies had been relentlessly unkind to the American mother. In the 1970's, more and more American women left home to join the work force.

> Mom is increasingly not found at home because she's out working, as well as attending meetings or shopping several nights a week. In 1975, for the first time in American history, a majority of the nation's mothers with school age children—ages six to seventeen—held jobs outside the home.... In 1975, 39 percent of mothers of children under six were working, more than three times as many as in 1948.... Of course, the increase of women in the work force is one of the most significant social and economic facts of our time. While the number of working husbands has risen from 29.8 million to 37.8 million between 1947 and 1975, or 27 percent, the number of working wives has shot up from 6.5 million to 19.8 million, or 205 percent—nearly ten times as much.[20]

While we cannot hope to find these figures or situations matched in motion pictures, the depiction of motherhood throughout the 1970's and early eighties does tend to suggest some of this social fragmentation and change.

Almost without exception, the castrating matriarchs of the sixties had been mothers first, last and always. Almost always shown about the home, almost never employed, they wore motherhood like a medal. In fiercely embracing what they saw as their sole reason for living, they sucked the life force from the very family that they gave birth to. In Annabel and other characters of the period, we confront mothers whom we can only condemn.

While the seventies showed itself not altogether willing to surrender such an image, it did develop an alternative view of motherhood. While screen mothers of the sixties single-mindedly embraced their calling, the seventies and eighties saw alternatives. In *Endless Love* (1981), for example, although Ann is a mother of three, she is by no means enthusiastic about it. While it may be argued that she merely shirks parental responsibility, it is equally true that she asserts her rights as an independent woman. When she finds herself pushed into assuming the posture of motherhood, she reacts negatively: "Oh my God! I'm sounding like a mother. Don't inflict that upon me, please."

In *Alice Doesn't Live Here Anymore* (1974), *An Unmarried Woman* (1978), *Luna* (1979), *Only When I Laugh* (1981), and other films, we encounter women who must manage the task of being wives, mothers and career people. If Hollywood writers had experienced difficulty in conceptualising career women as wives and mothers, television revealed similar problems. In the *Mary Tyler Moore Show*, Mary Richards had always had to opt for a career over a personal life. By 1981, however, viewers were permitted to see career women who could also lead fulfilling personal lives. In *Hill Street Blues*, Joyce Davenport operated successfully as both lawyer and lover, and in *Lou Grant*, Billie Newman managed to be both a good journalist and a wife. In the case of motion pictures, the point is not so much whether they manage or not as it is that they attempt to manage. Thus when Meryl Streep relinquishes her son in *Kramer vs. Kramer* (1979), she is doing much more than acknowledging that she has failed as a mother, she is in fact recognizing herself as a woman. For the first time in its history, Hollywood was liberating the movie mother from the home. More than thirty-five years had passed since Mildred Pierce confessed to knowing no other life than cooking and washing and having children. While the social role of women and our notion of motherhood has changed much since then, the movies have been slow to mirror the change. Caught in stereotypes and unconscious fears, our motion pictures have for too long done a disservice to American motherhood. Nowhere is the traditional screen mother's search for self more evident than in Beth Jarrett's poignant cry, "I don't know what anyone wants from me anymore!"

With the 1980's underway, we were at last able to see sympathetic portraits of heroines liberated from the home. although they stumbled and fell, although they sometimes made mistakes, they were at last able to exist as individuals with identities of their own. They had become wives and mothers before they had found themselves. Now they were free to become women. In walking out one door they were opening another. Beside them or behind them stood the film fathers.

4. Film's Failed Fathers

"What can you do when you have to be a man?"—Jim Stark in *Rebel Without a Cause*; 1955.

Throughout the thirties and forties, American film fathers alternated between working class villains and middle-class buffoons. The teenagers of the Depression era's dead end more often than not suffered from physical abuse or parental neglect. By the bobby-soxer boom of the next decade, fathers were increasingly depicted as hapless victims of some adolescent conspiracy. Busy at the office or running for one political position or another, they unwittingly neglected their children, with the result that it was often left up to their wives to translate teenage life for them. "What's happened to this family?" a confused Fredric March asks upon returning from the war in *The Best Years of Our Lives* (1946). Although his daughter tells him, "It's nice to have you around, Dad, you'll get this family back to normal," in post-war America the notion of normalcy was being re-defined. March returns to a family and a country that he has difficulty in recognizing. And nothing is more difficult for him than his children. Looking at Rob and Peggy he confesses that he finds youth "frightening."

The Best Years of Our Lives promised things to come. *Cynthia* (1947) found Elizabeth Taylor's screen mother condemning her husband's fear of life, of action, of anything that involved making a decision or taking a risk. For the most part, however, the decline of the film father was depicted in amusing terms beneath the froth and bubble of the domestic comedies that occupied the cinema of adolescence. This trend showed every sign of continuing unabated until midway through the 1950's when a relatively unknown actor from Indiana asked, "What can you do when you have to be a man?" In both *East of Eden* and *Rebel Without a Cause*, James Dean seized upon a theme that had emerged in the forties, launching an attack on the myth of masculinity. In the process he significantly re-defined the image of screen father and son.

It is impossible to consider the fifties without considering Dean. The decade presented the archetypal image of the disenfranchised adolescent, alienated from his family and in open conflict with his father. In many senses it was a regressive decade longing for the security of a more ordered past. The role of the father figure in this search cannot be ignored. The death of FDR in 1944 deprived a whole generation of Americans of the most enduring and visible symbol of the patriarchal order. When the war ended the following year, American men who had single-mindedly devoted themselves to one goal were asked to suddenly readjust to peacetime conditions. Such adjustments placed a major strain on the national psyche. The large-scale entry of women into the work force had significantly altered relations between the sexes. It is hardly surprising, therefore, to discover a new generation of American youth, growing up and wondering what it meant to be a man.

The 1950's opened with one of the most perennial and popular father figures the American screen had to offer. In *Captains Courageous* (1937), Spencer Tracy had played Manuel, a Portuguese fisherman who functioned as surrogate father to Freddie Bartholomew. In the following year he appeared in the Oscar-winning *Boys Town* as Father Flanagan, a priest who functioned as father figure for Mickey Rooney and the other youngsters of the famed Nebraska school. Then in 1950, as one of America's most popular film fathers, he teamed with one of the country's most popular screen daughters in *Father of the Bride*. Contemplating the approaching marriage of Kay (Elizabeth Taylor), Tracy faces the painful prospect of coming home each day and not finding her there. Looking back on his daughter's life, he reflects on her first permanent wave, her first party. From that moment on, he recalls, life for him and his wife had been one constant panic, filled with the ever present worry that boys would flock to her, and the more distrubing thought that they would not. Yet despite his fears, the confusion and chaos of the wedding day, and a sense that "things will never be the same again," a proud father watches his only daughter walk away like a princess in a fairy tale.

It was to be one of the last moments of family harmony and happiness that the fifties would afford film families, and film fathers in particular. As Tracy gave his daughter away, a generation of American parents, it seemed at times, were giving up on their own children. Dr. William H. Kiser, an Atlanta pediatric psychiatrist, commented:

> An adolescent is often a segregated individual. He needs a bridge to the adult world. The best way to provide that bridge is through the father and mother. I like to explain it as if these kids are like moths attracted to something that glows. If the father glows, a boy attaches himself to him and is guided by him. If the father doesn't glow, the youngster will attach himself to someone else — sometimes to a psychopathic youngster who glows in an evil way.... Unfortunately, too many American parents are too preoccupied with their own 'problems' to glow for their children.[1]

In the Trask household of *East of Eden* and the Stark family of *Rebel Without a Cause*, we confront film fathers who were incapable of "glowing" for their sons. From his first appearance, Cal Trask is seen as a misfit, a loner, a teenager caught between two worlds, hovering between the paternal environment of his father in Salinas and his mother's world in Monterey. Huddled and hunched up, he rides on top of a train, a solitary figure chilled by the wind and by the lack of human warmth and understanding in his life. A creature of the shadows, he stalks the night like an animal returning to rest at dawn.

In contrast to Cal, his brother Aaron (Richard Davalos) seems like a whole person. In love with Abbra (Julie Harris), Aaron appears blissfully content. When Cal comes upon the sweethearts, he darts and weaves his way between them, always on the outside, never part of the group; he remains on the periphery of the family. He has been out all night and his father Adam (Raymond Massey) is angry with him. "He's thoughtless and inconsiderate. I'm at my wit's end with the boy," he tells a neighbor.

When Cal tries to become part of his father's world, to share in his dreams and work, he quickly finds himself rebuffed. Adam is interested in an ice plant and dreams of being able to freeze vegetables so they may arrive fresh at the market. Cal is enthusiastic about the plan, seeing it as an opportunity to make money. "I'm not particularly interested in making a profit," his father tells him and the boy, feeling rebuffed, skulks off alone.

In the loft of the ice house, he paces restlessly, spying on Aaron and Abbra, sulking at his father's rejection. Watching his brother, whose head is cradled on Abbra's lap, the boy feels isolated and alone. Desperately missing the mother he never knew, he is jealous at the mother-surrogate his brother seems to have found in Abbra. Confused and angry, he begins to hurl ice down the shoot thus further angering his father.

Later, as a form of punishment, Adam has the boy read verses from the Bible. Though he has told Cal to read the passages without giving the scripture numbers, the boy deliberately disobeys him. Angrily his father turns on him: "You're bad through and through." In a sensitive moment, the boy's response reveals his innermost fears and feelings. "You're right. I'm bad. I've known that for a long time." Shocked by his son's words, Adam tries to reassure him. For a moment it appears that some form of reconciliation and understanding is possible between the two of them. But Cal has released the floodgates of his emotions. The fears and feelings tumble forth in a torrent and he needs answers, not reassurances. "Talk to me, Father! I gotta know who I am! I gotta know what I'm like!" He begs Adam to tell him about his mother. The boys have always been led to believe that she is dead, but Cal knows better. Desperately reaching out for answers, he demands more from his father than the man is capable of giving. Unable to contend with the wretched awkwardness of the boy's needs, Adam stiffly closes up. Disgusted and contemptuous, his needs once more denied, Cal rises to leave. As he gets to the door, his father calls after

him, "Cal, if you go out that door, we might never be able to talk again."
For Cal there is nothing left to say.

When war breaks out, Cal discovers a means to win his father's love
and approval. He becomes involved in agriculture, raising beans and
making a very handsome profit. While the war offers him an opportunity to
make money and win his father's approval, it affects Aaron in a different
way. "It just seems to affect him so personally," Abbra tells Cal. Cal can
stand in the street and watch the war rallies and parades and enjoy it with
the innocence of a child. But Aaron sees beyond the glamor of the uniforms, understanding that they disguise an ugly side of human nature.
"Nothing will ever make me go. I just don't believe it's right," he tells
Abbra. When the townfolk turn on a German who has lived among them all
their lives, Aaron is alone in coming to his defense. High above, suspended
momentarily from the hustle and bustle, Cal and Abbra spend a moment
together on a ferris wheel. Each surrenders briefly to their impulses and they
kiss, only to suffer immediate guilt and shame. "I love Aaron," the girl tells
Cal, and he feels rejection once again and a sense of having betrayed his
brother. When they see a fight below, he is quick in coming to Aaron's
defense. Again he meets only rejection. A pacifist, Aaron loathes the
thought of violence, but he has become suspicious of Cal's involvement with
Abbra. A violent fight breaks out between the two of them, brother pitted
against brother. "I tried to kill him," Cal drunkenly tells Abbra. Cal, desperate and hurt, is vulnerable to the girl's ministerings and she to his needs.

While Aaron becomes increasingly sullen, withdrawn and
suspicious, Cal and Abbra, like two children, happily set about a birthday
party for Mr. Trask. Cal has made his beans work and he intends to present
his father with enough money to make up for the losses he suffered in an
earlier business failure. Dressed in a suit and tie, bubbling and excited, he
awaits his father's homecoming, convinced that at last he will win his love,
respect and gratitude. Aaron hovers in the background as though waiting to
spring. As Cal is about to present his gift to an already delighted Adam,
Aaron suddenly announces that he and Abbra are engaged. "I can't imagine
anything better," his father tells them, totally unaware that all of Cal's plans
and efforts have been undermined. When the boy does step forward and
give the man his present, rather than being embraced, he finds himself once
more rejected. "I sign my name and men go out and some get killed and
some lie helpless without arms and legs. Not one will come back untorn. Do
you think I could take a profit on that?" In total disbelief and desperation,
the boy clutches agonizingly at his father, his body sagging under the
endless onslaught of denial.

When he played this scene, Dean improvised; the grasping at
Massey, the gut-wrenching emotion he projected was not called for in the
script. An element of the actor's personal life surfaced in the public performance. So strong was the identification between Dean and Cal that
director Elia Kazan felt they were one and the same:

> I chose him because he was Cal Trask.... There was no point in attempting to cast it better.... Jimmy was it. He had a grudge against all fathers. He was vengeful. He had a sense of aloneness and of being persecuted.[2]

While Dean thus brought to the character of Cal a special interpretation and understanding of his own, he also contributed greatly to a new image of the American male. Joan Mellen has written, in *Big Bad Wolves*, that

> Cal sobs from the depths of his being as only a fifties male could. His devastation echoes that of so many young people who could not, no matter how frantically they strove to wrench free of their parents and authority, locate an essential, life sustaining acknowledgment of their identity.... Dean added an enormous dimension to the screen male with his unprecedented freedom in acknowledging his hurt and disappointments so openly and without shame. His image confirmed and rendered acceptable the fact that men are tormented by feelings of rejection and loneliness as women.[3]

Unable once again to respond to the needs of his son, Adam stiffens and the boy stumbles in pain from the house. When the girl seeks to comfort him, Aaron in his bitterness tells Cal to keep away. "You're mean and vicious and wild. You always have been." Too full of pain to understand anything but his blind fury and desperate need of revenge, Cal determines to make his brother face the truth about their mother: "Can you look at truth just once?" He takes the boy with him to Kate's house and, opening the door to the office reveals the slumbering woman and thrusts his brother in. Kate awakens and her face reveals the horror with which she views Cal's action, for in revealing the truth to Aaron, Cal has destroyed his brother's world of ideals and illusions. Shattered from the experience, a drunken Aaron signs up and boards a troop train. With the train pulling out, the boy wildly plunges his head through the window and laughs maniacally, oblivious to the pain. "And Cain rose up against his brother and slew him and Cain went away and dwelt in the Land of Nod, somewhere east of Eden."

Aaron's departure causes his father to suffer a stroke. Incapacitated and almost incapable of speech, he is tended by Abbra. Cal, too, needs tending. Remorseful at his actions, he now feels responsible for his father's condition, but cannot break through the barrier that has always been between them. It is Abbra who finally makes him face his father. In the final moments of the film, the boy approaches the bedside and struggles to find the words as he has struggled all his life. It is an awkward and painfully private moment in which we become almost intruders. "Man has a choice, and it's the choice that makes him a man," the boy tells his father, assuring him that he has learned from him, that he does know that man has free will and is born neither good nor evil. Summoning all his strength, Adam manages a few words. He asks his son to dismiss the nurse and to look after him himself. For the first time in his life, Cal understands that he is wanted, needed and loved by his father.

Commenting on the film, Pauline Kael observed:

> A boy's agonies should not be dwelt on so lovingly; being misunderstood may easily become the new glamorous lyricism.... The romance of human desperation is ravishing for those who wish to identify with the hero's amoral victory; everything he does is forgiveable, his crimes are not crimes at all because he was so terribly misunderstood.... The bad things that he does establish him as a hero by demonstrating his need. (When Peter Lorre in *M* said he could'nt help what he did, who would have thought him heroic? We have come a slippery distance.) This is a complete negation of previous conceptions of heroism; the hero is not responsible for his actions – the crazy, mixed-up kid becomes a romantic hero by being treated on an infantile level. And the climax of the film is not the boy's growing up beyond this need or transferring it to more suitable objects, but simply the satisfaction of an infantile fantasy: he displaces his brother and is at last accepted by his father.[4]

Kael, of course, was not wrong. Cal Trask/James Dean, call him what you will, had presented an image of American youth that, if Hollywood did not understand, it could at least try to replicate. In so doing, they would be depicting more than an image; they would be re-examining an institution. For Cal Trask said something not only about a section of American youth, but about the American family.

On Wednesday, October 15, 1955, two weeks after Dean's death, a double page ad for *Rebel Without a Cause* appeared in *Variety*. "Jim Stark – a kid in the year 1955 – what makes him tick ... like a time bomb? Maybe the police should have picked up his parents instead." In the one ad Dean, the image of the adolescent, and the American family had taken a major step. If Cal Trask had appeared contemporary, there was to be no mistaking the nowness of Jim Stark's milieu. His very name, an anagram of Trask, was an extension of the character he had already established. The impact the film was to have upon the industry was as yet unseen. Dean's death had hardly caused widespread mourning in the industry. When he crashed his Porsche on September 30 he had only one film in release. He had not yet had time to make a major impact. Eden, although well received and ultimately gaining an Oscar nomination for Dean, had not yet succeeded in cementing his image or appeal in the minds of either the industry or the public. *Rebel Without a Cause* would.

Made for Warners and directed by Nicholas Ray, the film had been intended for Tab Hunter and Jayne Mansfield, but Ray had insisted on the then little-known James Dean and former child star Natalie Wood. As the film opens, Jimmy is alone and drunk, lying embryo-like in the street as he plays with a child's toy monkey. Picked up by the police, he is taken to juvenile hall. It is there we first encounter Judy (Natalie Wood). "He called me a dirty tramp! My own father!" she says in disbelief. Also at juvenile hall we meet Plato (Sal Mineo), a disturbed and fragile teenager from a broken home. His mother leaves him alone most of the time and today she has left him alone on his birthday. The boy, for reasons he does not understand, has killed a puppy. In quick succession we have been introduced to three well-off youngsters from well-to-do homes, all hopelessly confused and lacking in understanding. As *Variety* commented, "The shock impact in *Rebel* is perhaps greater (than *Blackboard Jungle*) because this is a pleasant middle-class community."[5]

When Jim's family arrives at the police station, we perceive immediately why the boy is in so much trouble. The family is a hotbed of simmering feuds and seething antagonisms. Beneath the tuxedoes, jewelry and expensive cigars, the Stark family is totally lacking in understanding and communication. The boy looks his father (Jim Backus) up and down, a drunken smirk crossing his face. "King of the ball," he calls his dad, seating him on a chair, and the man, somewhat bemused, relinquishes himself to the boy's game. "You think I'm funny," Jim snaps at him, his mood suddenly changing wildly. While his father tries to placate him, mother and grandmother each contribute their advice until no sense can be made of the jabbering voices. "You're tearing me apart," Jim screams at them in desperation. "I don't know what to do anymore except maybe die.... How can a guy grow up in a circus like this?" he asks the juvenile officer.

When a gang at his new school challenges him to a "chicken run," the boy wants to talk to his father. He has been in trouble with the law before. Indeed, they have been constantly on the move because of his inability to get on with people. Entering the family home, he encounters his father wearing a frilly apron, crawling on his hands and knees as he cleans up some food, terrified that his wife will hear. It is without a doubt one of the most humiliating images of the American husband the screen has presented. In the same year, the pervasiveness of such an image was reported in "The Decline and Fall of the American Father," which commented:

> Nowhere is this fall more clearly pointed out than in our entertainment media, which routinely show father as a foolish fifth wheel in the family group and a loud-voiced windbag.... Scarcely a night passes, for instance, in which you cannot see family life portrayed on TV in terms of the quiet triumph of the mother and children over the father.[6]

But if television showed a defeated father and a triumphant mother, it was pretty much saccharine coated and unlikely to offend. On the big screen, *Rebel Without a Cause* and films that would ape it were presenting an image of the American father and mother that were much more disturbing. "What can you do when you have to be a man?" Jim asks his father, desperately

Rebel Without a Cause (1955): **An emasculated father and a boy's desperate search for a masculine role model.**

hoping for advice. Instead he encounters a meaningless lecture on what "a wonderful age" it is. When his father's failure to respond sends the boy out to find his own solution, it leads to the death of another youngster.

Returning home, he finds his father asleep in front of the television that has ceased transmission. Jim rests on the couch, a bottle of cold milk pressed against his face. His moment's respite is shattered by the distorted image of his mother suddenly descending the staircase. Shot from Jim's viewpoint, his mother (Ann Doran) appears upsidedown. It is a cunning visual device that suggests the distorted relationships within the house. As the boy struggles to explain to his parents what has happened and how he feels, he finds himself and his needs totally subordinated to their concerns. Throughout much of the scene, his mother stands on the stairway dominating the action, with Jim caught in the middle, between the aggressive mother who stands over him and the ineffectual father below him. Arguing with his parents, struggling to get them to listen to him, the boy realizes how completely his mother dominates his father. "Dad, let me hear you answer her! Dad, stand up for me!" he pleads, grabbing his father and hurling him out of his armchair.

The urgency of Jim's need for a father was mirrored in the other two major adolescent characters of the film. As Judy, Natalie Wood portrayed a sixteen-year-old, loving her father and needing his love, but finding it denied. Her relationship with her father is full of sexual tension. In one scene at the family dinner table, she quarrels with him, a quarrel based upon her affection for him. Attempting to kiss him, she is told tersely, "You're getting too old for that kind of stuff, kiddo." Confused and upset, she tries to brush it off. "Girls don't love their fathers? Since when? Since I got to be sixteen?" She bends over and kisses him. As she does so, her father angrily strikes her. His reaction is clearly one of revulsion and it establishes an element of sexual attraction in the father/daughter relationship.

> The fights Judy has with her father are at least partly the result of a latent sexual attraction between them that often causes problems between adolescent daughters and their fathers.[7]

Thus the sexual disturbance in the Stark family, indicated by his mother's domination and the boy's aggression toward his grandmother, is repeated in Judy's house. The very first time we see the girl she is in the police station, confused and hurt because her father has rubbed her lipstick off. His action suggests an attempt to prevent her from growing into a woman, a desire to keep her a young girl. If she is frightened and confused by her father's behavior, then she seems no happier with her mother. When an officer says her mother is coming to pick her up, she becomes hysterical.

The third teenager encountered in the opening scene is equally troubled by his family and its failure to provide models, both social and sexual. John Crawford ("Plato") is the product of a wealthy but broken home. The boys spends most of his time deprived of both parents and is tended to by a maid. When it is suggested that he needs psychiatric help, the maid tells the police, "Mrs. Crawford don't believe in them." It is the boy's birthday but rather than spend the day with her son, his mother has left him alone again. When Jim Stark comes into his life, Plato finds the hero, father figure and role model he has been looking for. In a scene set at the high school, the boy opens his locker and we see a picture of Alan Ladd. It immediately calls to mind *Shane* and Joey's admiration for the stranger who taught him how to shoot. In Jim, Plato sees a similar opportunity. Later he mixes fantasy and fact and tells Judy that Jim is going to take him camping and teach him to hunt and fish.

The boy's relationship to Jim is worth looking at in some detail. In a school excursion to the planetarium, both Jim and Plato function as outsiders. Jim is isolated because of his newness to the school, and Plato falls far beyond the lipstick and leather jacket clique that seems to dominate Dawson High. While Jim seeks to crash the clique by making wisecracks, demonstrating that he's cool, Plato has no games to play and lies open and exposed like a raw nerve. Unable to relate to those his own age, he is equally unable to relate to the world and the cosmos beyond. As the voice of the lecturer informs the group that "Man existing alone seems himself an episode of little consequence," Plato crouches in terror beyond the seats. In the adolescent world, with ego dominant, "I" is the center of the universe and Plato, more than any screen teen to date, seems totally threatened. "What does he know about man alone?" the boy asks contemptuously. What is a lecture for the other students is real life for Plato.

It is Plato who warns Jim that Buzz and the other young toughs are out to get him. And it is Plato who remains his one declared supporter during the chicken run at Miller's Bluff. As Buzz and Jim warm up for the perilous plunge toward the cliff, Plato and Judy talk:

> *Judy*: Is he a friend of yours?
> *Plato*: Yeah, he's my best friend ... he doesn't say much but when he does, you know he means it. He's sincere.
> *Judy*: Well, that's the main thing.

Jim and Buzz walk toward the cliff that threatens their lives. They look down on the rocks that they know may soon destroy them. The anger of the afternoon's fight has abated. No longer enemies, they face each other as they face the cliff, with a sense of challenge but no enmity. The chicken run functions as a rite of passage, a means of proving one's masculinity. The taunt of chicken has haunted Jim throughout his adolescence. It has been the challenge to his manhood that has disrupted his schooling and gotten him into trouble with the law. Now it threatens his life. In a moment that recalls *The Wild One*, the two boys look at each other. "Why do we do this?" Jim asks. "You gotta do something," Buzz answers. In his leather jacket, he sounds like Brando's Johnny asking, "Whatta ya got?" when asked what he's rebelling against.

It is by no means insignificant that Buzz dies when his leather jacket catches in the car and prevents him from escaping before it plunges over the

cliff. The jacket is black, moody and withdrawn. Tough and armorlike, it
contains and restrains the personality it houses. Buzz is locked into it and
the image it represents for him. There is no logical reason for him to want to
participate in the chicken run, but he accepts it as unquestioningly as he
accepts his sexuality. Dean, on the other hand, is more volatile, more vulnerable and more questioning. It is he who asks what it means to be a man
and he who questions the ritual of the chicken run. His red nylon jacket was
to become an emblem with which thousands of American youngsters
aligned themselves. Bright, stark and open, it serves as a red badge of
courage. In the process, it is as ambiguous as the character himself. Sensitive and withdrawn, Jim Stark picks a peculiarly open and assertive coat in
which to clad himself. It is this sincerity and openness that attracts Judy to
him. While she has aligned herself with Buzz and the other gang members,
she has longed for something which they cannot provide.

Standing by the cliff, looking down on the rocks that have killed
Buzz, Jim stands by helplessly, uncertainly. Behind him in the distance,
Plato finally unlocks the fingers he has had crossed throughout the conflict.
Judy, her boyfriend killed, stands tenuously alone, looking down on one
dead love, reaching out to another. As she and Jim stretch out their hands
to each other, looking questioningly into each other's eyes, Plato comes
toward them and the trinity is formed. It is the birth of a new family with
Jim and Judy as parents, Plato as the child. "Gee, if only you could be my
dad," he tells Jim later that night.

The three return to their own homes, each to deal in their own minds
with the night's tragedy. Later, when the gang sets out to hound Jim for the
death of Buzz and the belief that he has informed on them, the three are
once again united. Unable to find Jim, the gang tries to find him through
Plato. Capturing him, they grab his address book which reveals Jim's
address. The boy's infatuation has thus directly threatened Jim. Jim,
however, is not at home. He and Judy have retreated to a deserted mansion that Plato had pointed out earlier in the day. While looking for protection, he has thus functioned as provider and protector. When Plato also
retreats to the mansion, the three function as a new form of family. Plato
lights a candle and escorts Jim and Judy about the house. It is a play scene
with serious significance. Jim and Judy act as prosepctive buyers, yet they
are buyers who cannot tolerate children. "No one talks to children, they just
tell them." The roles they assume reflect directly upon their own parents.
Indeed, in a complex commentary, Dean, by his own instigation, assumed
the voice of the near-sighted cartoon character, Mr. Magoo. (Magoo's voice
was played by Jim Backus who in this film plays Jim's ineffectual father.)

When police arrive at the mansion, Jim tries to calm the terrified
Plato. He tricks the boy into surrendering his gun and removes the bullets
from it so he can do no harm. The police, however, believe the gun is loaded
and Plato is shot and killed. Jim's parents are both outside the mansion as
Plato is killed. Wearing the jacket Jim has given him, the boy has assumed

Tribute **(1980): An advertising campaign that recognized that "being a father means more than having a son."**

Jim's character, coming as close to him as the screen could allow. Momentarily believing they have seen their own son shot, the Starks are relieved when they see Jim alive and well. Throughout the film, in carefully designed scenes, particularly in the staircase sequence, Jim's mother has dominated both husband and son. Now, inexplicably, she is banished to the edge of the frame. As Jim kneels over Plato's body, it is his father who for the first time takes the initiative. Reaching out to the boy he tells him, "Stand up and I'll stand up with you. I'll try and be as strong as you want me to be." On this dawn of a new day, the film promises hope through the return of the patriarchal order. In this way it closely mirrors *Mildred Pierce*; yet it promises what it cannot deliver. Given what we have seen of Jim's parents, it seems unlikely that any role reversal could take place, an idea suggested if not by the plot, than at least by the mournful Rosenman score at the film's conclusion.

As Cal Trask and as Jim Stark, James Dean had brought to the

American cinema a new image of masculinity. In part it was an extension of what Brando had delivered in *The Wild One*, and yet it was much more. As Johnny, the bike-riding rebel, Brando had portrayed a resilient yet sensitive male. He had shown an individual capable of sitting down and crying, "a man clearly in touch with his feelings and, as such, an appealing model."[8] The key word, however, is "man." For Brando was a man. Devoid of family, school and the trappings of adolescence, he functioned as a man alone. Dean, on the other hand, whether as Cal or Jim, and even later as Jett in *Giant*, suggested the vulnerability of adolescence. His appeal was in part a result of his own nature and a result of human nature. As a rebel in all three films, he established an image that still remains, as exemplified by references to him in rock recordings such as Bruce Springstein's "Cadillac Ranch," the Eagles' "James Dean," and David Essex's "Rock On."

While some film analysts have looked at *Rebel Without a Cause* as an extension of a trend begun with *Blackboard Jungle*, the truth of the matter was that the film dealt more with the family than with delinquency. As such, it initiated a new vision of middle-class suburban life and it was this image that was quickly seized upon and repeated in *The Unguarded Moment* (1956), *The Young Stranger* (1957), *Peyton Place* (1957), *The Restless Years* (1958), *Blue Denim* (1959), *A Summer Place* (1959) and *Imitation of Life* (1959).

The Young Stranger, for example, found Hal Ditmar sounding like Cal Trask as he asked, "Is it wrong to want your father to believe in you?" Within two years of the release of *Rebel Without a Cause*, *Variety* was complaining about "the seemingly endless spate of tales about teenagers and parents who don't dig them."[9]

5. Discovering Dad

*"I'm not disappointed; I love you." "I love
you, too"*—Conrad and Calvin Jarrett; *Ordinary People*; 1980.

The issues raised in the films of the fifties would have to wait another
decade to be addressed. Faced with a sustained portrait of paternal plight,
the industry escaped into fairy tale families (*The Sound of Music*; *Mary
Poppins*). The sixties opened by retreating backwards to an image of the
American family as it once was. In *Sunrise at Campobello* (1960), audiences
were presented with an image of a tightly knit, happy, and harmonious
family benignly ruled by a loving patriarch who had become, for a whole
generation of Americans, a familiar father figure. In the same year, the
nation embraced the Kennedys as the first family and embarked upon a
dazzling thousand days of Camelot.

But beneath the surface of the dream, like an assassin in waiting, lay
the nightmare. In the halcyon days of 1960, with the Bay of Pigs and Dallas
still ahead, one could look up, reach out, and believe. We were not yet a
nation of iconoclasts intent on creating heroes and then destroying them.
Marilyn Monroe, who would shortly become one of the first casualties of
the culture, was still alive. We could still look at FDR on the screen and
believe in our dreams. We had not yet, as a nation, heard of Lucy Ruther-
ford nor of Franklin's difficulties with Eleanor. We would learn that year
that the ordinary acts of life, like taking a shower, could become an encounter with the terrifying and, we would discover some three years later,
that a car ride through city streets could end a dream.

Although Franklin's mother hovers ever present in *Sunrise at
Campobello*, her influence, it is suggested, is limited. The young Roosevelt
boys, we are told, can talk her out of anything by simply speaking a few
words of French. While Eleanor plays the total mother, she makes it quite
apparent that in all matters, the ultimate decision-making process rests with
her husband. As the children argue over who is to play what role in the
family play reading of *Julius Caesar* she tells them, "Your father makes the
final decisions." Later, when they appeal to her in the hope that she will

overturn an unpopular decision their father had made, she tells them bluntly, "Your father closed the discussion some minutes ago."

But while Franklin proved to be the head of the house, the screen families for the remainder of the decade were mother dominated. Deenie's father sits passively by while his wife has the girl committed (*Splendor in the Grass*). Clinton's father commits slow suicide, drinking his life away in *All Fall Down*. Phillip Harrington's father alienates both his wife and son in *Five Finger Exercise*. Mick Kelly's father is an emotional and physical cripple no longer able to function as head of the house (*The Heart Is a Lonely Hunter*), and Elaine's father is subjected to his wife's endless infidelities in *The Graduate*. By the middle of the decade, in an article entitled "The Vanishing American Father," *Readers Digest* commented:

> The vanishing father is perhaps the central fact of the changing American family structure.... The American father has become a physical absentee. Preoccupied with his job, his community, his conventions and his suburban commuting, he sees his family only at the exhausted end of a day, on weekends or between business trips. He has become an absentee in a second, more important sense too. He is no longer the source of authority of the family. The American wife now has the thankless task of exercising the authority – disciplinary, intellectual, emotional – which once was the father's. But while she reigns, she cannot rule. With rare exceptions, there is no effective emotional authority in the American home."[1]

More than fifteen years had elapsed since James Dean had asked, "What can you do when you have to be a man?" With the seventies under way, Hollywood had not yet found an answer. It would take a major assault on the nation's psyche to provide a response. In June, 1972, writing in *Commonweal*, Henry Nouwen observed that "We are facing a generation which as parents but no fathers."[2] The screen reflected the changing nature of the American family. "Father, you don't know what time it is," Oliver Barrett III told Ray Milland in the 1970 smash hit, *Love Story*. "That bastard, I'll show him; I'll become a big film star.... The real truth is he just doesn't care," Sally Bowles says of her father in 1972's Academy Award winning *Cabaret*. Though neither film dealt with adolescents, they both did deal specifically with the generation gap and with young people unable to establish meaningful relationships with their parents.

If the parents of children in their twenties were failing, then the initial glimpses the movies provided of parents with adolescent offspring were hardly more positive. "We're failing, we have to face that," Julie Harris tells her husband in 1970's *The Family Next Door*. Her husband, totally incapable of responding sensitively to his teenage son and daughter, only alienates them. "The almighty dollar is your way of judging everything," his daughter condemns him, as she escapes into drugs.

In *Taking Off*, the pressures and problems of middle America became the target for Milos Forman's satire. When fifteen-and-a-half-year-old Jeannie finds her parents too much to handle, she leaves home, lured by drugs and the "free life." A distraught father hunts her, only to encounter an organization known as "The Society for the Parents of Fugitive Children." In America circa 1971, running away from home was a national pastime.

In dealing with film families, the early seventies represented a nation on the run. It is not surprising to encounter during this period a series of films depicting children and adolescents in a negative light. If the children of the sixties had been victims of neurotic families, then the families of the seventies seemed to suffer from a spate of satanic children. *The Exorcist* (1973), *Carrie* (1977), *Damien: Omen II* (1978), and *The Fury* (1978) all dealt in images of disturbed and disturbing youngsters capable of wreaking havoc. In part, these films were a response to the unconscious fears that had haunted America since the sixties. The young seemed to be out of control, marching to the beat of a different drum. At the same time, zero population growth and an anti-child movement had become a pervasive philosophy. In May, 1975, *Psychology Today* reported that "the best of all possible worlds for most Americans is to be newly married and not have children.... Almost as soon as a couple has kids the happy bubble bursts."[3] Commenting on the spate of horror films so popular throughout the period, Amitai Etzioni, a professor of sociology at Columbia, said they appeared when "we were at the height of the anti-child feeling in this country."[4]

The horror films were part of Hollywood's response to the generation gap. Another reaction involved a small group of films that presented a new definition of family life. If the traditional family unit was no longer viable, the industry seemed to suggest, new units could be created even when individuals were not related. *Harold and Maude* (1971) advanced the philosophy that "everyone has the right to make an ass out of themselves; you can't let the world judge you too much." Unable to make any sense of his home life, Harold establishes a relationship with an octegenarian who refuses to acknowledge social conventions. Unable to reconcile the difference between children and their parents, Hollywood responded with a series of films in which youngsters skipped a generation and found understanding with grandparents or older figures. *Kotch* (1973) featured Walter Matheau as a widower who has become a burden for his family. When he encounters a pregnant teenager, he finds a purpose in life and helps the girl prepare for the coming of the baby. In helping Erica and her child, he provides the security that she has been denied and cements a place for himself in the future. "He was old and ending, and kids and babies were new and just beginning.... He'd have made you one hell of a grandfather," the girl writes in a letter she intends to give her son when he grows up. In *Harry and Tonto* (1975), Art Carney gave an Oscar-winning performance as an old man who finds more companionship with a cat, a runaway, and an acid-taking nephew than with his own family.

While the horror movies and new family films were one response to the generation gap, the largest single response was to retreat. The youth films the studios turned out in the late sixties and early seventies failed to chalk up the expected revenues. By November 1971, attempting to assess what was doing well at the box office, *Variety* reported that "Thus far ... nostalgia seems to be more of a proven hit than anything else. *Summer of '42*, *The Last Picture Show*, and *Carnal Knowledge* all share that common denominator."[5] Nor was the nostalgia wave confined to the film industry. In the wake of the Vietnam war, faced with the failure of the New Frontier and the Great Society, the nation turned away from its present problems to look back upon an age when things seemed somehow simpler and better.

K-Tel had a field day, releasing album after album of hits from the fifties and sixties. Eddie Fisher admonished us to "Turn Back the Hands of Time." While Punk and New Wave were struggling to break through, on college campuses from Melbourne to Madison, rock groups like Daddy Cool, Dr. Bop, and Sha Na Na found there was a ready market for the old sound. Don McLean lamented the day the music died in a tribute to Buddy Holly. The Eagles, David Essex, Harpo, and other pop and rock stars sang about James Dean. Theaters sprang up around the nation specializing in double bills of old movie classics. Bogart became a cult figure.

On television, *Happy Days'* Ron Howard made the transition from the big screen's 1962 adolescent of *American Graffiti* to Milwaukee's Ritchie Cunningham and the America of the Eisenhower years. Middle America became the setting for the equally successful *Laverne and Shirley*, which once again proved that money was to be made in looking backward. And there, for almost a decade, coming into our living rooms once a week with a vision of life that recalled the Hardy's Carvel, were John and Olivia Walton with their happy, happy brood. Michael Landon successfully moved from the Ponderosa to *The Little House on the Prairie*, and updated versions of the same theme appeared in series such as *Apple's Way*, which more than hinted that father knows best.

By the latter part of the decade, *Family* led us into the living room of Kate and Doug Lawrence, where television audiences were provided with one of the most realistic depictions of the problems of a middle-class family. While the Lawrences often seemed to be in a state of psychoanalysis rather than normal interaction, there was no doubt that the issues that confronted them were like those confronting families across the nation.

It was a peculiar irony that, given the more liberal code allowed the big screen, the film industry could not bring such characters to life. Unable to deal with the present, they escaped to the past. Wallowing in a morasse of waning political fortunes, Jimmy Carter decided in 1979 that he too could seek solace in the past. America, he suggested, had a crisis of confidence, the gravest crisis it had faced since 1945. Asked to respond to his low standing in the polls, the President chose to compare himself to Harry Truman, a man who won against seemingly insurmountable odds.

Throughout the seventies, from the highest office in the land on down, it was as if the nation as a collective whole had decided to return to "the way we were." But the past which Americans immersed themselves in was a past they could only see through rose-colored glasses. It was, as the *New York Times* scolded, "mostly fantasy." It was not what the past had to offer but what the present had failed to deliver that motivated the wave of nostalgia. It was, according to the *Times*, "what Americans have done to themselves that makes them look to a golden age that never was."[6] In looking back, Jimmy Carter failed to come to terms with the present. He paid for it with his political life. In movies, looking back was equally dangerous. While *Red Sky at Morning* (1971) and *Sounder* (1972) needed to step into the past to encounter a positive relationship between father and son, the issue would not be resolved until the industry confronted the issue head on.

The image of the American father was firmly wedded to the image of American masculinity. The failure of the screen father was so often an extension of his failure as a husband. Jim Stark's terror of being called "chicken" was an outgrowth of the contempt he felt for his "pussy-whipped" father. While the term is never used in any of the films we have considered, there is no doubt that the husbands and fathers who dominated the cinema of adolescence throughout the fifties and sixties were indeed pussy-whipped. When Jim asks his father to stand up for him, he is asking him to assert himself as a man.

In looking at the changing image of the American father throughout the 1970's and early eighties, it is impossible to divorce this from a changing notion of masculinity. While John Wayne began the decade by winning an Oscar for having "true grit," as the decade progressed it became increasingly impossible to accept such a macho stance. Perhaps more than any other figure in American film, Wayne had represented machismo with the oftstated notion that "a man's gotta do what a man's gotta do." Closely associated with the Wayne image went the military milieu. Indeed, throughout the Second World War and later, Wayne came to represent an image of sacrifice, courage and rugged individualism. In *They Were Expendable* (1945), *Sands of Iwo Jima* (1949), and *The Alamo* (1960), he personified American masculinity. While Hollywood turned its back on the Vietnam war, Wayne was there at the front with *The Green Berets* (1968).

But while the image lingered, the social conditions that sustained it were changing. The youth movement was not prepared to unthinkingly embrace war. In rejecting the draft, they rejected the war machine and asserted a more independent sexuality. "Make Love Not War" and "Women Say Yes to Men Who Say No" were two clear indications of the link between sexuality and the war. The massacre at Mai Lai and the trial of Lieutenant Calley further called into question the whole issue of discipline, authority and command.

With the war over, the American nation was forced to realize that

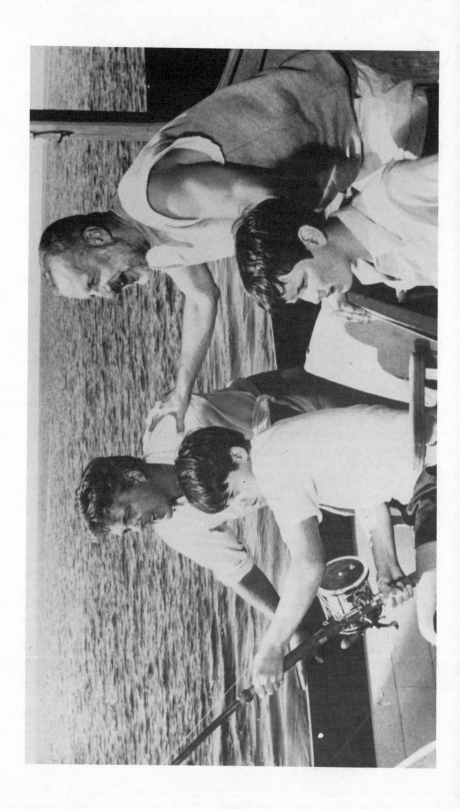

for the first time in the history of the country it had not won a war. Another wound had been inflicted on the myth of manhood. Watergate severely eroded the traditional belief in the presidency and further damaged respect for the patriarchy and national symbols of authority. In 1979, when the embassy in Iran was seized, network news proclaimed "America Held Hostage!" For more than twelve months, the nation seemed impotent, unable to do anything to rescue its citizens. The traditional notion that strength, power and justice would prevail took another beating.

The search for leadership and a new definition of manhood was reflected in the popular music of the day. Kenny Rogers had a big hit with "Coward of the County," and the Charlie Daniels Band scored with the patriotic "In America." The movies also began to re-define the notion of masculinity. Reviewing *Islands in the Stream* (1977), *Variety* wrote:

> Remember when manliness was delineated in terms of straight shot booze, the fondling of high powered rifles, the presence of 'dames' and an implicit social infrastructure based on racist/sexist/patriarchal underpinning.... The strength of *Islands in the Stream* is instantaneously its commercial failing, it gracefully demolishes those macho posturings that, in the era of Howard Hawks, John Ford, Bogart, Cagney and their peers, were enough to establish a definite character. Yet since society has not yet reached consensus on new symbols, it cannot do more than lay bare an exposed soul.[7]

Directed by Franklin F. Schaffner, *Islands in the Stream* was based on a Hemingway book begun in the 1940's but left unfinished at his death in 1961, apparently due to the fact that he found it too painful to complete. His widow Mary, aided by Scribner's, edited the material and the book was released in 1970. Autobiographical in content, it traces the relationship between painter Thomas Hudson (George C. Scott) and his children. Having left the United States, he has become a metal worker and taken to residing on Bimini Island in the Bahamas. Twice married, he is the father of three sons: Tom, age nineteen (Hart Bochner), fourteen-year-old David (Michael-James Wixted) and ten-year-old Andrew (Brad Savage).

Having not seen the boys in four years, his life revolves around his work, drinking, and his passion for the sea. When the boys arrive to spend their summer vacation with him, he does not go to meet them. Their suits and ties are a reminder of the formal world he has left behind. The oldest and the youngest boys are quick to greet their father, but David is hesitant and stand-offish. That night as they lie awake in bed, David tells Tom of his discomfort. "It doesn't make any sense, Andy and I being here." The boy believes that Tom, as the first-born son and the child of their father's

Opposite: Father and son in a Hemingwayesque encounter as the movies sought to redefine masculinity (*Islands in the Stream*, 1977).

first wife, is the only one the man really cares about. He remembers as well
the bitterness of home life when his parents were still married. "Did he ever
hit your mother? Well, he hit ours." Tommy tries to defend his father,
explaining that he has mellowed, but David remains deeply resentful. "He
hasn't changed, he's still a mean bastard." The three boys engage in a pillow
fight. When their father enters, David's pent-up emotions and resentment
explode and, with tears in his eyes, he hammers the pillow into him again
and again.

Tom takes the boys out to sea with his friend Eddie (David Hem-
mings). He is horrified to see a shark moving towards Tommy who is in the
water. Although he grabs a gun and fires at the shark, his fear for the boy
shatters his composure, causing him to miss as the shark continues on its
perilous course. Only the intervention of the cool-headed Eddie saves
Tommy, while at the same time winning the admiration of young Andy who
announces that "It was the greatest thing I ever saw in my life."

That night, on the veranda of their island retreat, the family are
reminded of the danger closing in on them as the night sky lights up from
the explosion of a torpedoed freighter. In the morning the flotsam and
bodies wash ashore. Hudson's island sanctuary has been visibly touched by
the world beyond. As much as he tries to prevent the boys from seeing the
grim realities of the dead bodies, he cannot escape the knowledge that his
paradise is lost. Looking at the body of a boy not much older than his
oldest, he realizes that the war threatens not only his peace but the security
and safety of his own loved ones. In a moment of shared companionship
with Tommy he tells him that he still loves his mother, explaining that
perhaps they just loved each other too much, demanded too much of each
other. He introduces the boy to Lil, a whore with whom he is having a relationship. "A friend; she doesn't give it away free though." "Oh, that kind
of friend." It is a moment of masculine understanding that signified the
boy's coming of age in his father's eyes.

For Hemingway, the nature of manhood was a popular and
recurring theme. *Islands in the Stream* features a scene that the author had
used as the source for *The Old Man and the Sea*, and one which graphically
illustrates the struggle of the adolescent to achieve manhood. While the
family is out on the ocean, David hooks an enormous fish. Strapped into the
harness and struggling with the monster, the boy battles for long hours, but
although his hands are lacerated, he still refuses to give in. "He'll let that fish
kill him just so he can show Papa he can take it," Andy tells Tommy.
Despite the gruelling pain, David hangs on determinedly while his father
watches the endurance his son suffers in his name. "He's the one with the
hook in his mouth. I'm giving him a beating," the boy insists. Struggling
with the fish, David finds in the pain and the battle a depth to himself he had
not known before. At the point where the fish is almost landed, the line
breaks and it goes free. The boy's ambivalent response is a classic moment
of adolescent confusion, with the boy still experimenting with his role in life

and the feelings that assail him. "In the worst parts," he tells his father, "when I was the tiredest, I began to love him more than anything on earth. I'm sorry we lost him, glad he got away." "You're a good boy, Davey, and I'm proud of you," Hudson tells the boy, hugging him. In the battle with the hidden monster from the sea, the boy has exorcised the hidden fears from his past that have haunted his relationship with his father. It is, however, a typical Hemingway moment of macho accomplishment. The boy has reached his father by becoming his father, by measuring up to the terms he set down. By the end of the decade, such ordeals and tests of endurance would no longer be met.

The boy's battle to grow up is set against the growing battle on the world stage. The sight of the torpedoed freighter and the arrival of refugees from Europe convinces young Tom that he has a part to play in the war, and he tells his father he's going to Canada to be a fighter pilot with the RAF. His approaching departure prompts him to talk to his father about David. "I know you love him the most. 'He's the best of us; you ought to." And so, though Davey felt unloved and an outsider, he had occupied a favored place in his father's heart all along. When the summer ends, he and Andrew have to return. At school, they begin to hear from their father. Their visit has awakened in him his love and a sense of responsibility. He opens up to them, telling them of his love for the sea. "She's my home, my religion. She's eternal. You moved into a part of me that, when you moved out, felt empty." The emptiness is magnified by the death of Tommy. Shattered and feeling vulnerable for the first time in his life, he decides to return to the United States to be with his sons. Enroute he attempts to help a group of refugees and is killed in the process. A tough man, he had tried to run from a world of emotions and responsibilities. By the time he discovered he could not run, it was too late. There is not a great deal that one can find to admire in Tom Hudson. His enduring quality is his strength, but it is not like David's strength, tempered with love and sensitivity. It is brutal, an overt display of masculinity that has too often shrunk from compassion. It is men patterned after Tom Hudson that have created the conflict that engulfs the world and which finally destroys him. In David, we have the promise of a future generation who will know how to fight but also be capable of tears, a boy who knows the good things in life but understands too that it is often made up of mean bastards.

In *Saturday Night Fever* (1978), John Travolta played Tony Romero, an Italian-American who had to come to terms with his own masculinity. Life exists as a battle for Tony and his friends. "It's a dog-eat-dog world." "They got it all locked up." "It's a stinkin' rat race." If life on the streets of New York is tough for Tony, then coming home offers little respite. "I feel like my whole life I've been told I'm no good in the family," he tells his older brother. At the dinner table the boy stands to clear the dishes. "What are you doing? Girls do that!" his father tells him angrily. The boy has come home delighted with himself for getting a raise. Rather than finding himself admired, his father derides him for being so "shit-ass happy over a crummy $2.50 raise." It is a world in which there is little love, self-esteem or family unity. Tony has spent his entire life without the family support we so often take for granted. His brother Frank, the pride of the family, throws in the priesthood. He has learned that he has to be true to himself and that remaining a priest simply to please his family is a betrayal of both himself and his religion. "Do what you think is right, not what they keep trying to jam into you," he advises Tony.

As much as Tony rejects his father, it is this image of masculinity that dominates his life, the hallmark of which seems to be "promoting pussy." Superficially resembling the macho lifestyle, Tony's life in fact represents a breakdown in the image. Said Travolta, "The kicks are maybe in a more surface type of thing.... There's no Hemingway type thing going on here." For the remainder of the film we see Tony attempting to shape a self he can live with. Caught between the conflicting values of the family, the peer group, and his slowly awakening sensitivity, he attempts to become that peculiar combination of man capable of being both strong and gentle.

In the same year, Eric Roberts played adolescent David in a story of a boy who similarly found himself pressured by his family. Paramount's *King of the Gypsies* raised similar issues of masculinity, independence and family responsibility. Set in a Gypsy community, it is liberally sprinkled with an ethos of aggressive masculinity and violence. "All the rest of your life you live with it or fight it." "Even before I was born I was in trouble." "They want their kids smart and tough." "I loved my mother but she couldn't stop him from knocking us over when he got drunk." It is a world of forced marriages, hard drinking, stealing, and the passion of music, travel and romance.

At the age of twelve, David flees the Gypsies when his grandfather suggests he should take a wife. Streetwise but able to neither read nor write, he survives by a series of cleverly devised insurance frauds. But he cannot escape his responsibilities, and his grandfather is determined that the boy succeed him as king of the Gypsies. "You got the tribe, you got the family." For David, the honor comes more as a burden. "Why did I have to be his hope when I was going to be my hope?" It is not his born destiny to be king. The role rightfully belongs to his father who, by his behavior, has forfeited his own father's trust.

When we see David at home, we come to understand the life he is running from. His father largely ignores him and takes it as his right to hit his wife. When the boy tries to prevent his mother from receiving another beating, a violent fight breaks out with his father, who attacks him with a knife. Menacing the boy, his father demands, "Are you my son?" When David denies that he is the son of such a man, his father rips the clothes from his wife's body, forces the boy upon her and orders him to "fuck her." The boy survives the encounter only by leaping from a window.

He abandons the gypsy life, takes to singing in an Italian restaurant, dates blondes with names like Susan, Debbie and Sharon, and dreams of a life in Hollywood where he can renounce his heritage. But the past is in his blood and if he is prepared to forget it, his family and the members of the tribe are not. His mother tells him that the king is dying and that he will inherit the ring and medallion that will make him king. "We live in a democracy, there are no kings.... Give it to anybody with respect for what you are," the boy tells her. David, however, finds himself drawn to the deathbed of his grandfather, where the responsibility for the tribe is handed over to him. "Take care of the girls, make sure they don't reject the family. Make sure they hold to the old ways." Like it or not, David finds himself destined to lead the Gypsies into the twentieth century. But he will not assume the burden. He publicly gives the symbols of authority to his father and informs the Gypsies that he is leaving them and going to California.

His father, however, not content with the fact, feels that the boy's presence will always undermine his authority. He hires hit men to kill his son. David could be safely away, but the ties of kinship detain him at gunpoint. He rescues his sister from an arranged marriage to save her from what their mother has endured. Their father chases them, ramming their car and killing the girl. David has been pushed to the breaking point. Bursting into the family home, he kills his father with a shotgun as the solidarity of the tribe closes in on him, protecting him from the police but condemning him to a life from which he cannot escape.

Warner's *Bloodbrothers* (1978) once again raised the issue of masculinity and the violent nature of the home. *Variety* called it "an ambitious if uneven probe into the disintegration of an Italian-American family."[8] "Why," they asked, "should filmgoers pay to see what they can already hear in the next apartment?"[9] It is a good question but one which can be answered. Robert Mulligan's film is an important and worthwhile contribution to the depiction of the American family for a number of very basic reasons. First, it was one of the earliest films to look seriously at domestic violence. Second, it broke from the industry's obsession with white, middle class American families and showed an image of the Italian-American family which, while hardly a positive image of that segment of the population, at least broke from traditional stereotypes. In the presence of Richard Gere, it also helped develop an actor who, while most loudly acclaimed two years later in Broadway's *Bent* and Paul Schrader's *American Gigolo*, impressed enormously in this role of a sensitive late adolescent caught between his future and his family's past. In *Looking for Mr. Goodbar*, *Days of Heaven*, and *American Gigolo*, Gere had played characters on the precipice of chaos, caught in a violent world that offered merely an illusion of control. Mulligan's film afforded him the opportunity to explore a more sensitive role.

As Stony DeCocco, he plays the son of an aggressively masculine father (Tony LoBianco) and an equally aggressive uncle (Paul Sorvino). Faced with witnessing their lifestyle and the unhappiness it brings, the boy discovers that he must break from it and be himself. Pauline Kael dismissed Gere as an imitator of James Dean. The real comparison, however, was not between Dean and Gere but between the characters they played. Watching Cal Trask do battle with his father in *East of Eden*, Kael had herself commented on the unsatisfactory resolution of the boy's conflict. He had assumed a false victory over a pseudo maturity. Stony DeCocco, on the other hand, achieved real independence both physically and emotionally. His break from his father stands as a significant moment in the cinema's presentation of father-son relationships. In Stony DeCocco, Cal Trask finally grows up. The boy who had wanted his father's love so badly that he destroyed his brother for it has become the young man who loved his brother enough to try and save him from a father whose love was flawed.

Released in 1978, *Bloodbrothers* was a particularly appropriate contribution to a subject that was receiving more attention in the American media. Writing in January of the previous year, Urie Bronfenbrenner had this to say:

> Child abuse by parents has become a national problem. A 1970 survey projected that at least two million battered child cases a year may be found annually now; nearly 200,000 infants and children a year are being killed by their supposed caretakers. A more gruesome trend shows that the killing of infants under one year of age has been increasing since 1957. The infanticide rate has risen from 3.1 per 100,000 in 1957 to 4.7 per 100,000 in 1970. Sadly, ninety percent of these incidents take place right in the home; the most severe injuries occur in single parent homes and many brutalities are inflicted by the frazzled mother herself.[10]

If for no other reason than this, *Bloodbrothers* demands a place of recognition alongside *To Kill a Mockingbird* as a film that saw a problem and attempted to address it.

The film opens in a working man's bar. The aggressively masculine ethos dominates the conversation with talk of the search for a chick with "a tongue like an anteater." In his own bar across town with the younger set Tony, like his father, is hot and horny. Nineteen years old, frustrated and full of explosive tension, his first appearance recalls his character in *Looking for Mr. Goodbar*. Looking in the bar mirror, he sees his former girlfriend dancing with another man. The violence bursts from him and he has to be restrained by his friends. From the first moment then, the relationship between sex, violence, and love is established.

The movie crosses back and forth between the Saturday night exploits of the boy and his father and uncle. Just out of high school, Stony has not yet decided what he wants to do. His family, however, have no doubts. "He's too smart for college; it's four years of fucking around," they agree as they plan an apprenticeship for him. Like David, Stony's life seems to be predetermined for him. If he has no control over his future, he seems equally incapable of controlling his present. Restrained briefly in the bar, he later follows Sherry and her new boyfriend home. Throwing the man out, he slaps Sherry and then finds himself trapped in the building by the boyfriend and his cronies. A quick phone call brings his uncle swinging a chain in his defense, as they vanquish the villains and enjoy their triumph. "Women love violence. Four guys fighting for her, she must have been dying for it," Chubby tells him. Stony, however, is not so sure. "You're sick," he tells his uncle. It is the cue for the boy to unburden himself of some of the self-doubts and uncertainties that afflict him. Standing in the dark of the street he begins to ask his uncle about sex and how to treat a woman. "She doesn't come. I don't understand, I tried everything." Stony's inability to provoke orgasm in his partner has obviously damaged his concept of his own masculinity. If he needed consolation and understanding, in his uncle he finds little of value. His aunt Phyllis came only three times in 23 years, he is told, and the subject is dropped.

The first image of the DeCocco family together establishes the tension pervading the family. It is breakfast time. Stony's father, Tommy, is still in his shorts. The boy enters and nurses his young brother Albert (Michael Mershewe) on his lap. Their mother Maria (Lelia Goldoni) angrily berates the young boy for not eating while her husband blames the boy's fragile frame on her. It is Sunday, family day, a day that usually means driving about searching for a G-rated movie. It is a ritual that Stony is growing tired of. But this Sunday his father and uncle have something else in mind. They drive the family to a cemetery to show a plot they have brought, "so we can stay together." Standing on the hillside, Stony's father and uncle reflect on their childhood and their own father. A tough man, he was "a mean bastard with his hands," but he kept them fed and together throughout the Depression and they loved and respected him for it.

The next time we see young Albert, he once again becomes the center of family conflict. Left at home to finish his breakfast, he has become preoccupied with television. When his mother returns to find that he has not eaten, she explodes angrily, clutching at herself and screaming. "Why do you take such pleasure in torturing us?" she demands, forcing food into the boy's mouth until, frightened and overcome, he faints.

At the hospital, the doctors agree that the boy is suffering from "pure shock.... That boy's been terrorized." Disturbed, Stony is nonetheless capable of understanding what motivates his mother. "She does it 'cause she loves him," he tries to tell the doctors. Maria agrees to give the boy Valium, but reacts negatively at the prospect of his undergoing therapy. "What are his little friends going to say when they find out he's seeing a shrink?" When Stony tries to calm her, she becomes so agitated that she throws the Valium away and Albert is left without medication.

Stony takes the boy home, but at the entrance to the house Albert becomes frightened and he throws up. His absolute terror of facing life at home can no longer be hidden. Dismayed at his brother's condition, Stony turns on his mother angrily. "What have you done to him? What have you done, you bitch? What have you done to my brother?" In his own anger, Stony has come perilously close to hitting his mother and he fears the awesome anger bottled up within him. The anger that has engulfed the family threatens now to engulf him. He returns to the hospital and talks to a doctor about his own anger.

In the doctor he finds an adult with whom he can talk and who will listen to him. He has filled in his college entrance papers but not mailed them. At the point when he thinks he may become an electrician like his father, he admits that he got a kick a couple of summers ago out of being a camp counselor for kids in "Joisey." When the doctor offers him a position as a recreation assistant in the children's ward, Stony accepts. His father, however, is far from enthusiastic about the idea. He has just managed to get the boy a union card. He's going to be a chip off the old block. "A job like this, it's everything.... I want what's best for you," he tells the boy as he musses his hair affectionately, delighted to be welcoming him into his world.

Stony tries to explain that he wants to work with kids, but his father is not willing to listen. "Recreational assistant is woman's work.... I can still kick your fuckin' ass all over this room." But Stony is too old now to simply acquiesce to his father's wishes or his strength. "Don't you ever touch me like that again," he tells him, establishing the physical and psychological barrier that separates them. Standing in the doorway to the boy's bedroom, strategically positioned between the house where he remains the boss and Stony's room where his authority has dissipated. Tommy makes a concession, suggesting that the boy spend a couple of weeks in each job.

In the children's ward, Stony proves a natural with the kids. He has authority but it is based on love and respect. He tells them stories of Indian tribes, assuring them that "The more bloodbrothers you got, the better off you are." His relationship with the children contrasts to the way his father deals with the young. A perpetual adolescent, the man has never grown up. Aided and abetted by his brother, he drinks his life away, pining for a silky Korean girl from 25 years ago. "You only get one shot in life—you better not fuck it up." He manifests the symbols of family unity such as the compulsory Sunday outing, but there is little depth beneath the outward show. Sexually neither he nor his brother have matured. They chase women relentlessly with no regard for their own families. Flashing at a beautiful woman is par for the course. Treating them as human beings with feelings of their own is totally foreign to them. It is a man's world in which Tommy can continue to believe that "a father and a son is the greatest thing in the world."

The hospital has awakened in Stony the compassion and sensitivity that he had previously reserved for Albert. When we next see him in a bar, it is quite a transformation from his first scene. He meets Annette, a girl from a rough background who was put in a home at fifteen. She senses a hidden depth in the boy. "There's somethin' chewin' on you. You know there's somethin' out there besides playin' cool and actin' macho and makin' bucks and gettin' yourself laid." She is not wrong. Stony likes the job at the hospital and wants to stay but, true to his word, the time has come for him to try a couple of weeks with his father and uncle. Knowing his worth, the hospital agrees to let him go for two weeks when he explains, "Ever since I was a kid, they got this hard hat waiting for me like it was a crown and I'm heir to the throne or something."

On the job he runs the gauntlet that is the usual initiation rite for a new brother. Despite the harassment he keeps his cool and refuses to blow his stack. Capable of making it in the overtly masculine world of his father, he knows too that he has the strength to be a man with feelings he does not have to be afraid of. The few moments of sensitivity we see in his father and uncle are reserved for other men. They take Stony to a bar where they are giving a party for the crippled owner. Presenting him with a four-speed wheelchair, they join together and sing "When Irish Eyes Are Smiling." "And that's what it's all about," Stony's father tells him.

For Stony, however, there has to be more from life. There can be pride in work but it must be the work you have determined for yourself. There can be sex but it must be sex balanced with love. There can be family love and loyalty but it must exist in practice as well as principle. In an interview with Ralph Appelbaum, Robert Mulligan talked about youngsters like Stony, faced with deciding what sort of future they want:

> I feel that the only people who escape that — and they're the blessed ones — are those who have a talent, whether it's for music or painting or architecture or engineering or math or something that puts focus in their life very early on. The rest of us have to stumble our way into what we are and what we hope to become, because we don't know. And that's the kind of pain I can relate to. Not to be able to articulate at nineteen or even twenty that this is what I want to be.... Now Stony doesn't have a dream, he doesn't know what he wants to do because he's living in a box, in a very limited structured world that says to him that this is what you do at nineteen or twenty: your father gives you a union card and that's life. You've got it, you're all set, don't worry about it. But the minute he takes the card he is locked into it and yet he can't articulate, 'No, I don't want the card.' Because he doesn't know what the hell he wants to do."[11]

The boy knows he does not want to work with his father but he does not want to reject him in the process. Annette talks to him about going to college and all the while he can only feel that somehow, somewhere out there beyond the Bronx there is a life waiting to present him with opportunities that he has never had. Ensnared in a life that relentlessly demands that he make decisions without providing him the means to arrive at them, he retreats to the bars and the tension-filled individual we have witnessed in the

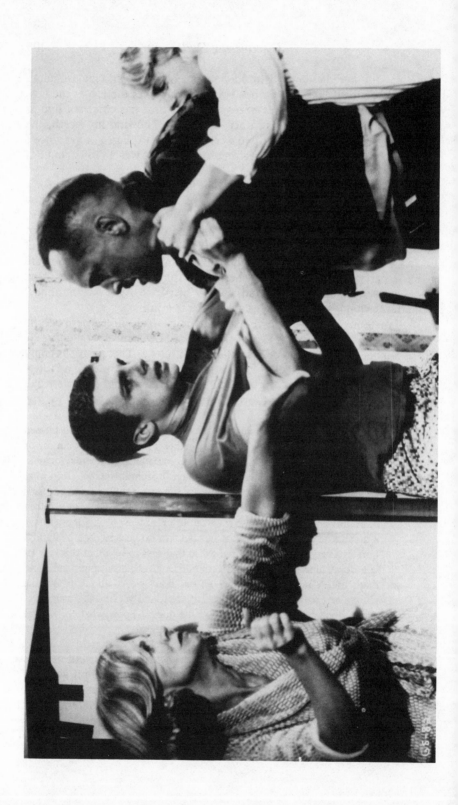

earlier scenes. Disgusted with him, Annette declares that he has "turned into a fully blooded DeCocco, fighting and boozing and chasing snatch."

Against this backdrop of Stony struggling with his own sexuality, we see in closeup the shabby suspicion and betrayal that dominates his parents' sex life. When Maria discovers her husband's infidelity, she allows herself to be degraded by a sordid relationship with a man for whom she has no feelings at all. Her husband finds out and bashes her violently while a terrified Albert hides in his room. And yet for all the horror and repugnance of the beating, we come to understand something about the man and his inability to control himself.

In the character of Tommy DeCocco, Mulligan has skillfully etched an individual whom we can simultaneously admire and despise. If his wife is a victim, then he himself is a victim of his own upbringing. Only in understanding him can we fully comprehend the antithesis that is Stony. While Tommy causes pain, it is pain bred of his own suffering.

> It's his kind of pain. He doesn't know how to handle it. That kind of suspicion, that macho pride has been violated, he thinks. There's also that sense of loss. Here he is at 45, whatever years old and he's beginning to look at his life and wonder what it's all about. Is life still getting drunk on weekends and buying some broad in a hotel room? And then to wake up on Sunday and play the papa of the family and go to church? You see, there's an emptiness there and a fear that goes on in that kind of man.[12]

Nowhere is this fear more evident than when Tommy wakes up in the hospital. It has taken four cops to get the handcuffs on him and now, in the sober light of day, he must face the awful realization of what he has done. "I just want to crawl in a fucking hole and die," he tells Stony. Through his father's pain and his mother's fear, the boy begins to crystalize in his mind a sense of, if not what he wants, then at least a knowledge of what he does not want. "I love them and I keep thinking maybe I can help them out," he explains to Annette. But the boy cannot help his parents. As Mulligan has suggested, "They're locked into a system that was put on them by the lives they grew up in, by their fathers who were tough men and demanded a certain type of behavior. And now they're acting it out again."[13]

No sooner is he released from the hospital than Tommy, spurred by the insinuations of his fellow workers, turns violent again. Ranting about the excess of permissiveness in his home and in the nation, his temper gets the better of him once again. Rescuing his brother from his room where he is crouching, embryo-like in terror, Stony leaves home. But he will not just

Opposite: A final fling for the machismo of fatherhood. "If there's one thing that I want to give my son, it's the gift of fury ... gobble up the world. Eat life or it'll eat you" (*The Great Santini*, 1980).

run. There is in his nature too much character and too much decency to simply take off. He will leave his father and his family as a man, but a man on his own terms. He enters the barroom where his father sits, prepared to face the man on his own turf. "I came to say goodbye. I came to tell you I love you. I ain't against you or nothing." He leaves with Albert as they head away from town in a cab. Behind them in the street his father breaks down and buckles up in tears. "It pays to have kids," he says bitterly.

The Great Santini featured a brilliant performance by Robert Duvall as a living anachronism. Totally obsessed by his life in the Marines, he cannot distinguish between being a father and being a soldier. "I want you to look on me like I was God.... If I say something, you pretend like it was coming from the burning bush." "If there's one thing that I want to give my son, it's the gift of fury ... gobble up the world ... eat life or it'll eat them." But his son Ben cannot live his father's life. He sees through the alcohol, the aggression and the macho facade. Drawing upon his father's courage and convictions, he is able to look at the man and understand him for who and what he is, with all his faults and failures, without wishing to emulate him.

Breaking Away further strengthened the growing bond between film fathers and sons. Dave's father initially believes "He's worthless, that one — lazy freeloader. I tell you, I die of shame every time I see him." But in the course of the film, both characters come to grow and mature and better understand each other. The Academy Award-winning screenplay presented an image of a father neither weak nor wise, neither too tough nor overly tender, who could let his child grow and become what he wanted. In mutal affection and understanding, father and son look upon each other and learn from each other's lives. While Ben achieved his independence upon his father's death, and Stony left home to achieve his, Dave established independence within the family fold, where he may not always be understood but where he will be loved.

Finally, in *Ordinary People*, we see one last image of the son who found himself through the father. In the closing moments of the film, as Beth Jarrett leaves home, Calvin (Donald Sutherland) sits on the front steps with his son Conrad. Beth has failed as both wife and mother. Unable to handle a mess, she likes everything clean and neat. When emotions and pressures close in on her, she has no way of dealing with them. When her oldest son died, part of her died with him. "It was the best of you that you buried," her husband tells her. She leaves because she has nothing to offer, because she cannot face the task ahead.

In therapy, still shaky from his suicide attempt, Conrad needs the support of his family. He has learned not to expect anything from his mother. His strength and his future rests with Calvin. "You ought to do that more often. Haul my ass a little, get after me," he tells his dad. "I used to figure you had a handle for everything, you knew it all." While Calvin enjoys the boy's respect, he will not allow him the comfort of illusions. He knows from his own experience that he has lived a lie too long and he wants

Ordinary People (1980): Mary Tyler Moore as Beth Jarrett, a mother who no longer understands what people expect of her.

his son to have a better start to life. "Don't admire people too much. They'll disappoint you sometimes." But Conrad invests his trust and his emotions well. "I'm not disappointed. I love you." "I love you too," Calvin replies.

It had taken fifty years for the American cinema to realistically look at the American family and present it with all its strengths and faults.

Shock, sensation and sentimentality had too often obscured the mirror into which we gazed. Either idealized or grossly distorted, the mirror had taken us first through the looking glass into fantasyland, and then confronted us with a portrait of Dorian Gray until we shrank away in horror and disgust.

Long dominated by an image, the industry had refused to confront the issues. With the 1970's under way, vast changes in American society slowly infiltrated the cinema. The feminist movement began to manifest itself in movies. Films such as *Norma Rae* presented strident, more independent women. Like two sides of a coin, any basic change in one could not but bring about a reciprocal reaction in the other. Hollywood by implication could not re-define the American wife and mother without re-defining the American husband and father. If the American screen father had an easier time of it than movie mothers, he was still forced to struggle at times. *Middle Aged Crazy* found Bruce Dern screaming, "I don't want to be the daddy." It was, however, a role and responsibility he could no longer avoid.

While there is growing evidence of a new and more mature rendition of the American family, it is equally apparent that many of the old prejudices remain. While mother is at last liberated from the home and able to establish an independent life and career of her own, the suggestion remains implicit that she needs a man in her life. Thus in *Alice Doesn't Live Here Anymore*, while Alice asserts a new independence, she still succumbs to a man's advice. When David (Kris Kristofferson) encounters Alice's son, he tells her, "You spoil him rotten. He's got the foulest mouth of any kid his age I've ever seen." The woman is allowed her momentary act of assertion, telling him, "How dare you tell me how to bring up my child!" But in the end she realized that both she and her son need a man. In opting for the patriarchy, Hollywood thus resorted to its traditional response. Both *Kramer vs. Kramer* and *Ordinary People* clearly imply that while women need time to find themselves, men are more together. If there is a crisis in the family home, the suggestion goes, it can be overcome by the father and son, but only when the wife and mother is absent.

6. From Mentors to Murderers

"You're dangerous and unwholesome and children should not be exposed to you" —
Sandy to Jean Brodie; *The Prime of Miss Jean Brodie*; 1969.

Our experience of school is, after the family, the most universal and tribal involvement in which we participate during our lifetime. "Never again are we ranked so precisely by those around us and on so many scales.... What high school has become in fact and in memory is a self-contained community, a tribe with its own special rituals and status symbols, a tribal gathering where teenage Americans act out their puberty rights and wrongs."[1] If we are to take literature, cinema and television as examples of our preoccupations, we spend much of our time, after leaving school, reflecting on our experiences there, a process by which Frank Zappa has observed high school becomes more than a place, it becomes a state of mind. Sociologist Lloyd Temme says, "I believe the rest of our lives are spent making up for what we did or didn't do in high school."[2] Psychologist Erik Erikson believes that "adult values grow directly out of high school."[3] It is little wonder then that the mass media reflects and reinforces our preoccupation with school.

In England, television shows such as *Whacko, Please Sir, The Fenn Street Gang*, and *Glittering Prizes* have located themselves within the school and post-school experience of their main characters. In Australia, *The Class of '74, Certain Women*, and *The Restless Years* have all brought to the small screen television series largely centered around school. The growth in the Australian film industry in the 1970's also found room for such school fare as *The Mango Tree, The Getting of Wisdom, Picnic at Hanging Rock*, and *The Devil's Playground*. But it is the United States where the real high school cult is most evident. Springing from the school-based *Welcome Back Kotter*, John Travolta made the successful transfer from television to Rydell High in the film *Grease* (1978). *The White Shadow, The Facts of Life*, and a list of other American television series all deal in one way or another with school experiences. It is, however, on the big screen that one finds the most

111

interesting and pervasive depictions of school life—one which, incidentally, influenced television's depictions.

The celluloid classroom has never been a stranger to film audiences, but whereas once it was largely confined to adaptations of best sellers like *Goodbye Mr. Chips* (1939) and *Good Morning Miss Dove* (1955), the film industry's whole-hearted search for a youthful audience, added to the baby-boom which filled theaters and schools alike, elevated high school to a cult and a craze from which we have never fully recovered. *High School Caesar* (1960), *High School Hellcats* (1958), *Platinum High School* (1960), *High School Confidential* (1958); these were but a few of the billboards that the fifties and sixties screamed of. At home on our smaller screens we could enter the school environment of *Our Miss Brooks*, *Dobie Gillis*, *Mr. Novak*, or *Room 222*. Series such as *Father Knows Best*, *The Patty Duke Show*, *The Brady Bunch*, and *My Three Sons* constantly allowed both teenagers and adults alike to experience something of school life as the media envisaged it. Wherever film or television action has concerned itself with adolescence, the location has inevitably moved to the school ground or the classroom.

In the 1970's George Lucas gave further impetus to a trend that needed no encouragement when he made *American Graffiti*. It was, said the director, "a ten year reunion with myself, or rather with my teenage fantasies."[4] Continuing the trend, the highly acclaimed *The Paper Chase* (1973) moved from the large to the small screen and concerned itself with the law school experiences of a group of late adolescents and young adults. In 1978 the most popular movie, according to the People's Choice Awards, was *National Lampoon's Animal House*, which took an irreverent look at fraternity life in the early sixties. So well received was the film that life imitated art and the film's toga party sequence inspired similar events such as that held at the University of Wisconsin in Madison, where ten thousand students and friends joined in the high jinks.

Nor has the celebration of school simply been confined to the visual media. The lyrics of popular recording hits abound with references to school life. "Teacher's Pet," "To Sir With Love," "Don't Stand so Close to Me," "See You in September," "Smoking in the Boys' Room," "Be True to Your School," and the Chuck Berry classic, "School Days": all chronicle the adolescent educational encounter. Perhaps the ultimate rock and roll tribute to school came in 1972 when Alice Cooper released "School's Out," in which the album cover came in the shape of a school desk complete with report card.

It is in the celluloid classroom, however, that one can best see the sustained interest school has maintained for the mass media and the developments that have taken place in one industry's response to it. In looking at school on the screen, it is apparent that the stories divide themselves rather neatly, if not equally, into two sections. On the one hand, in dealing with school, Hollywood and indeed the film industries of other nations seem to have concentrated on the teacher as hero. Where the teacher is not exactly presented in such admirable terms, he or she still tends to dominate the action. These films thus center upon the impact of one particular teacher on a group of students. The other, less numerous type of story line usually concerns itself with the trials and tribulations of one youngster or group of youngsters in a school. Since the cinema of adolescence informs us not only about the young, but also the institutions through which we socialize them, it is equally important for us to consider the depiction of teachers, principals, coaches, and schools in general as it is for us to concentrate on the students.

The sustained failure of the film families, particularly throughout the fifties and sixties, opened the way for the screen schools to function as a perfect forum within which to articulate and address the concerns of adolescents. The result was the emergence of the teacher-hero, in which the teacher, operating as parent surrogate, sought to redress the problems caused by parental neglect and failure. While the depiction of school on the screen can therefore be seen as a logical outcome of the depiction of the family, its roots are deepset and can be traced to more than one source.

Literary tradition, for example, played no small role in the depiction of school. Edna Lue Furness, in her article, "The Image of High School Teachers in American Literature," had observed that "writers seem to have a penchant for giving the impression that our high school teachers are social misfits, lovable old bears, fuddy-duddies, ineffectual quacks, rag ends of unsaleable males and unmarriageable females, someone who is a school teacher and nothing more."[5] As we shall see, such an image found its way inevitably to the screen. As early as 1933, Shuttelworth and May in their study, "The Social Conduct and Attitude of Movie Fans," found that movies depicted college professors as incompetent, lazy, foolish, or lacking in intelligence. The teacher-hero format, rather than repudiating such an image, merely served to strengthen it, for in order for the teacher to emerge as hero, it was necessary for other teachers, and in particular for principals and administrators, to be depicted as villains. At its most simple level, this format led to a formula in which teacher meets class, teacher wins class, teacher loses class, teacher wins class back. *To Sir With Love* (1967), among others, noticeably complied with this formula.

Yet despite the prevalence of this format, subtle changes can be traced over a period of some fifty or more years. These changes reflect much more than changes within the nation's schools or in Hollywood's attitude towards the schools and teachers. While the industry claimed, in films like *The Blackboard Jungle* (1955), to reflect real conditions in the schools, images revealed in the celluloid classroom can be seen to represent much more than the state of the nation's schools. The depiction of school on the screen, like the depiction of the family, serves as an image of society as a whole. Both the family and the school are microcosms of society. What goes on in one is intimately related to what occurs in the other. In depicting school life Hollywood, consciously or unconsciously, touched upon concerns, fears, attitudes, and preoccupations that went well beyond the boundaries of the schoolyard and spilled out into the wider society beyond. The changing image of the school, and particularly of the school teacher, can therefore be read as a reflection, albeit a distorted reflection, of changes not only within the American school system but within the nation itself.

Most astounding of all these changes is the increasingly negative portrayal of the school teacher. Between 1935 and 1977, for example, one finds irrefutable evidence of an increasingly negative depiction of the teacher. It is a process by which the image of the teacher moves from mentor to murderer, from scholar to scapegoat. In the end the teacher is reduced to victim, voyeur, seducer, and killer. It is an image which single-handedly destroys the oft-made claim that films mirror reality, or that art imitates life. For while these films may reflect conditions and incidents within a few schools, they can in no way be regarded as representative of the American educational system. In seeking to repeat such images, Hollywood displayed its typical proclivity for sensationalism. To understand such negative images, one needs to understand the source from which they had emerged.

In 1935 Monogram Films made *Hoosier Schoolmaster*, a post-civil war account of a soldier turned teacher in rural Indiana. "School teachers don't last very long around here. You don't know what you're up against in this district, young man. The boys have driven off the last two school-masters, and they licked the one before them like blazes." While the words may sound like something from *The Blackboard Jungle*, the urban battle-ground was still a long way off and for the most part, exchanges between pupils and teachers in films of the thirties remained civil, respectful and warm. But if the classroom had not yet become a scene of conflict, one can still locate in these films evidence of the trend that came to dominate the schools on the screen for the next half-century.

Hoosier Schoolboy (1937) was another Monogram production. It featured Anne Nagel as Miss Evans, a novice teacher taking up her first appointment in the rural town of Ainsley. The image of the new teacher arriving in a strange and often inhospitable environment became one of the staple elements of the school movies. Ainsley is in the middle of a milk strike which severely dislocates the community. No sooner is she off the train than Miss Evans finds herself dragged into the conflict. Accused of being an agitator, she is almost forcibly placed back on the train and sent on her way. Only when she produces her credentials do the hostile strikers back off and begrudgingly allow her to remain, though still asserting, "You don't look like a school teacher to me."

Upon commencing teaching, she finds herself drawn to Charkie Carter (Mickey Rooney), a troubled youngster from the wrong side of the tracks who seems to be constantly in trouble. Keeping the boy after school, she tentatively tries to get through to him. "I'm not only your teacher, I'm a

Goodbye Mr. Chips (1939): **The quintessence of the movie mentor.**

friend. That's really my job.... I think you're a regular fellow." In supporting the boy, Miss Evans goes against the attitude of the headmistress and the other staff members. Suspicious of her as an outsider, and jealous of her good education, the other members of the staff reject her as "one of those upstart teachers who got a degree at Columbia." Rather than helping her adjust to the new school and town, they hope she'll "get her ears slapped down." Not only does Miss Evans challenge the traditional teaching methods, but she breaks customs in the town. Wishing to meet Charkie's father, she goes home with the boy one evening. Although he warns her "people won't respect you none if you're seen going over here," she refuses to be intimidated by local gossip, and dismisses Ainsely as "the sinful city of the misunderstood." As the story progresses, she successfully challenges the school and the community, demonstrating that her methods can work. In the process she saves a boy from being thrown on the junk heap and brings dignity to his father, who has always been treated as a social outcast.

Both films are important, for they establish themes that were to long dominate the depiction of school on the screen. As the teacher/hero, Miss Evans is a very early example of how such a format served to denigrate the rest of the teaching profession. As an outsider entering a strange environment, she invoked an image not only of traditional American antipathy to intellectuals, but also of suspicion of newcomers and intruders. This theme was to become particularly prevalent throughout the fifties.

The thirties, even in the form of one of the screen's most popular teachers, further reveals the long tradition of the celluloid classroom. MGM's *Goodbye Mr. Chips* (1939) was popularly acclaimed and resulted in an Oscar for Robert Donat's portrayal of the beloved master of Brookfield. But Mr. Chipping, despite his oft remembered popularity, is an abject failure as a teacher. His first day in the school is a disaster from which the headmaster has to rescue him. Fluctuating from one extreme to the other, Chips fails to exercise authority in one scene only to become a Caligula of the classroom in the next. His success comes in spite of himself, in spite of his colleagues, and in spite of the principal. When he emerges as a fine teacher, he does so upon the advice and guidance of his wife, a woman who has no background in teaching at all. The teacher-hero therefore once again emerges by becoming the non-teacher, the master who breaks with tradition and establishes his own style. Such a situation repeated itself time and time again in the fifties and sixties.

Throughout much of the thirties and forties, school existed as an incidental backdrop, seldom occupying the foreground of our motion picture screens. Yet even in these glimpses, one can see the gradual drift to the drama that consumed the classroom in years ahead. *These Three* (1936) found teachers as victims of gossip and innuendo spread by students. *Angels Wash Their Faces* (1939) featured Margaret Hamilton as a school teacher no more favorably presented than her role of the wicked witch of *The Wizard of Oz*, made in the same year. The Henry Aldrich series,

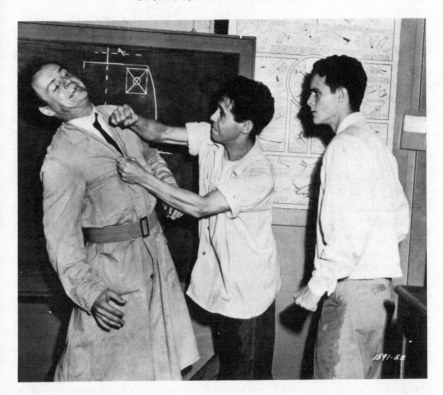

City Across the River **(1949): The teacher as victim in the first major battle of the blackboard jungle.**

throughout the forties, showed Henry as the victim of Principal Bradley and teachers like Mr. Crossley. *That Hagen Girl* (1947) repeated the image of teacher as heroine by surrounding her with a headmistress and staff too narrow-minded and prejudiced to reach out and help a tormented teenager.

In October 1946, a Sacramento conference on Life Adjustment Education reported the case of Jack, a sixteen-year-old delinquent with a record of truancy, running away from home and breaking into shops. "To him," the conference was told, "school was a hopeless coercion and a place of continuous defeat."[6] While Jack was to become a familiar film figure in the following decade, he first found his way into the celluloid classroom in 1949. *City Across the River* was one of the few films throughout the forties to face the problem of juvenile delinquency. When it did so, it encountered it in the classroom.

Set in Brooklyn, the film dealt with youngsters lacking parental guidance. With little or no discipline at home, they come to school as an unruly mob. In an industrial arts class, we watch as the students gain the upper hand, driving their teacher from the room in despair. Order is restored by the principal. But this is no simple book-throwing youthful high jinks like that encountered by Chipping. The principal calls it "the worst demonstration I've ever experienced." "You have to be firm with them," he advises the teacher. But the teacher knows that firmness has to come from more than just the school, it must come from the family and from society as a whole. "Firm? I can't slug them, I can only reason with them. It's like a boll weevil with a pack of wild animals. That's what they are, a pack, once they get that gang spirit, that arrogance. Sometimes I think the only solution is to clean out all the people and to drop an atom bomb on that whole slum."

Later, when two of the boys return to the school, they plead with the teacher not to bring their parents in on the problem. Genuinely afraid of their parents, the boys become increasingly desperate at the teacher's failure to consider their concern. When he threatens to have them arrested for loitering, the boys' fear consumes them and in the ensuing fight, they accidentally kill their teacher. As he slumps to the classroom floor dead, the image of the teacher as victim had reached its ultimate level.

While such an image became more and more evident throughout the next decade, *City Across the River* did more than set the stage for schools of the 1950's. By invoking the boys' fear of their families, as well as the image of the city slums, the film was a rare and timely reflection of concerns that exploded in headlines in the Kefauver investigations of the early fifties. While *The Blackboard Jungle* (1955) is often cited as an example of Hollywood's concern with controversy, the film was six years behind *City Across the River*, which itself was Hollywood's belated acknowledgement of a problem that had persisted throughout the forties.

The Blackboard Jungle, in fact, while it may have grown out of Evan Hunter's novel and reflected conditions in certain American schools, cannot be fully understood by looking at the social conditions from which it sprang. For if it served as a testimony to certain social conditions, it equally owed its existence to cinematic tradition and developments. When "Rock Around the Clock" exploded from the screen at the opening of the film, it did much more than anounce the arrival of rock and roll, or of Hollywood's realization that the nation's schools were in trouble. It announced that the film industry had found another social concern from which to reap a profit.

Between 1940 and 1949, the problem film had become a successful and controversial staple of the industry. *The Grapes of Wrath* (1940), *Lost Weekend* (1945), *Gentleman's Agreement* (1947), *The Snake Pit* (1948), *Pinky* (1949), and *Knock on Any Door* (1949) had dealt with such issues as racism, alcholism, mental illness, and juvenile delinquency. In typical Hollywood fashion, all of them dealt with the issues as if they had just been discovered. While *Grapes of Wrath* dealt with the plight of dispossessed farmers in the Depression, Hollywood's screens throughout that period had been peculiarly silent on such an issue. Similarly, while juvenile delinquency had been rife throughout the war years, it was not until the end of the

The Blackboard Jungle (1955): Darryl F. Zanuck complained that "it could only give an erroneous impression of the American school system."

decade that films like *Knock on Any Door* seriously addressed the question. *The Blackboard Jungle*, therefore, stemmed from a short-lived but profitable tradition of turning controversy into profit.

Based on the novel by Evan Hunter and directed by Richard Brookes, it introduced us to North Manual High, a product of the New York City school system, where Richard Dadier (Glenn Ford) encounters cynical teachers and rebellious students. The pupils who inhabit the hallways of North Manual are like nothing we have seen before. What *City*

Across the River threatened is at last delivered. When the boys killed their teacher in the earlier film, it was an accident. At North Manual High the threat of death and violence is painfully present. The young people we encounter in this film are strangers—alien, hostile, and threatening. The street is their home, their turf, their territory. Although the principal assures Dadier that there is no discipline problem at the school, our suspicions are aroused when he has him recite the St. Crispin's battle speech before entering his classroom. Despite the early attempts the students make to razz Dadier, he copes reasonably well, passing their behavior off as youthful exuberance. But underneath their glib remarks that indicate a survival of the flippest, there lurks a more sinister element. "Did you ever try to fight 35 guys at one time, Teach?" one of the kids asks defiantly.

Dadier, however, will not be intimidated. If the kids want to challenge him, he is prepared to rise to the challenge. "Take your hat off, boy, before I knock it off," he threatens one student. But these kids aren't playing at being tough, they are tough—children of a concrete jungle raised in a frightening urban environment where social Darwinism prevails. School is something that they put up with. They have no expectations of it and it apparently has none of them. "The garbage can of the educational system," is how one teacher regards the school, warning Dadier, "Don't be a hero and never turn your back on the class." The prospect of graduation never exists for these pupils as a real possiblity. "They just get to be eighteen and then they make room for more of the same kind," Dadier is told.

Our first vision of the teacher as victim occurs when a young teacher, Lois Hammond, is almost raped in the school at the end of the day. She is saved only by Dadier's intervention. It is a brutal and frightening scene as he pursues the boy through the corridors, finally grabbing him as he leaps through a window. As he drags the boy back inside, the student's face is cut on the jagged glass. Dadier's actions are taken by his class as a sign of aggression, an act of betrayal in which he clearly aligns himself with the establishment. If the students had previously been unwilling to learn, they are now openly hostile. He is forced to run the gauntlet of their tense bodies, terse expressions, and palpable dislike.

Seeking a brief respite, he visits a neighborhood bar with Josh, another young teacher, wryly wondering if "there are any alcoholics among high school teachers." Josh tells him of the plan he has to try and interest the kids by reaching them on their own level. He has a valuable collection of records and hopes that he can get on the same wavelength as the students by appealing to their interest in music. On their way home from the bar, both men are set upon by students who beat them viciously. In a peculiar comment on the incident, *Parents Magazine* suggested, "Mr. Dadier invites the beating given him by the boys from his class by becoming intoxicated at a bar in the school neighborhood."[7]

In the characters of Josh, Dadier and Miss Hammond, *The Blackboard Jungle* presents three visions of the teacher as victim. While they are victims of the boys' attacks, they are also victims of a more subtle nature. Dadier's own education seems to have failed to prepare him to deal with the realities of teaching. Returning to his university, he seeks out a former professor. "What's the point of teaching if kids don't care about education?" he asks the man. "You were my professor in college. You should have taught me how to stop a fight in a classroom, how to deal with an I.Q. of 66. If I'm going to be a lion tamer, I should teach with a chair and a whip." The culture shock the young teacher has suffered is not merely the result of running into a bunch of street-wise kids, it is a sense of being totally inadequate to the task. In response, his professor shows him a well-behaved class of clean-cut, bright-faced youngsters who sing "The Star Spangled Banner." Clearly, the implication is that the boys he teaches are not representative of American youth. While such an observation may be correct, it by no means alleviates Dadier's need to find a way to deal with them and his belief that they, like all young people, are entitled to an education. Boys like Greg Miller (Sydney Poitier) have potential, but they need special care and encouragement to bring out the best in them. Greg and the boys sense the indifference of the staff. "Nobody gives a hoot; not the other fellas, not the teachers, not even my parents."

Dadier, however, does care. Even when Josh is attacked again and his record collection destroyed, Dadier will not give in. He knows the cynicisim of the staff and he knows the way they feel. He listens as they despairingly tell him he can't beat the system. "They outnumber you, they outweigh you, and they outreach you ... besides, they've got clobbered at home and in the streets and they're used to it." If school is the survival of the fittest, then it is the kids who will survive. But Darwin said more than that, he said it was a struggle for the survival of the fittest. For many of the teachers at North Manual, there is no struggle, only capitulation, and it is this attitude that incenses Dadier. Accusing the staff of being slobberers, clobberers, grumblers and sleepers, he fully embraces the image of the teacher as hero by alienating himself from the rest of the staff. If he is to succeed, he will do it as his screen predecessors have done, without the assistance of faculty or administration. And yet it is not that easy. While Dadier gets through to Greg Miller, and anticipates McLuhan by winning the class over with movies, he does not succeed with all the boys.

When the roughest element in the class intrude upon his personal life, he seriously considers resigning. In a moment of despair he realizes that people really don't care. Teachers, he acknowledges, occupy a low position on the social ladder, paid $2 an hour like a soda jerk or a baby sitter. It is no accident that when he returns to the classroom he does so at his wife's instigation. "We all need the same thing. Patience, understanding, love; you've got that to give them," she tells him in an extension of the role of Mrs. Chipping.

The Blackboard Jungle clearly conformed to a familiar pattern of depicting school on the screen. At the same time, it brought a much more realistic image of teaching to the public's attention. Declaring itself a reflection of real conditions in certain sections of the educational system, it opened with a prologue that proclaimed, "We in the United States are fortunate to have a school system that is a tribute to our communities and our faith in American youth.... We believe that public school awareness is a first step to a remedy for any problem." There is little doubt that some of the concerns reflected in *The Blackboard Jungle* mirrored conditions in American schools.

By the mid-fifties, the function of American education was coming under serious scrutiny. As early as 1940, a committee, looking at ninth grade courses across the nation, had declared that "it seems legitimate to conclude that there must be something radically wrong with a curriculum that runs directly counter to compulsory school attendance laws and the purposes which a public school ought to have in an age when young people are forced into schools by economic and industrial conditions."[8] Life adjustment education grew out of the belief that schools were not adequately catering to the needs of all students. The post-war baby boom also significantly affected the ability of educators to teach. In 1945, the elementary and secondary school population was 26 million. By 1955, it had reached 36 million, and by 1960 it was expected that it would reach 42 million, a 61 percent increase on 1945. Such a rapid growth placed a serious strain on both the human and physical resources of the schools. Social problems like juvenile delinquency and integration also made their mark upon the nation's schools. In March 1954, in an article called "Our Schools: Afraid to Teach?" *Colliers* observed that teaching "seems to have fallen into disrepute."[9] The following year, the cover story in the January issue of *School and Society* proclaimed, "American Education in Crisis."[10]

While MGM seemed content to invoke altruism as a justification for their controversial hit, others in the industry were not so enthusiastic about the project. After seeing the film, Fox chief Darryl F. Zanuck, in a letter dated January 19, 1956, wrote to Dore Schary:

> I felt when I originally saw the picture that in spite of its quality, it could only give an erroneous impression of the American school system to European audiences. I also felt that it would be welcomed with open arms by the Communists ... the leading red paper in France, L'Humanite, gave a big splurge to the picture on four consecutive days.[11]

Evidence that Zanuck was right can be found in an issue of *School and Society* dated February 16, 1957. In an article entitled "German and Austrian Reaction to 'The Blackboard Jungle'," it was reported that European teachers and educators did not accurately perceive the meaning of the film, and were constantly asking, "Are the young people in America really like that?" and "Is that what schools in America are really like?"[12] *Parents Magazine* asserted that "the film's message is plain—the teaching profession must be made to attract superior human beings, for the mediocre have nothing with which to inspire their pupils and arouse in them the desire to learn."[13] If that was the idea behind the film, for many it was obscured in the image. With the explosive sounds of Bill Haley's "Rock Around the Clock," the film, particularly for the young, sounded a clarion call, an anthem of anarchy that led to riots and violence in theaters across the nation. If Hollywood had seriously wanted to address an issue, it seems that once again ideology had been lost beneath image.

The Blackboard Jungle embodied all the key elements that were to dominate the celluloid classroom in the years ahead. As the teacher-hero, Dadier was an extension of both Chips and Miss Evans. The kids, for their part, were the logical result of film's failed families. The principal and the rest of the teaching staff continued traditions established at least twenty years earlier.

For the remainder of the decade, the image of school and school teachers largely conformed to this pattern. At Madison High (*Our Miss Brooks*; 1956), the staff notice board "reads like a communique from the front," and Connie Brooks struggles to give students "a bank account from which they can draw ideas." *The Unguarded Moment* (1956) found Miss Conway sexually threatened by a young student and struggling with the unsympathetic principal of Ogden High. Santa Bello High in 1958's *High School Confidential* found Miss Williams as the victim of her delinquent students. *Rebel Without a Cause* (1955) was no more positive in its depiction of school teachers. While Dawson High appears orderly and respectable on the outside, it is riddled by cliques and gangs. On an excursion to a planetarium, in a gesture that sums up the decade, an elderly woman teacher relinquishes all pretense to control. "What's the use?" she laments as the students stream past her.

If the screen's schoolrooms seemed to be failing to responsibly deal with the young, they must be considered at least in part to be an accurate reflection of conditions within American education. When the Russians successfully put Sputnik into space in 1957, they issued a serious challenge to Americans' belief in their own superiority. Rear Admiral Rickover jarred Americans from complacency by a scathing attack on the education system. In the past, the schools had placed emphasis on socialization in order to meet the task of Americanizing the large number of migrants who filled the classrooms. Such a task had resulted in a softening of the curriculum, with the result that the nation was now paying the price and falling behind the Soviets in technological advances. Life adjustment education, said *Cosmopolitan*, produced "shallow citizens with flabby minds, tragically ill-fitted to meet the new stern challenges of leadership in the struggle for tomorrow."[14] The spectre of violence and delinquency had also served to erode confidence in the schools. "Hoodlums in the High Schools" appeared in *Catholic World* in April, 1959. "It is no exaggeration," the author asserted, "to say that practically no learning takes place in 50 percent of our classrooms from ninth through twelfth grade.... The sincere, capable and hardworking pupil is penalized by a school system and a philosophy of education which cannot be productive of other than blackboard jungles."[15]

Hollywood's response to the schools, while growing in part out of headlines of the day, stemmed also from a deep-seated social attitude toward the teacher. In September 1956, for example, *Atlantic* reported that:

> Americans have fixed the schoolmaster in a lowly status because he has fallen markedly in their estimation in the last fifty years. The lawyer, the newspaperman, and the doctor are active and powerful. *Mr. District Attorney*, editor Steve Wilson of *Big Town*, and *Medic* get things done. But who can respect *Our Miss Brooks*, a female eager to be married, but unsuccessful and therefore condemned to remain in the classroom; or male counterpart, the ineffectual, bumbling *Mr. Peepers*? Such people, incapable of the real work of the world, deserve no more than amused tolerance. "He who can, does. He who cannot, teaches," goes the old saw; and the nickname "the Professor" is used with comic disparagement. The caricature is certainly out of place in a society the welfare and security of which depend upon its laboratories and its libraries. It is the product of crass materialism but it is nonetheless widely held; and it determines American attitudes toward the profession. In every community there are teachers who love their work and are conscious of its importance. But increasingly, and tragically, they find themselves surrounded by colleagues who accept the popular image of themselves. Deprived of status and prestige, they acquiesce in the lowly role society assigns them.[16]

The film industry merely served to perpetuate such an image. The paradox, however, was that at the very time when the screens most exuded images of weak or embattled teachers, public confidence in teachers was quite strong.

In March, 1959, a report on the "Status and Job Satisfaction of Public School Teachers" reported that "the public school teachers, for whom the 'general public' is a most vital reference group with respect to their own status, appear to underestimate their standing accorded them by the general public."[17] Teachers, the article went on to report, were rated higher by the general public than four fields in the medical profession.

The fifties, and particularly *The Blackboard Jungle*, cemented a tradition that had evolved over a period of twenty years. For the next twenty years the depiction of the school on the screen would, to a greater or lesser degree, represent a variation on the image as defined by *The Blackboard Jungle*. It would be erroneous, however, to give one film so much weight, or to isolate it from the social and industrial conditions that created it. Heralded as it was by rock and roll, the film appealed immediately to youthful audiences who reached adolescence during the fifties. Declining box office receipts and the challenge from TV had left the industry eager to capture this young audience. Sensational stories torn from the headlines were one means of attracting attention.

But *The Blackboard Jungle* did much more than seize upon a timely issue or the booming youth market. It hit a hidden nerve in the American psyche. The themes and issues raised by the film extend much further than the boundaries of North Manual High and pervade motion pictures throughout the decade. Whether in westerns, war films, science fiction, or Biblical epics of the era, one encounters the same preoccupations. North Manual High School and those like it are mere microcosms of society. The lethargy, cynicism, and indifference of staff and administration all have direct parallels in the townfolk of *High Noon* (1952). The administrators and agents of authority that Dadier, Conway, Brooks and others challenge find their counterparts in *The Caine Mutiny* (1954) and *Mr. Roberts* (1955). The teacherhero, challenging a hostile power structure, is equally evident in *The Robe* (1953), *On the Waterfront* (1954), and *Ben Hur* (1959). Finally, the suspicion of the teacher as an outsider and a newcomer has its parallels in the fear of aliens in films such as *The Thing* (1951), *Them* (1954), and *The Invasion of the Body Snatchers* (1956). Such common concerns remove the celluloid classroom from a state of splendid isolation and locate it clearly within the mainstream of American film.

While such images may initially be read as reflections, if not representative reflections, of the American school system, they must also be read as the product of deeper social and cinematic concerns. HUAC, the bomb, McCarthyism, and Korea all had a significant impact on the American psyche in the 1950's. Fear, uncertainty, suspicion, hysteria, corrupt authority, and the struggle of the individual to survive are key elements not only of the school films, but of almost every genre the decade delivered. Such pervasiveness serves to explain at least in part the continuation of such images in the celluloid classrooms of the sixties.

To Sir with Love (Columbia; 1967), despite its conventionally contrived formula of teacher meets class, teacher wins class, teacher loses class, teacher wins class back, had everything going for it. Like *The Blackboard Jungle* and *Because They're Young* (1961), it strengthened its appeal to the youth market by the inclusion of a pop star or two and a hit record. British singer Lulu featured in the film and sang the title song. Poitier moved from the role of student in *The Blackboard Jungle* to the Dadier-inspired role of Mark Thackeray. Set in the swinging London of the Carnaby Street era, and with the good looks of Christian Roberts and Judy Geeson, not to mention the racial theme, the film was relevant to both American and British audiences and did well at the box office. Like *The Blackboard Jungle*, the opening sequences of the film are used to establish the social environment and the homes from which the students come.

Thackeray travels the East Ham bus on his way to school. On board, two middle-aged cockney women discuss their sex lives. "I'll send my Alf around, he's not bad when he gets going," one tells the other. The conversation

serves to reflect the sexual frankness and the honest if somewhat crude approach to life of the locals. Entering the rather squalid schoolgrounds with their outside toilets, Thackeray encounters a youngster slouched against a wall, cigarette dangling from his mouth. "Lookin' for someone, mate?" the kid asks, totally unintimidated by the presence of the figure of authority. When he enters the staffroom, it is apparent that we are in another urban battlezone. "So you're the new lamb for the slaughter," Theo Weston greets him. His predecessor, he quickly discovers, has fled the school and is pouring out his woes to the divisional officer.

And yet, while North Quay appears to be simply an extension of North Manual High, the teaching philosophy that pervades is distinctly different. The school is run by neither fear nor intimidation. "There's no form of corporal punishment or any punishment," Thackeray is informed. If Theo Weston is the familiar cynic, then there are other characters who at least give the impression that they are trying to get through to the kids. The deputy head is Grace Evans, a woman who seems genuinely concerned with the education and welfare of the students. When we first meet her she is preparing a bath for one of the girls whose body odor has incurred the rancor of other students. "Personal hygiene problem. Fourteen and helpless!" The principal, too, appears as a more fully rounded character than those we have previously seen. "Most of our children are rejects from other schools.... The local authorities are not entirely on our side.... Success or failure will depend entirely on you," he tells his newest member of the staff.

Entering his classroom for the first time, Thackeray attempts to establish order and to call the roll. He is greeted by a sea of apathetic faces, bodies slouched in seats. Attempting to commence a reading class, he is disrupted by Denim (Christian Roberts), who sits in a back desk playing with a rubber striptease doll. If Denim is to be the thorn in Thackeray's side then Pamela Dare (Judy Geeson) appears to be his star pupil. She willingly volunteers to read and does more than an adequate job. Between Denim and Pamela, however, exists the rest of the class, who provide a range of academic ability and behavior problems.

One of the film's problems emerges in Mark's first encounter with the class. Given what we are told about the demise of his predecessor, given what we have heard about the lack of discipline in the school, it seems unlikely that these students would readily comply with the directions of a newcomer. Yet when Thackeray tells them to copy down their arithmetic tables, they seem strangely willing to do as they are told. Too much of the initial resistance is left to Denim. While we are told that "these kids come from homes where an order is usually accompanied with a blow; one rude word to their parents and they know the roof will hit them," there is little to

Opposite: *To Sir with Love* (1967): An appealing but all too simplistic story that conformed to the familiar format: teacher meets class, teacher wins class, teacher loses class, teacher wins class back.

suggest that they expect Thackeray to behave in the same way. Nonetheless, from the outset the majority seem willing to do as they are told.

What Thackeray finds himself faced with is a class largely willing to be led by either a teacher or the peer group leader. The battle lines are drawn and Thackeray quickly perceives if he cannot win Denim over, then he will lose the whole class. While the others acquiesce to his request to "do exercise four, five and six," Denim and Potter slam their desks, arrive late, talk in class, and generally establish a disruptive presence. Unable to cope with them, Mark turns to Grace Evans for advice. "Weston couldn't care less about them and that's no good," she tells him. "They're good kids, Mark, most of them, but if you don't solve them, they'll break you and damn quickly." Weston, on the other hand, can only be cynical in his response. "These little bastards have a multitude of tricks. What they need is a bloody good hiding.... They'll happily be part of the great London unwashed; illiterate, smelly, and quite content.... Education's a disadvantage these days."

Caught between Weston's cynicism and the sensitivity of Grace Evans, Thackeray is forced to find a middle ground on which, if he cannot teach he can at least negotiate a truce. When he goes back into his classroom, his desk collapses beneath him, the kids having sawn through a leg of it. Grabbing the severed leg, he waves it slowly at them. For a moment he seems threatening, on the point of losing control of himself. Then quietly, forcefully, he tells them to "take your proper places," and again the kids passively comply. The following morning, as he enters the school building, a water bomb narrowly misses him. Losing his temper, he angrily enters the classroom where he discovers that the kids have thrown a tampon in a trash can and set fire to it. Totally outraged, he explodes in anger. "All you boys, out! The girls stay where you are. I'm sick of your foul language, your crude behavior, and your sluttish manner.... Only a filthy slut would have done this. I don't care who's responsible. You're all to blame!" he tells them, storming out of the room.

In the staffroom, Mark rages not at the students but at himself, furious that he has allowed a bunch of kids to provoke him. In the midst of his outpouring he suddenly realizes that he's been treating the class as kids when in reality they are a group of young adults, almost ready to go out into society and enter the work force. It is a significant realization. Discussing the way in which high schools respond to students, noted educator James Coleman has commented, "They are shielded from responsibility and they become irresponsible. They are held in dependent status and they become dependent. They are kept away from productive work and they become unproductive."[18]

Thackeray returns to the class and throws his textbooks in the trash can. "These are out, they're useless to you," he tells the students. From now on, they are told, they will be treated as responsible and reasonable adults. "Soon boyfriends and marriage will concern you. No man likes a slut for long." The girls will be addressed as Miss and the boys will be referred to by their surnames. "Toughness," he tells the boys, "is a condition of the mind," and he expects them to shape up. He throws the classroom open to the sort of issues and questions that concern the students; "life, survival, love, death, sex, marriage, rebellion, anything you want." He tutors the class in grooming, personal appearance, etiquette, and basic survival skills. Equally as important, he recognizes that the school is part of a community and he wants to take the class out into the community. While the administration is initially reluctant, he convinces them that the class can be trusted in public. He thus offers the students a sense of pride and responsibility. While the majority of the class responds positively to the new methods, Denim goes along only grudgingly, and until he is won over, the victory will never be complete.

A gym teacher provokes an incident with one of the class members. Bullying the boy, he forces him to perform an activity that results in the boy being hurt. Inflamed by the behavior of the teacher, Potter grabs a piece of wood and menacingly advances towards him. Only the intervention of Thackeray saves the teacher from a beating. In saving the gym teacher, Mark has aligned himself, in the eyes of the students, with the enemy. When he insists that Potter apologize to the teacher, he enrages the class, who cannot understand how he can defend a man who was so clearly in the wrong. "There's never been a teacher that you could trust. We're only safe together, against them like it's always been." Not only does Thackeray lose the support of the students, he also finds that the administration deserts him. The gym teacher resigns and the principal tells Mark, "I'm afraid the adult approach hasn't worked. It would have been better to let things be." Even Pamela Dare deserts him when he takes her mother's side in a domestice dispute. Totally rejected by students once his friends, now his enemies, Thackeray seems headed for resignation, prepared to give up teaching for an engineering position in the Midlands.

Substituting for the gym teacher, he finds himself confronted by Denim, who puts on boxing gloves and wants to go a few rounds with him. Although the boy expects to hurt Thackeray, he quickly finds himself on the floor, as Mark connects with a fair but solid punch. It is a turning point in the relationship between the two antagonists. Denim respects the fact that the man not only has principles but guts and strength as well. When his friends tell him it was just a lucky punch, he tells them that Thackeray "could have done me with one hand behind his back." Having won Denim, he has by implication won the class, but the means by which he wins them clearly locates him in the same group with Dadier, Hendrie and the others.

By throwing out the books, he demonstrates once again that the best teacher is not a teacher at all but a rebel who bucks the system and goes it alone. While Grace Evans and some of the others suggest a middle ground among teachers previously absent from the screen, they rather rapidly disappear into the background. Given that Thackeray is by profession an engineer and not a teacher, the image of the teacher as outsider is once again emphasized. Finally, Thackeray succeeds not by employing books, not by listening to the advice of his colleagues, and not by anything he initiates in the classroom. He wins by throwing a punch. It is Thackeray the boxer, not Thackeray the teacher, who ultimately succeeds with the class. When he knocks the boy down he establishes his physical as well as intellectual superiority, a point which would be the central theme in the television series, *The White Shadow*.

In the same year that *To Sir with Love* found its way to the screens, Sylvia Barrett took the Dadier route through the New York school system in Warner's *Up the Down Staircase*. Based on the novel by Bel Kauffman and directed by Robert Mulligan, it featured Sandy Dennis as the young school teacher trying to establish herself at Calvin Coolidge High. Faced with homeroom, English 322, and 40 pupils, from the very beginning she gets off on the wrong foot and has to be asked, "Do you realize you're going up the down staircase?"

Although the school is named after a man who campaigned under the banner of normalcy, Calvin Coolidge High School seems more redolent of depression. The principal, Mr. McHabe, believes that "if you try running this school with ideas, you'll have riots in the classrooms. Fear, that's all they understand." However much we may reject his philosophy, and Sylvia is plainly disturbed by it, we are assured that "this place was chaos before he came here." The rod of iron with which McMabe rules the school may bring law and order, but it is apparent that it brings little in the way of learning. The problems confronting Sylvia Barrett and the other teachers are not unlike those we have seen before. A black teacher tells her, "White kids don't trust me and the Negro kids think I've sold out to the whites." The kids themselves have no easier time of it. One girl is beaten by her father. A boy is on probation and another falls asleep in class because he works all night in a garage. Sylvia, like Thackeray, discovers that she is immediately placed in the enemy camp by the kids. "I am some kind of enemy, the butt of some enormous joke."

Yet she continues to try to get through to the students in the only way that she understands, by human warmth and compassion. Closer to Dadier than Thackeray, she knows that the school system is wrong but is uncertain as to what to do about it.

In the character of Mr. Barringer we are presented with a response that Sylvia cannot accept. Distanced, objective, and coldly analytical in his approach to the school, Barringer is a variation of the cynical teachers who had for so long populated the school on the screen. He functions not as a human being with whom the students can relate, interact, and identify, but as a dispenser of information and facts. Less man than machine, he recognizes the system for the threat it is and retreats in order to save himself. When a girl develops a crush on him, his response is harsh, cold and indifferent. Shattered by his reaction, the girl attempts suicide. Sylvia condemns him for failing to deal responsibly with the girl, but Barringer will not be blamed. Anything he had done, he tells her, would have simply "encouraged an erotic teenager." Given a choice between her survival or his own, he chose to save himself. "Some of you may prefer to leave by the window; I'd prefer to leave by the door."

Up the Down Staircase added grey to a moral landscape where black and white had too long dominated. It also presented the figure of a female teacher who could succeed. While the movie felt obliged to include the sexual threat (a seemingly obligatory incident since *The Blackboard Jungle*), it was a much more positive rendition of the woman teacher than the screen had seen in twenty years. Acknowledging the image, Richard Schickel, in a review for *Life* magazine, linked Sylvia Barrett with the schoolmarms of westerns:

> The only feminine myth we have developed in America that is comparable to the Western good badman is the one about the schoolmarm—idealistic, virginal, surprisingly strong beneath a sweet exterior—who, against seemingly hopeless odds, brings civilization to the wilderness.... Our new wilderness is the jungle of the cities, our new villains are the bureaucrats with the grey flannel brains who conspire against the true education while pretending to advance it.[19]

Only twice in the history of the Academy Awards has the role of school teacher won the coveted Oscar, once for Robert Donat's performance as Mr. Chips and again in 1969, when Maggie Smith won for her outstanding performance in *The Prime of Miss Jean Brodie*. Released by Fox and directed by Robert Neame, the screenplay was written by Jay Presson Allen based upon her play from the successful Muriel Spark novel. Like *To Sir With Love, Because They're Young, High School Confidential*, and *The Blackboard Jungle*, the film was well represented musically by the Rod McKuen song "Jean," which was equally successful come Oscar time. While the character of the song seems a romantic figure, the Jean Brodie we encounter in the film is much more ambiguous, moving the school on the screen into that grey area which *Up the Down Staircase* had revealed.

The film opens at Marcia Blane School for Girls in the Edinburgh of 1932. It is a school that *Time* magazine characterized as "a chalkdust bowl," where "the staff is a frightened gaggle arranged in perfect pecking order" and the "girls throw themselves into adolescence as if they were breaking the sound barrier." Alongside the chalky characters of the majority of the staff, Jean Brodie sparkles with vigor and passion. A commanding presence, she more than recalls the formal classroom of Miss Dove. Her rules are fixed, precise, and not to be challenged. Miss Dove and Miss Brodie, however, are as alike as cheese and chalk. Brodie not only has rules, she has opinions—opinions about everything and everyone. Rather than helping the girls to develop interests of their own, she sees her function as providing them with

The Prime of Miss Jean Brodie: **A teacher, dangerous and unwholesome.**

interests. She is, as she tells her girls, "in the business of putting old heads on young shoulders ... and you are the creme de la creme. Give me a girl at an impressionable age and she is mine for life." It is a telling and frightening insight into a disarmingly appealing character, for Brodie wants much more than to teach the girls, she wishes to indoctrinate them so that they will emerge as imitations of herself.

Dedicated to the girls in what she calls her prime, she steadfastly ignores the curriculum, thus aligning herself with Thackeray. Whereas he replaced traditional classes and methods with a course in survival aimed at preparing the students for the demands of the real world, Brodie shuns reality, surrounding the girls instead with a world of romance and rebellion. Not only does she subvert the curriculum, but she undermines the order of the school by establishing a conspiratorial air in her classroom. "Prop up your books against instruders," she warns the girls, asking them to help her deceive headmistress Miss MacKay. While the rest of the school assembles in the dining hall for meals, Jean and her girls enjoy lunch outdoors, leaving the staffroom a hotbed of gossip about the Brodie set. In taking her class on excursions and field trips, Brodie forges another link with Thackeray, but whereas education and responsibility had been Mark's goal, Jean's prime interest is the continued indoctrination of the girls. Unable to separate her private and public life, she sets herself up as a role model for the girls. It is not long before the impressionable youngsters begin to speculate about her lovelife and her relationship with another staff member. A weekend visit to the home of the school music teacher quickly inflames the students' imagination, and gossip is rife amongst them as they discuss Brodie's sexual liaison with the man.

Constantly suspicious of the woman's behavior, Miss MacKay misses no opportunity to challenge the girls and find out what really goes on in class. The students, however, are a loyal and dedicated bunch. One teacher has observed that Brodie has them well trained. It is a not inaccurate observation, for Brodie's discipline is highly regimented and reflects her admiration for Mussolini. Miss Brodie, the girls tell the headmistress, "makes history seem like cinema." It is an incisive comment, for Brodie, whether she is aware of it or not, transforms fact into fiction. The romantic images she creates for a vulnerable adolescent audience may be entertaining, but when an audience exits from the comfortable dark security of the theater, they are jolted back to reality by the brightness beyond the silver screen. If the audience begins to identify more with the world they see on the screen than the one in which they live, the results can be positively dangerous.

"Goodness, truth, and beauty come first," Brodie has told the girls, but there are times when those three are at odds with each other and, obscured in romance as her lessons are, Brodie has offered the girls no means with which to make reliable and responsible judgements. Brodie sees goodness and beauty in the fact that Mussolini had made Capri into a sanctuary for birds—that single act seems to have obscured for her the truth of his fascistic regime. If as an adult she chose to ignore such a situation, it was her prerogative; however, when she edits such a fact from the information she imparts to the girls, she must stand condemned as a teacher. Criticized for her methods, she declares, "I'm proud to think that my girls are more aware ... to me education is simply a leading out of what is already there."

Brodie is clearly misguided about her own intentions, her own methods, and their outcome. While she says she helps the girls to develop their own ideas, it is blatantly obvious that she forces her own opinions upon them. When a girl suggests that DaVinci is the greatest artist, clearly a subjective matter, Brodie dismisses the response, insisting that the correct answer is Giotto. While the girls may be different to the rest of the school, they are hardly perceived as individuals. Brodie sees each one of them as an extension of herself, believing that she can somehow predestine them to achieve what she expects of them.

When Miss MacKay finds a note implicating Brodie with the music teacher, she realizes that the students have long been aware of the affair. Mortified that "infants should be knowledgeable," she insists upon the woman's resignation. Jean, however, will not be intimidated. With all the fire and self-righteousness that she can summon, she prepares to defend herself against what she regards as character assassination. "You will not use the excuse of that pathetic, that humorous document to blackmail me. I will not resign and you will not dismiss me, Miss MacKay.... If one word of this outrageous calumny reaches my ears I will sue. If scandal is to your taste, Miss MacKay, I shall give you a feast.... I am a teacher first, last, and always. I influence them to be aware of the possibilities of life, beauty, honor, courage. I have dedicated, sacrificed my life to this profession — I will not allow myself to be crucified!" It is a brilliant speech and one which the rebel in all of us must applaud, but there is something faintly ludicrous about this woman. The very words she chooses to refer to herself — assassination, sacrifice, crucifixion — all indicate the messianic madness with which she approaches teaching and the romantic posture she wishes to assume.

In her assessment of herself and her function, however, Brodie is plainly misguided. Marcia Blane is more than a school for her, it is a stage on which she can strut and fret, full of sound and fury, magnified by the passivity of the characters around her. She could teach at a school which would condone her progressive methods, but she chooses to remain at Marcia Blane because there she is always center stage, and because there she can fulfill her rebellious nature by challenging authority. Faced with the opportunity to marry the music teacher, she rejects him. Not for her the marriage bed with the ties, responsibilities and shared life that it implies, for Brodie stands alone not merely as the foremost performer on the stage of life she has constructed but also as the director, attempting to arrange the lives of those she sees around her.

Her manipulations and machinations drive one student to Spain and the civil war where she is killed. Brodie's romantic musing and her belief that "Franco's army contains all the best elements" convinces the girl that she too "must be prepared to serve, suffer, and sacrifice." Inspired by the words of her misguided mentor, she rushes to her death. Wishing to live vicariously through the girls, Brodie conspires to have one of them occupy the bed of her former lover. But Brodie is forced to realize that she is not God and she cannot control destiny.

When one of the girls finally tells Miss MacKay the truth about Jean, her time as a teacher is over. In characteristic fashion she accuses the girl of assassinating her, but Sandy will not accept the condemnation. She at last knows Brodie for what she is, "a ridiculous woman" forever assuming attitudes and striking poses. The girl is right. Brodies is not simply ridiculous, she is pathetic. We may feel sorry for her and believe her to be misguided, but the truth of the matter is that she has contributed to the death of a student, been guilty of indoctrination, and with great impropriety has opened her personal life to the students. Romantic vision, dedication to causes, unconventional teaching methods, and extracurricular activities — all of these are acceptable, and there are moments in the film when we feel disposed to cheer Jean and to encourage her crusade against the dried-up and lifeless forces that run the school. In the end, however, for all her lifelessness, Miss MacKay is vindicated. While we may not like her, we know that she is right and Brodie must go.

As the film closes, the school bids farewell to its senior girls who are "about to take your place in a larger, more dangerous world." Marcia Blane has trained them, they are told, and their training will stand them in good stead in that world. One wonders, however, if the world beyond the classroom can be more dangerous than the one they are leaving. In their years at the school the girls have experienced sex, death, and disillusionment. More powerfully, however, they have been exposed to the systematic and subtle indoctrination of a figure with whom they were enamored. "Give me a girl at an impressionable age and she is mine for life," Brodie has declared. In rebelling against her, Sandy has experienced only momentary freedom. As she leaves the school for the last time, she hears Brodie's words and we know that the girl will never escape the hold the woman has over her. In the same year that Brodie came to the screen, *Mental Hygiene* carried an article on "The Influence of the Emotionally Disturbed Teacher on School Children."[20] If Jean Brodie was to be taken as representative, the influence was indeed profound.

Although Jean Brodie claimed that she was betrayed and assassinated by one of her own, her character assassination seemed insignificant alongside the murder evident in Lindsay Anderson's *If* (1969). The insurrection of the students of this film was contemporaneous with the appearance of armed students in the streets of Paris, and on the campuses at Cornell and Columbia. College House, indeed the entire school in *If*, is corrupt. Supported by a prefect system that indulges in vice and violence, and a caricature collection of staff members, it represents a crumbling order. When Mick Travers and his young student companions challenge the system, we are meant to applaud their attempt to clean up corruption. "One man can change the world with a bullet in the right place," Mick comments, but it is hardly a point of view we can endorse. In a final scene that must have appealed to the rebel in every adolescent, Mick stands on the roof of the school and he and his friends open fire on the teachers and visiting dignitaries below. Shot through the head, the principal falls to the ground in what is surely the ultimate image of the teacher as victim.

The violence and disruption of the English film was a timely reflection of conditions of the day in school and society. The assassinations of Martin Luther King Jr. and Robert Kennedy the previous year were surely called to mind by Mick's statement. Riots at the Democratic National Convention in Chicago and widespread unrest across the nation was reflected in the schools, which served as a microcosm of society. If parents were concerned with the behavior of young people on the streets of the nation, they were equally concerned by their behavior at school. In 1969, in national Gallup poll surveys, parents rated discipline as the major problem facing American schools. In eight of nine Gallup polls conducted between 1969 and 1977, discipline continued to be cited as a major problem. In May, 1969,

in a cover story called "Collision Course in the High Schools," *Life* magazine reported the changing nature of students and schools. A Lou Harris
poll found that "they are willing to be taught but not be told."[21] While
parents felt lack of respect and discipline was a major concern, the students,
surprisingly enough, complained more about leniency and sloppily enforced
rules than they did about arbitrary strictures. The issues that had served to
dislocate the nation and fracture the families found their way into the school
system, which could not for long remain immune to the changing nature of
youth.

In February 1969, the United States Supreme Court, in the case of
Tinker vs. Des Moines Independent Community School District, handed
down a landmark decision defending student rights. Supporting the right of
students to wear arm bands protesting the war in Vietnam, the court determined that students did not surrender their constitutional rights upon
entering the classroom. In Breen vs. Kahl, a federal district court in Wisconsin ruled against the school's attempt to enforce grooming, suggesting
that they could not demonstrate that long hair was a disruptive influence. In
August 1970, *School Review* reported,

> Frightened and bewildered teachers are uncertain about the releveance
> of what they are doing and resented by their students. Administrators
> feel trapped between local Birchites attacking sex education programs
> and seditious students fomenting, so it is believed, rebellions against
> between parents complaining about school taxes and the breakdown
> in discipline and teachers now divided not just on issues of curricu-
> lum and discipline, but on the purposes and worth of education
> itself.[22]

Yet despite all of this, the Harris poll still found parents favorably
disposed to teachers, who were perceived as go-betweens in the generation
gap. "That much maligned figure, the teacher," reported Harris, "not only
draws respect and affection from parents and children, but is revealed to be
a catalyst to bridge the generation gap."[23] As the seventies got under way,
Hollywood responded to teachers and the schools as they had responded to
the families. Caught up in a long tradition of stereotyping, they repeated
time-honored formulas, or grabbed at superficial headlines without
exploring the issues beneath them.

A typical case in point was *Halls of Anger* (1970). Publicity for the
film declared it to be "a long hard look at the current high school scene
where white and black students are in daily confrontations which have led
to school closings across the nation." The movie featured Melvin Lockhart
as Quincy Davis, a former basketball star turned teacher. Comfortable in
his present teaching position, he is offered the job as deputy principal at
Lafayette High, a school with 200 whites and 3,000 blacks.

By invoking the busing issue, Hollywood had uncharacteristically

Halls of Anger (1970): **Trapped in the traditional stereotypical depiction of school life, the film was unable to successfully explore the issue of busing.**

hit upon a timely and controversial theme. In March of the same year, *Time* ran a cover story on "The Retreat from Integration." Edith Green, Chairperson of the House Select Subcommittee on Education, had declared, "We simply cannot afford to let our classrooms turn into battlefields."[24] In announcing that he was once more running for governor, George Wallace promised to "get our schools back from the federal government."[25] In 1970, when *Halls of Anger* was released, the whole issue of busing and integration was explosive.

In introducing the character of the black teacher, Hollywood had taken up where *To Sir with Love* left off. By making him both a sporting hero and an administrator, it seemed to be exploring new avenues in the depiction of the school on the screen. This was to be no novice teacher coming into a strange environment, but a respected and experienced teacher whose racial and sporting credentials would give him an added advantage with the largely black student population. And yet, despite its potential, *Halls of Anger* could not salvage itself from Hollywood's traditional response to the schools. Davis is no sooner in the school than he is in confrontation with Principal Wilkerson, a man more intent on maintaining order than on education. "In order to teach we have to stablize. As vice principal, your main job is to keep the lid on."

Student J.T. Watson becomes for Davis what Denim was to Thackeray and Greg Miller was to Dadier, a pupil whom he must get through to in order to establish his credibility. When the principal makes it clear that he wants to get rid of Watson, he and Davis dispute the whole process of education. "You'll only be passing the problem onto the streets," Davis argues angrily. For Wilkerson, however, that is not an issue—the world of the school and the world beyond its boundaries exist as two separate and unrelated places. Quincy, on the other hand, realizes that society's problems are invariably manifested in the school and that both school and society must work together to solve them.

Like almost every other school film that Hollywood had dealt with, it simply reduced major issues to a clash of personalities. The teacher is good, the principal and the administrators are bad, and somewhere in between there is a collection of cynical and shellshocked teachers no longer capable of fighting. Typical of them is English teacher Lorraine Nash. Although she cares about the kids, she no longer has the energy to fight for them. "There are no answers, not with those old fogies downtown running the show," she laments. For Lorraine, like Josh and countless others, the answer is to quit.

In terms of the racial issue and educational inequality, the best that can be said for the film is that it at least acknowledged the presence of the problems. While it always tended to dismiss the issue as a matter of blacks versus honkies, the film was at least courageous enough to acknowledge the existence of a separate and viable black culture. Mixing black and white kids through the busing process would not make them equal, the film made clear. "Just because you don't know the meaning of words like thermofax and Utopia doesn't mean you can't cut it," Davis tells them. Cutting it, he understands, depends upon whether you come from Georgia or Connecticut. If they can't make it with the white man's culture, then they have a culture of their own that they have the right to be proud of. So far, so good.

The problem with *Halls of Anger*, however, is that it continually promises more than it can deliver. While it touches upon issues, it seems to be forever backing away from them. It is a hodgepodge assemblage of every cliché the film industry had ever visited upon schools, teachers, and students. For every new element, it had a tradition. The confrontation in the gymnasium between Denim and Thackeray was repeated in a basketball game, Quincy going one on one with Watson. In the end, the teacher wins the student over by allowing him to paint a mural of black heroes in the school hallway. Like *To Sir With Love*, the film requires one final confrontation in which the administration condemns the new methods. "You failed, Mr. Davis," the principal declares after Watson, like Potter, becomes involved in a fight.

With the influence of *If* and the real life campus turmoil that had culminated at Kent State, the film closes with the students rioting and calling for a strike. As a helpless principal watches the order he had established crumbling, it is apparent that Davis represents the new order. What he promises, however, is the same as Dadier, Thackeray, Barrett and the rest: patience, understanding, and love. While they are admirable and worthy approaches to teaching, neither *Halls of Anger* nor any other film throughout the seventies realistically explored ways in which such goals could be achieved in the bored black jungles of the inner city schools, or in the havens of white flight where so many students fled in the wake of busing Indeed, Quincy Davis was one of the last visions of the teacher/hero the decade had to offer. As Hollywood saw it, both schools and schoolteachers were in an increasingly untenable position.

Pretty Maids All in a Row (1971) starred Rock Hudson in a black comedy about a high school counselor who seduced and murdered his students. The sexual involvement between teacher and student had its roots in the fifties, but was developed in England during the sixties. Saunders had found himself propositioned by a young student in *Spare the Rod* (1961); in 1963 Laurence Olivier played a school teacher, in *Term of Trial*, whose career is destroyed when one of his students accuses him of molesting her. *The Prime of Miss Jean Brodie* featured, in addition to Brodie's attempt to manipulate the lovelife of a student, the sexual relationship between art teacher Teddy Lloyd and one of the Brodie bunch. While the screen teachers of the fifties and sixties had been the victims of over-imaginative and erotic youngsters, the teachers of the late sixties and seventies succumbed willingly or actively sought to seduce their young charges.

On both sides of the Atlantic, British and American filmmakers shared a similarly bleak view of the teaching profession. *Unman Wittering and Zigo* (1971) looked at a school system in which the students were ruthless and corrupt. Having killed their previous teacher, they set about terrorizing his replacement who finds himself the victim of their brutality and sadism. Wrote Judith Crist, "It carries Vigo's *Zero for Conduct* and Lindsay Anderson's *If* ... from infancy and fantasy to the cold light of contemporary realism, going from horror in the nursery to subtle terrors in the classroom. And it brings us to the final sad farewell to Mr. Chips."[26]

Equally disturbing was the vision of teaching presented in Paramount's 1972 production of *Child's Play*. Directed by Sidney Lumet and based on Robert Morasco's Broadway success, it was a horror-thriller set in a Catholic boys' school. When Paul Reis returns to his old school as the physical education teacher, he finds it pervaded with an ominous air. One student has a broken hand; several others have been beaten up for no apparent reason; obscenities are scrawled on the buildings; and artifacts used in religious services have been desecrated. The peculiar events continue to dominate the school as another boy is beaten and tied to a cross in the chapel. When an elderly Latin teacher suicides, we discover that the bizarre events have all been orchestrated by another teacher whose popularity has enabled him to wage a malicious and vindictive vendetta against his rival. The boys who do his bidding are more extensions of the Brodie bunch, and a frightening reminder of the teacher's ability to mold the minds of impressionable adolescents. As one reviewer observed,

The primitive tribal activities of the young savages of *Child's Play* are
not spontaneous or random expressions of social regression. They aren't
a return to instinctive cruelty, sacrifice, ritual and violence but a conscious manipulation of the hero-worshipping young by a beloved dema-
gogue — a mystic, deranged, perverted fuehrer whose power base is the
male mystique, whose role is father/guru, whose game is espirit de corps,
whose fraternal method is blind loyalty.[27]

For the remainder of the decade, both school and schoolteacher alike
came in for increasingly negative treatment. The teacher/hero was no
longer viable. *Conrak* (1977) introduced us to what appeared to be the traditional figure of the teacher/hero. As teacher Pat Conroy, John Voight
brought wide-eyed optimism to the classroom and a belief in the decency of
kids. True to tradition, he discovers that his methods are not popular with
his superiors. "You're in a snake pit, son ... put your feet on them and keep
it there. They need the whip." While the film's point of view supports
Conroy's contention that these kids need tender loving care, such a program is impossible in the celluloid classrooms of the seventies. Conroy finds
himself dismissed and out of work, a decent teacher who lost his job
because "he doesn't work with the chain of command ... he wants to change
everything." The defeat of Conroy represented a victory for Theo Weston
and the cynics who had for so long plagued the teacher/hero. The one
teacher in *Corvette Summer* (1978) turned out to be a common crook,
involved with a former student in a car theft racket. *American Graffiti*
(1974) showed us a teacher who felt condemned to small town obscurity and
who skirted the edge of a relationship with one of his students.

By the end of the decade, the cinematic classroom resembled an
urban battleground. *Rock and Roll High School* (1979) and *Over the Edge*
(1979) both ended with rioting students setting fire to the schools. In reviewing the latter, *Variety* said, "It won't be long before the PTA stops
scolding television and begins pointing a finger at the neighborhood
theater."[28]

In the case of school on the screen, television seemed to be imitating
the themes and plots developed by the film industry. Ken Reeves, the bas-
ketball-playing teacher of *The White Shadow*, was a white extension of
Quincy Davis. The sexual liaisons between students and teachers that had
emerged since the late sixties found their way to television in the following
decade. In "Whispers," a 1980 episode of the series *Family*, teenage Buddy
finds herself attracted to one of her teachers. The girl is shattered when she
discovers that the man is already sleeping with another student. A 1980
episode of *The White Shadow* found seventeen-year-old Salami involved
with one of his teachers, "You come by tonight and we'll see what we can do
about curing your insomnia," she tells him.

Screened in 1979, made-for-television movie *Coach* once again dealt
with the student/teacher relationship. Publicity in *TV Guide* read:

She taught the boys how to play the game and ended up breaking the forbidden rule. She was a hard-driving basketball coach. She was also a woman with every right to have a love affair. But not with a student — a boys so young, so innocent!

Yet while the publicity argued that the relationship was wrong, that was certainly not the implication of the film. There was even a scene in which teacher and student make love in a shower in the school gym. Another made-for-television movie, *Thin Ice* (1981), also sanctioned the relationship between teacher and senior student. Series such as *Shirley*, *Family*, and *Eight Is Enough* featured teachers among cast regulars. Without exception, their experience of school conformed to Hollywood tradition and they were left to struggle against both staff and students. Advertising for *The Survival of Dana*, a 1979 TV movie, indicated the industry's traditional preoccupation. "The class of 1980 — they're majoring in vandalism and violence," *TV Guide*'s ad proclaimed.

A 1978 CBS special asked, "Is Anyone Out There Learning?" Among other shocking statistics contained in the program was the revelation that 70,000 teachers a year in the United States are the victims of physical assault. *Bad Boys USA* was a documentary made for television which concentrated on Bryant High School in New York's Queens. "The don't care, all they come to get is their pay," the kids say about their teachers. After seeing the program on national television, parents, students, and teachers at the school were so disturbed by the image of the school that they made their own program to correct that image. Introducing the new program, a professor rightly asked, "What was the impact of this type of image making on the school?" It is a question that must be seriously addressed when we consider both the film and television industries' depiction of the teaching profession.

While Hollywood has demonstrated that it can produce forceful films about school, it has also demonstrated a lamentable tendency to ignore issues and concentrate its drama on a clash of personalities. The teacher as hero, while dramatically interesting, can only render a disservice to the teacher profession as a whole. Neither heroes nor villains, teachers are three-dimensional human beings with the same flaws and faults as others. In attempting to locate them within a recognizable environment and confronting them with the day-to-day issues that teachers face, Hollywood has been remarkably unsuccessful. While sex and violence may sell well at the box office, they are not the staple components of a teacher's day. In seizing upon such incidents, the film industry serves to limit debate on one of the most pressing problems of the day.

Discussing the media's role in helping us to better understand schools, the chairman of the Washington Education Association said, in 1964,

Mr. Novak: **An award winning television series that attempted to correct the negative depiction of school, teachers and students.**

The effect that *Mr. Novak* has had in focusing public attention on education shows that when responsible men in broadcasting so choose, the mass communications media can be a potent instrument for generating public understanding of our schools.[29]

The success of *Mr. Novak* was no accident. Creator of the series Jack Neuman painstakingly researched the series for authenticity and with a view to correcting the injustice he felt the media had done to teachers. Addressing a professional group in April 1964, he said,

> The school teachers that I talked to were suspicious if not downright hostile. I couldn't blame them. Motion pictures and television have treated education as farce comedy too many times. I said I was going to make a high school teacher the most popular hero ever seen on film. In short, I wanted to see if a man without a gun, a badge, a horse or a stethescope could capture a few million hearts. I also wanted to put the distorted image of the teenager back into a proper and authentic perspective. [30]

In the years since *Novak* the distortion of teacher and student has continued unabated with little farce comedy. Alongside the killers, criminals, seducers and victims the teachers of the screen have now become, even farce seems preferable. Forced to confront the image of themselves that Hollywood projects, teachers might well think of Sandy's words to Jean Brodie, "You're dangerous and unwholesome and children should not be exposed to you!"

7. Halls of Anger?

A student bites a teacher. The school psychologist goes berserk. The substitute teacher is a certified lunatic. And students graduate who can't read or write—Advertisement for Teachers, 1984.

School is the child's first experience with an institution created by society just to serve him so that he, in turn, will serve society. More than anything else it will shape his view of society and his behavior in it. If he remains anonymous there in his first encounter with the wider world, he will come to expect that this is how life in society will unfold. If in school he finds understanding, stability, security, and personal attention to his individuality, he'll believe these will be available to him in society and will strive for them.[1]

If the schools on the screen are to be taken as representative of the schools of his nation, then American adolescents have seldom been afforded understanding, stability, or security. With very few exceptions, Hollywood's vision of the student's encounter with education has almost totally ignored the primary function of the school and concentrated instead on images of an urban battleground, or a gathering place for the rituals of puberty. Into this situation came Jack Neuman and *Mr. Novak*.

Writing to the producers of the program, a junior from Evanston High, Illinois, said, "Being a high school student and having experienced many of the situations you present, I am able to identify with the marvelous actors and the problems portrayed."[2] A girl one year out of high school told them, "Everything is exactly how it is in school: the teachers, casual principal, students, furniture and parents."[3] Teachers, too, considered the series to be an accurate reflection of their profession. The show was honored by the National Association of Secondary School Principals, the Citizenship Committee of the National Education Association, the Iowa State Education Association, and other professional bodies and organizations.

It is not difficult to see why Novak was so well received. In putting the program together, Neuman travelled from California to New York, visiting 50 high schools across the country, talking to principals and first year teachers. The bulk of programming was based on those discussions. Two high school teachers and one principal wrote scripts for the series, and technical directors on the production staff included a vice-principal and an English teacher. The authenticity that resulted enabled both teachers and students to see an image of themselves with which they could identify.

In putting the series together, Neuman clearly understood the sterotypes that had long dominated the media's depiction of education. He understood too the domino principle by which distortion in one area inevitably resulted in distortion in a related area. The teacher/hero format by necessity resulted in reducing the principal and other teachers to villains. On more than one occasion it also resulted in undermining the already severely tarnished image of family life. Finally, as Neuman acknowledged, it resulted in a rather jaundiced view of adolescents. In dealing with the family unit, the cinema of adolescence had repeatedly located young people within a social environment in which they were denied a voice, and from which they had to battle to break free. Parents, as we have seen, often hindered rather than helped the growth process of their children. When Hollywood transplanted these teenagers from the home environment to the classroom, it brought with them the same dramatic format and stemmed directly out of the industry's depiction of family life.

In *Because They're Young*, for example, Buddy's mother tells Mr. Hendrie, "He hates me, he knows what I am." In the same film, Gritt quarrels with his father: "Go ahead, slug me. You've hit me before, you with your big hands and tight fists, you don't care what happens to me, you never did." Hendrie as the teacher is thus permitted to intervene in the life of his students because of the nature of their home lives. The depiction of school on the screen is obviously umbilically wedded to the treatment which the film industry had afforded the family. In the celluloid classroom we are given an insight into the way in which Hollywood conceives of the adolescent's experience of school. Instead of teenagers battling parents, what we largely find is adolescents forced to combat or ignore a demeaning and alienating school system, equally remiss in supporting them in their odyssey to adulthood.

The link between school and the family, school and society, is evident on the screen as early as the 1930's. In *Hoosier Schoolboy*, Charkie Carter finds himself harassed and persecuted at school. "There ought to be two schools, one for our set and one for his kind," one of the other students says, adding significantly, "mamma says." The boy is made to feel unwanted and inferior because his father is considered to be the town drunk. In fact, he is a war hero suffering from shell shock. No one in the self-righteous community, however, has taken time to look into the matter or to render assistance to the veteran. The school, rather than providing the boy with an education and dealing with him equally, simply reinforces the prejudices of the town. It becomes a place where the boy come to believe,

"Maybe I ain't no good." If Cal Trask had come to such a conclusion as the result of his home life, then the school relentlessly hammers the same message home to young Charkie. While *Goodbye Mr. Chips* introduced us to students like Peter Colley, who obviously enjoyed their experience of school, it also made it apparent that without the intervention of the teacher/hero, many of these young people would find school a painful and worthless experience.

Throughout the 1940's the adolescent's experience of school, at least as Hollywood saw it, seemed to be steeped with awkward, humiliating and embarrassing moments. Fox's 1940 production, *High School*, starred Jane Withers as Jane Wallace, the daughter of a wealthy rancher. Raised on a ranch and without the guidance of a mother, the girl has embarked upon adolescence, rather wild and headstrong. Her father sends her to Jefferson High School in San Antonio with the hope that she'll learn to behave "like a young lady, not like a cowhand." Jane's problems at the school are a result of her over-confidence, her different background, and the time required to adjust to a new environment and find new friends. As the new kid on the block, her problems are typical of those encountered by Jim Stark and Will Henderson in the next decade. The connection between school and home is equally apparent. "Her father's been too busy, too crazy about her to give her any discipline." Used to ruling the roost and getting her own way, the girl is forced to realize that in the high school social scene she is just another face. Desperately wanting to join the Lassoo Girls, she finds her ego and cockiness an obstacle she has to learn to overcome. Ultimately the girl is accepted by her peer group, but not before one humiliating rebuff after another, a lot of tears, and one attempt to drop out.

Both the Henry Aldrich and the Andy Hardy series showed the painful side of school life. Henry is constantly hounded by Mr. Bradley, the school principal. His peers ridicule him and even his sister refers to him as "the class clown." For Henry, Centerville High is simply an extension of home, a place where he must always struggle to succeed and make people believe in him. Carvel High can be equally disappointing for Andy Hardy. In *Andy Hardy's Private Secretary* (1941), Andy is president of his high school graduating class and spends much of the movie in frenzied activity, planning the passing out ceremony. During his English exam he daydreams and plans advertisements for the graduation program. During dress rehearsal, in front of his friends and peers, his teacher arrives to tell him he has failed and cannot graduate. "You've been so fascinated with all the glitter, you didn't bother with the gold," his father tells him sternly.

Nobody's Darling (1943) found Janie Farnsworth (Mary Lee) struggling for acceptance with both her parents and her peers. The daughter of two movie stars, she attends Pennington School, populated to a large degree by the sons and daughters of Hollywood luminaries. The girl's parents have little faith in her ability to act and resign themselves to the hope that she might at least marry well. Unable to prove herself at home, the girl is forced to use school as a place to assert herself. Desperately intent on getting a part in the school play, she attempts to make herself noticed by glamorizing herself. False eyelashes, low-cut gown, and spike heels, however, rather than winning her the role, manage to produce only laughter from her fellow students, and the girl is humiliated.

That Hagen Girl (1947) was another story of adolescent alienation at home and school. Directed by Peter Godfrey, it starred Shirley Temple as the teenager tormented by a past she could not understand. Eighteen-year-old Mary Bates lives in Jordan, Ohio. From the time of her birth, mystery has surrounded the girl and she is plagued by the stigma of illegitimacy. Trying to fulfill one of the major developmental stages of adolescence and establish an identity for herself, the girl finds that she has no foundation on which to build. "Who am I? Please tell me the truth," she pleads, wondering, "How can you be somebody if you're nobody to begin with?" The school, rather than helping the girl, simply reinforces the suspicion and prejudices of the community. At a high school dance, a boy forces his intentions upon the girl in a corridor. When the headmistress, Miss Grover, encounters the couple, she takes the matter to the school board, claiming the girl is in breach of acceptable conduct. An extension of the townsfolk, Miss Grover observes that knowing who the girl is, they really couldn't expect much better behavior. Distraught and confused, the girl runs away to Chicago, only to be brought back home by the police. The incident has merely fueled the fires of gossip and Mary finds she has become the subject of adolescent bull sessions in the boys' locker room, while parents worry about what sort of influence she will have on their children. "Mary's so unhappy. She needs a chance and the town isn't giving her one," a teacher pleads, trying to support the girl and encourage her to try out for the school play. Given the opportunity to star as Juliet, Mary finds the hostility and suspicion from the community brings pressure to bear on the school, and she is removed from the production.

What the girl finds herself suffering from is a process described by Edgar Friedenberg in *The Vanishing Adolescent.* "The high school," he wrote, "still reflects and transmits faithfully the esteem or disparagement in which the community holds its students and their families. All aspects of a youngster's life in high school, not just his social life outside the classroom, are strongly influenced by his family's social status."[4] Throughout the 1930's and 1940's the celluloid classroom reveals itself as a reflection of the community beyond. The adolescent's experience of school is seldom related to formal learning, and the lessons encountered are often bitter and painful. Nonetheless it would be erroneous to suggest that Hollywood seriously addressed itself to the nature of schooling. Centerville High and Carvel High are largely extensions of the bobby-soxer cult, and the kids we see there are mainly concerned with malts, matinees, and the latest dance craze. They seem singularly unconcerned with lessons, teachers, or graduation. School for these young people is merely an extension of their social life.

What is most surprising about this is the relationship between school and the war. While we might have expected to see films in which the young were inquisitive about the war, in which schools and teachers discussed history, outlined foreign policy, helped the young to contribute to the war effort, and to understand the conflict going on about them, screen schools, like screen families, largely ignored the war and its impact upon youth.

There are, of course, moments in which the school setting is used as a rallying point. In *Andy Hardy's Private Secretary*, school is clearly cited as the road to democracy. "When I see our kids walk into the big free high school together," a character comments, "I know what's wrong with the United States of America: absolutely nothing!" In *Henry Aldrich for President* (1942), Henry runs for a class president against a wealthy snob. Campaigning on behalf of Henry, a girl declares," ... a snob, a small town plutocrat who insults your intelligence by trying to buy your sacred right to vote by a measly ice cream. Let's not forget, folks, that this is wartime and we're fighting dictator powers. America can use every plug it can get, especially from fresh faced vibrant youth, to plug its democratic system." Such connections, however, are rare and, despite the traumas of girls like Janie Farnsworth and Mary Bates, school seldom seems to intrude upon the life of the young throughout the thirties and forties.

In contrast, the European cinema seemed much more aware of how dominant school could be for the young. In France, Vigo's *Zero for Conduct* (1933) dealt with a student rebellion. The relationship between school and society was immediately perceived by French authorities and the film was banned until after the liberation. In Sweden, *Torment* (1946) depicted school as a brutalizing experience, the students subjected to the sadistic control of a master who drove them to exhaustion. When the young hero collapses, the doctor tells his father, "They suffer from eyestrain, anemia; half of them are turning homosexual ... each teacher thinks his subject is more important than the other.... Don't push him too hard, he's going to find it hard enough to come to grips with reality." While such a vision of school life would not come to the American screen for many years, the release of *City Across the River* in 1949 abruptly terminated the vision of school as an extension of bobby soxer society.

Tom Brown's Schooldays (1951), though set in England in the nineteenth century and itself a re-make of a Billy Halop-Freddie Bartholemew movie of the thirties, was decidedly contemporaneous to the mood of the 1950's. A logical outgrowth of both *Torment* and *City Across the River*, the film finds young Tom and his friend East at the mercy of corrupt seniors like Flashman, and merciless masters who proclaim, "Birching will continue to flourish, gentlemen.... Though tempest roar and every earth do quake, a man of thee or else thy end I'll make." Tom and the other boys in such a school are looked upon as "spotty and unpleasant denizens of pond life." They are subjected to sadistic and barbaric phasing rituals including being held against an open fire.

Phasing and brutality were also evident in Calder Willingham's stageplay, *End as a Man*, which dealt with life in a military academy and came to the screen in 1957. Violence thoroughly pervades the school environment throughout the decade. In *The Blackboard Jungle*, racial hostilities between students explode in verbal violence with taunts of "mick," "nigger," and "spic" bandied about the classroom. Artie West, armed with his flick knife, is as large a threat to other students as he is to Dadier. "Did you ever try to fight 35 guys at one time, teach?" he taunts Dadier. Totally beyond redemption, he is a product of both school and society, and his presence is an indication of the powerlessness of his peers. His defeat, while designed by Dadier, is engineered and executed by the intervention of other students. Dadier has pleaded with them to "learn to think for yourself." When they overpower Artie in a classroom brawl, they have learned their lesson, but it has been a violent one in which neither books nor blackboard have been useful.

The same situation is present in *High School Confidential*. The classroom belongs to tough-guy J.I. Coleridge, who pays only lip service to teacher Miss Williams, and reduces lessons to the hip street lingo of his gang of leather-jacketed friends. The remainder of the class appear to be willing accomplices in his games, and devote more energy to chicken runs and dope smoking than they do to their studies. If the school has failed, it is plainly seen as an extension of the community. Indeed, at the film's conclusion, when Mike Landon and the other formerly passive jocks come to the aid of the law enforcement agencies, the battle (guns and all) moves from the classroom to the town.

The Restless Years (1958) advertised itself as "the story of a town with a dirty mind." If Liberty as a town is dirty, then the school is clearly not immune to the dirt nor to the violence that pervades films of that period. On parent night a fight breaks out in the school, and when one boy is wrongly blamed, his father turns angrily on the school board—"If you make that boy suffer, I'll find you and break your neck. That's a promise!"

Reach for Glory (1963) once again linked school, violence, and the military. A British film, it was set in England during the Second World War and concerned a group of boys who become increasingly unable to distinguish fact from fantasy. When they inadvertently kill one of their own number, their stunned leader turns upon school officials, tearfully seeking an answer, "If it isn't war, why are we wearing these uniforms, why do we spend three days a week learning the parts of a rifle? If they don't want us to use the bloody things, why do they teach us how to?"

School is once again the setting for death in Paramount's 1972 production, *A Separate Peace*. Like *Reach for Glory*, the film dealt with the school life of a group of adolescents during the Second World War. Shot on location at Phillips Exeter Academy in New Hampshire, the film explores a love/hate relationship between its adolescent heroes, Gene and Finny. The Devon Academy is for Finny a place of fear, anger, and senseless rivalries.

Despite the pressure of examinations, athletic competition, and a full school schedule, the war beyond increasingly impinges upon the school, penetrating the ivy-league isolation and affecting the boys. The turmoil and dislocation of the outer world is reflected in the inner turmoil which Gene experiences in his feelings for Finny. Introverted and scholarly, he finds himself attracted to the out-going and athletic Finny, a born leader who seems to inspire those about him. Yet despite the deep and trusting friendship that grows up between the two sixteen-year-olds, there is a darker side to the relationship. In Finny, Gene sees everything that he is not and that he wishes to be. Indeed, he finds himself increasingly surrendering his time and his personality to the carefree whims of his friend. Increasingly Finny manages to intrude upon Gene's life, to dislocate his schedule, his routine, his personality. "Examinations, books — this is a school, not a playground," Gene complains, tired of Finny's endless games and escapades.

It is during one of these games that Gene pushes his friend from a tree, crippling him for life. The surface camaraderie of the boys has given way to the jealousy and discontent that has haunted Gene all along. While Finny has been a good friend, he has also been a rival, a personality so dominant that the identity projection he elicited from Gene threatened to stunt the boy's growth. In toppling his friend from the tree, Gene has attempted to liberate himself. It might also be argued that his action is a response to his growing awareness and fear of the homosexual overtones of their relationship. While nothing overt ever takes place between the two boys, much of the film is shot and played like a love story. Shortly before the tree incident, the boys spend a night together on the beach. "I hope you're having a pretty good time here," Finny says. "After all, you don't just come to the beach with anyone ... in this teenage period of your life, the proper person to come to the beach with is your best pal, which is what you are." Whatever the reason that motivates Gene's action, he is subsequently subjected to feelings of guilt, to persecution and harassment by other students, and driven to a desperate attempt to confess to Finny.

When Finny is publicly forced to face the reality of the situation, he cannot deal with it. Attempting to flee, he falls down the stairs and later dies on the operating table. Like Piggy in William Golding's *Lord of the Flies*, Finny dies when he learns the truth. Piggy had come to understand that the beast he and his young friends feared was in reality their own savage inner natures. Finny is unwilling to face such a reality. "You were always savage underneath," one of the boys tells Gene. It is a truth and a realization about human nature that Finny cannot live with. In a world torn apart by war, he remains an innocent, unable to grow, unable to survive in such a society. His death saves him from the savagery of the world around him; it also brings the war into the school. "This is one of those things that I think boys of your generation are going to see a lot of," the doctor tells Gene.

Bless the Beasts and Children (1971), *Red Sky at Morning* (1971), *Carrie* (1977), *Fraternity Row* (1977), *My Bodyguard* (1980), and *Teachers*

(1984) perpetuated school as a violent playground. When it has not been the setting for intimidation, confrontation, and physical attacks, the school has served to isolate and humiliate the student. Natalie Wood runs in tears from the classroom in *Splendor in the Grass* (1961). Billy Casper is repeatedly humiliated in *Kes* (1970). Sonny and Duane are harassed because of their failure to perform on the football field in *The Last Picture Show* (1971). Conrad Jarrett and most of the swim team find themselves subjected to the insensitive cajoling of their coach in *Ordinary People* (1980). Henry Steel finds himself subjected to brutal punishment on the instructions of his basketball coach in *One on One* (1977).

Edgar Friedenberg has noted that, "What is learned in school, or for that matter anywhere at all, depends far less on what is taught than on what one actually experiences in the place."[4] In the celluloid classroom, students seldom seem interested in books, classes, papers, or anything vaguely related to the academic program. With the rare exception of Francie Nolan (*A Tree Grows in Brooklyn*; 1945) and Matilda (*The Effects of Gamma Rays on Man-In-the-Moon Marigolds*; 1972), students seem singularly uninspired by school. While Matilda may be intrigued with the fantastic world of atoms, molecules, and an endless universe mystically held together by a mysterious life force, her screen peers are preoccupied with more libidinal pursuits.

In 1959, one educator complained of the "constant classroom strutting, particularly by the boys, after the manner of peacocks in the barnyard.... A walk through the corridors of some schools is like a trip down lover's lane.... For these students, the only school activities of interest or importance are the socials or dances." The schools, he believed, were centers where Johnny and Mary are "hurried into sexual precocity by elders more concerned about their social acceptability than their academic acceptability."[5] *Red Sky at Morning*, *The Last Picture Show*, *Splendor in the Grass*, and *Pretty Maids All in a Row* all reflect such adolescent preoccupation with matters less than academic.

When sex and social activities do not form the basis of the young person's school life, sport functions as the major area of interest. In *Saturday's Hero* (1951), John Saxon played Steve Novak, who was faced with a choice between academic and sporting success. "Get wise!" a character tells him, "It isn't education that interests Americans, it's heroes. Any street corner in America, ask a guy who his Congressman is, he can't tell ya. But ask him who's the all-American, that's the pass key!" Whether through running (*Our Winning Season*; 1978), basketball (*One on One*), wrestling (*Take Down*; 1979), or some other sporting activity, the school provides a forum in which the adolescent can prove himself.

If the screen seems to place too much emphasis upon the role of sport in the school program, there is ample evidence to support such an image. In *Growing Up American*, Alan Peshkin reported his research of school life in a small American town. Mansfield, he declared, "is a football town.... More

The Effect of Gamma Rays on Man-in-the-Moon Marigolds (1972): A rare image of school providing a positive experience for a young student.

than just an athletic event, a football game is a significant social occasion, during which a variety of personal and communal needs are satisfied and reinforced. The football games provide unsurpassed opportunity for recreation and social interaction, and for promoting and expressing community pride and loyalty. On these five nights, more than any other time, the school can be seen as the heart of Mansfield."[6]

The celluloid classroom, then, exists as a place where adolescents live and learn with almost complete disregard for the curriculum and the academic program. While such a state may be lamentable, it has more than a little basis in reality. In April 1978, *The High School Journal*, in an article that compared school to jail, observed that "Prisons get bad guys out of the way and high schools get teenagers off the street."[7] In November of the same year, the same journal reported that "our educational system actually serves to deaden human consciousness."[8] Philip Cusick, in his study, *Inside High School: The Students' World*, documented similar alienation and disenchantment with the school program. The students' "most active and alive moments," he wrote, "were spent not with teachers and subject matter affairs but in their own small group interactions."[9]

In bringing such an image of school life to the screen, Hollywood, it must be said, has managed to reflect a general attitude and situation.

While the celluloid classroom can thus be seen as indicative of some of the conditions in secondary education today, it would be wrong to suggest that the images and individuals Hollywood presents us with are representative. Every day, class after class, semester after semester, year after year, millions of young Americans pass through the educational system in an orderly and successful manner. Along the way some of them drop out; some feel alienated. For some, school is a lonely and frustrating experience compounded by the pressures of peers and puberty. For others, many more than the screen would suggest, school is a stimulating and exciting time that opens new vistas, new horizons, and prepares them for the world of tomorrow.

If the film industry has been guilty in producing a rather negative image of school it is not alone. The most popular album of 1980 was Pink Floyd's *The Wall*, in which a group of English school children declared, "We don't need no education," and their vicious teacher was depicted as the henpecked victim of a psychopathic wife.

In his book, *Is There Life After High School?*, Ralph Keyes suggests that many writers used their material as a means of getting back at their unhappy experiences of school. Whatever the reason, movies have seldom been able to realistically capture either the adolescents' or the teachers' experience of school. While individual films have been forceful, even informative, the reliance on formula, stereotype and conflict have resulted in an unrepresentative vision of American secondary education.

For whatever its faults, and given its failure to respond rapidly to the changing nature and needs of the young, the American high school system has played an integral role in shaping the character of the nation. While it is dramatically interesting to depict the teacher as hero and the school as a battleground, for the average student the day-to-day encounter with school takes him through halls of neither anger nor anguish. In depicting school as a constant storm center or as an adolescent nemesis, the film industry once again abandoned reality in favor of sensationalism, presenting as it had done with the family a lop-sided and distorted view of American life.

8. Dead Ends and Death Row
1931–1949

> *"We must build in this child a respect for law*
> *and order and above all a respect that will*
> *guard her in the future from being a social*
> *outcast"*—Judge, in *Beloved Brat*; 1938.

Reviewing *The Warriors* in February 1979, *Time* magazine commented,

> Director Walter Hill does not seem to know much about contemporary
> teenage hoods. The gangs in this film differ only slightly from the Dead
> End Kids of the thirties or the Jets of *West Side Story*, or even the Sweat-
> hogs of TV's *Welcome Back Kotter*[1]

The review places *The Warriors* and the depiction of juvenile delinquency within Hollywood's tradition of stereotyping, but the film was interesting for other reasons. Employing a provocative advertising campaign,
Paramount released the movie in some 670 theaters across the nation. The
poster used featured a picture of armed youngsters, strident and defiant as
they stare back at onlookers. "These are the armies of the night. They are
100,000 strong. They outnumber the cops five to one. They could run New
York City. Tonight they're all out to get the Warriors."

Both the film and the elaborate publicity campaign were more
successful than the producers may have wanted. Within a week of reviewing
the movie, *Time* reported three murders inspired by the film. A California
farm town, a Palm Springs drive-in, and a Boston street had provided
strikingly disparate backgrounds for frighteningly similar outbreaks of
violence. Faced with such incidents, the film's distributors scrapped the
lurid advertising campaign and offered to pay for extra security at the
theaters where the film was playing. While seeming to respond with a social
conscience, the industry was able at the same time to reap the handsome $10
million grossed by the film in its first two weeks.

The concern expressed at the violence which followed the release of
The Warriors helps to further locate the movie within the mainstream of the
Hollywood tradition. The gangster genre which had emerged most successfully

in the thirties had provoked similar complaints. While pocketing the profits, Hollywood had responded in the first instance by suggesting the films were realistic depictions of social problems, and later by having the movies end with the death of the gangster who had been glorified for the majority of the film. In provoking violence *The Warriors* simply followed a long established tradition in the relationship between the screen and juvenile crime.

In October 1942, for example, *Variety* had reported that late movie screenings were seen as a menace to kids. Movie houses, the report indicated, were increasingly becoming a scene of the source for outbreaks of juvenile crime. In *Movies, Delinquency, and Crime*, published in 1933, Herbert Blumer, in a flawed but fascinating study, looked at the impact of the movies on juvenile crime. A seventeen-year-old Italian male told him, "The gang pictures came out and soon had our bunch standing on their heads. They took on the nicknames of characters in the pictures and it wasn't long before we went out on raiding parties of chicken coops and small stores and getting away with ease."[2]

The Warriors, therefore, rather than representing a new and startling trend in filmmaking, was firmly rooted in Hollywood's response to both crime and the juvenile delinquent. First the characters, as *Time* noted, were shallow stereotypes with their counterparts well in evidence in other movies. Second, the film afforded the industry the opportunity to turn controversy into profit while at the same time seeming to have a social conscience. Third, by depicting and inciting violence the film continued a trend that had existed for more than five decades. But while *The Warriors* and films like it clearly owe something to the gangster genre and to the film industry's reliance upon format and formula, they are also the logical outcome of Hollywood's response to both the family and the school.

Abandoned by parents and pedagogues alike, filmdom's teenagers found themselves in a moral vacuum devoid of appropriate adult role models upon whom to base their behavior. In *Dead End* (1937) and *Angels with Dirty Faces* (1938), the major role models for the Dead End Kids are the gangsters Baby Face Martin and Rocky. Ten years later, in *Knock on Any Door* (1949), the screen adolescent is still without any adult guidance. With both the family and the school failing in their task of socializing young people, John Derek can find no better philosophy to adopt than to "live fast, die young, and have a good looking corpse."

Between 1930 and 1980 Hollywood's depiction of the juvenile delinquent has largely stemmed out of its rendition of both the American family and the American school system. *Are These Our Children?* (1931) presented Eddie Brand, a lower middle-class teenager from a broken but loving home, who becomes first delinquent and then a killer. The boy's plunge into crime seems to be triggered when he fails to win a debating contest at school. In *King Creole* (1957) Elvis Presley played a young man skirting the edge of delinquency because of the weakness of his father and an unsympathetic and hostile school administration. Finally, *Over the Edge*

(1979) combined the failure of family and school as co-conspirators in the process of producing juvenile delinquents. When the middle-class kids of the film band together in open opposition to their parents and teachers, they set fire to the school in which these twin targets of their hate are meeting. In that single incident Hollywood united two of the key contributing factors to its depiction of delinquency over half a century. Whether Jets or Sharks, Wanderers or Warriors, the gangs and cliques that have so occupied the film industry emerge in essence because of the failure of any social system to absorb them or channel their interests. Having robbed its teenagers of a childhood, depriving them of the pillars of school and family, Hollywood backed itself into a corner in which the peer group emerged as the dominant setting within which these screenagers were socialized.

But while the peer group may provide security it is essentially detrimental to adolescent development and stands in the way of the passage to adulthood and autonomy. Marsland and Perry, in "Variations in Adolescent Societies," have pointed out that

> The young person most powerfully identified with an exclusive youth culture is also most likely to be anomic, or lacking in identification with the generally established culture and in anchorage in the social structure which carries that culture.[3]

The Hollywood delinquents, whether those of the thirties, the fifties, the seventies, or any of the periods in between conform perfectly to such a description. Alienated and hostile, these adolescents are adrift in a turbulent social sea with little prospect for rescue.

More important, however, than the sense of alienation these young people feel is the sense of alienation that pervades these films and is communicated to young audiences. In the delinquent stories, Hollywood inherits the legacy of its previous depiction of adolescence. Having systematically deprived its celluloid sons and daughters of positive images of parents and pedagogues, it found itself forced to turn them over to the pervasive influence of the peer group. In the process it also abandoned its young audience to their own social group, inviting them to identify with the alienated delinquents of the screen. While the gangster genre has largely ceased to exist, films dealing with juvenile delinquency have a cyclical existence, and seem to emerge briefly but successfully throughout each decade. *Saturday Night Fever* (1978), *The Wanderers* (1979), *Over the Edge* (1979), *Walk Proud* (1979), and *Boulevard Nights* (1979) all testify to the sudden and short-lived nature of such cycles. While the success of *Saturday Night Fever* encouraged producers to go with other gang related themes, such an assumption merely tells why Hollywood makes certain movies rather than explaining the images these movies deal with.

One of the most startling but least known films to deal with juvenile delinquency was Wesley's Ruggles' *Are These Our Children?*, which

Are These Our Children? (1931): A flawed but fascinating film. It remains the only movie in which a teenage character is executed by the state.

incorporated the legacy of the gangster genre with Hollywood's depiction of both family and school. It remains to this day the only Hollywood film in which an adolescent is executed by the state. Greeted by the *New York*

Times as an "accurate lithograph of the feverish New York scene that will not be lost on New Yorkers,"[4] the film dealt with juvenile violence in the Big Apple. But if youthful delinquency was the key issue of the film, it was more than a little related to Hollywood's depiction of the adult gangster. Released in November 1931, the film had been preceeded in January by *Little Caesar* and in April by *The Public Enemy.* In its depiction of adolescent crime, the movie owed more than a little to its cinematic predecessors. The Cagney vehicle had opened with a statement from the filmmakers suggesting that the movie represented an attempt "to depict honestly an environment that exists today in a certain strata of American life, rather than to glorify the criminal of hoodlum." While *The Public Enemy* implied that Tommy Powers was the product of his environment, such a suggestion was rendered meaningless by the fact that while Tommy and his brother both sprang from a common background, only one of them went crooked. The reality therefore was that the life of crime was embarked upon as an act of free will, as indeed it was in the case of Rico in *Little Caesar.*

Free will also seems the most logical explanation for the life of crime embarked upon by high school student Eddie Brand in *Are These Our Children?* Such a view is more than implied by the statement RKO attached as a prologue to the film. "Youth, love and happiness—these make the world go round. To all each day comes choice—every hour we must decide. One way leads to shadows, the other into peace and light." Eddie Brand is a good looking, clean-living, decent, and well-behaved boy. While he has no parents, his home life seems warm and convivial. Raised by his grandmother, the boy has seemingly always been a loving and obedient child dedicated to his sweetheart and to his younger brother. His plunge into crime stems, it seems, from the bizarre fact that he loses a public speaking contest. Speaking on the merits of the constitution, the boy is shattered when he fails to win. In the tradition of Rico he dreams of being a big shot, of seeing his name in the papers. As Rico found himself drawn to the night life of the Palermo Club, so Eddie finds himself attracted by the allure of the Orient Club. Both Eddie and Rico initially entered these night-spots as outsiders and both quickly assumed leadership of the group. Both Eddie and Rico initially reject alcohol and both are finally undone by alcohol and consuming ambition. Indeed, in Eddie's case the murder he commits is a drunken one, when he opens fire on a family friend who refuses to give him a drink. Both Tommy Powers and Rico paid the ultimate price for their violence. In conforming once again to the pattern established in the earlier movies, Eddie too must die. But while Tommy is killed by a rival gang and Rico is gunned down in a battle with the police, Eddie is sentenced to death and is executed by the state.

It is impossible to discuss *Are These Our Children?* without acknowledging its debt to these early classics of the gangster genre. But while it owes much to the characters and situations of both *Little Caesar* and *The Public Enemy,* it also owes more than a little to Hollywood's traditional response to both school and family. While Eddie ultimately acknowledges free will, confessing, "I picked the wrong side," the filmmakers attempted, albeit weakly, to suggest the cause of his criminal activities. When the boy goes to trial, newspapers and the church insist that "this young boy is a product of our civilization." If Eddie is sick, the implication goes, then the society that produced him is also sick. Yet when we first encounter Eddie he seems far from disturbed. While he obviously is attracted to the provocative rhythms of jazz, he is the sort of boy who is kind to a stray dog, who calls his girl-friend regularly, and who seems at home at the kitchen table with cookies and milk. In what way can Eddie and his society be considered sick? There is no satisfactory answer to the question.

Alcohol is obviously a curse and leads to the boy's downfall but the film is hardly a defense of Prohibition. The boy's grandmother believes the peer group is to blame, pleading for the judge to "send him away where he'll be free from such bad influence." During her testimony she also raises the spectre of the fractured family. Eddie's mother, we discover, died two years earlier, and his father deserted. Yet rather than provide plausible explana-tions for the boy's behavior, these responses appear to be little more than the confused musings of the scriptwriters who seem unable to suggest any cause for juvenile delinquency. "Those crazy kids, the things they do these days are awful," a bystander comments.

Eddie and his gang are seen in some ways as products of the lost gene-ration, kids out of control with no morals or values. "Sheiks, Flappers Jailed in Killing," the newspapers headline when they are arrested. Like Rico, Eddie wants the good life. "I thought I was smart. I thought I had to get money and drink." But whereas both Rico and Tommy embark upon a life of crime with their eyes open and both films see them as opportunists out to succeed in a country that cherished the struggle of the individual, Eddie stumbles into crime. It isn't simply that he is naive. In dealing with juvenile delinquency, Hollywood itself was naive.

It is no accident that Eddie became the first and last teenager in Hollywood history to find his way to the electric chair. Hollywood killed him because crime had to be punished. But watching the end of the film as a heavenly choir sings and Eddie lovingly embraces his younger brother, it is evident that the producers had backed themselves into a corner. This boy has been redeemed. He is repentant. He is sorry for his crimes and he de-serves to live. Unlike Rico or Tommy, the boy has seen the error of his ways. His death is as illogical as the flimsy causes of his criminality. *Are These Our Children?* is a startling and exciting film that merits more attention than it has been given by either critics or the general public. More than anything it shows the industry's confused response to juvenile delin-quency in the early thirties.

One other film from the early thirties clearly demonstrates this confusion. *Wild Boys of the Road* (1933) was directed for Warner Brothers by William Wellman. An excellent study of the impact of the Depression upon juveniles, it provided a fascinating image of lower middle-class life and the plight of the nation's youth. As such it stands apart from the depiction of juvenile delinquency throughout much of the thirties. *Mayor of Hell* (1933), *The Devil Is a Sissy* (1936), *Dead End* (1937), *Boy of the Streets* (1937), *Boys Town* (1938), *Crime School* (1938), and *Angels With Dirty Faces* (1938) dealt almost entirely with working class environments and working class youngsters, and were almost always played by the Dead End Kids, Jackie Cooper, Mickey Rooney, or Frankie Darro.

But *Wild Boys of the Road* differed from the majority of juvenile delinquency movies in another way too. Not only did it shift the emphasis from working class to middle and lower middle-class environments, it actively located the story within the Depression milieu. Throughout much of the decade, in its typical fashion, Hollywood responded to controversy by ignoring it. The gangster films that had been so successful for the period were stories ripped from yesterday's headlines. The heyday of the mob and racketeering was over before Hollywood responded to it. Equally, controversial anti-war films such as *All Quiet on the Western Front* emerged well after the last battle cry had sounded and the nation had embarked upon a period of isolationism. In *Wild Boys of the Road* Hollywood came close to confronting the reality of the Depression. Commenting on one scene in the film, the *New York Times* suggested that "no sequence in recent pictures provides so much realism."[5] But while the film at least in terms of its image-making seemed realistic, the ideology it espoused was less so.

Based on the Russian film *Road to Life*, the film concentrated on a group of young people forced by economic hardship to leave school and home to try and establish financial independence. Eddie Smith (Frankie Darro), Tommy Gordon (Edwin Philips), and Sally (Dorothy Coonan) team up on board a freight car and begin their trek across the country in search of work. The youngsters are cast together within the protection of the peer group because of the failure of both school and family to adequately deal with the Depression. The failure of the school is clearly demonstrated when Tommy is refused admittance to a school dance because he cannot afford it. Clinging to the rules and regulations of the past, the school penalizes pupils who, through no fault of their own, are unable to cope financially. The failure of the family is equally evident when Eddie confronts his tearful mother and, realizing the difficulties that lie ahead, sells his car, thus usurping his father's role and assuming the role of provider.

The failure of the major social institutions to deal with the Depression is one of the most crucial points made by the film. This failure provides the very motivation the young people have to leave home. Yet as the film progresses it becomes apparent that it cannot seriously address the very issue it has raised. Affecting a semi-documentary style, the movie featured a montage of countless nameless faces intercut with shots from the March of Time, the feet of the nation's youth marching over a map of the United States. The Depression as both the subject and the setting of the film appeared timely and realistic. In March 1933, for example, American City reported,

> Boys in large numbers have left their homes under stress of economic
> circumstances, and are bumming their way from city to city in search of
> work or at least sustenance.[6]

The National Committee on the Care of the Transient and Homeless reported a transient population of 1,250,000 of which 135,000 were boys under the age of 21. Eddie, Tommy and Sally thus represented a very real segment of American youth faced with an equally real problem of poverty and homelessness.

But while their situation and circumstance are real enough, the solution proposed by the moviemakers is decidedly unsatisfactory. Having established from the outset that school and family were failing to deal with the needs of the young, the filmmakers seemed incapable of providing a satisfactory solution for these needs. Brought before a court, Eddie angrily condemns the judge and those he represents. "You're sending us to jail because you don't want to see us. Well you can't do it because I'm not the only one! There's thousands just like me and there's more hitting the road every day. Go ahead! Put me in jail! Lock me up! I'm sick of being hungry and cold. I'm sick of freight trains. Jail can't be any worse than the street, so give it to me!" Moved by the boy's plea, the judge who had earlier declared, "You're an enemy to society and I have to keep you off the street," assumes a more benign attitude. Dismissing the charges, he sets out to find work for Eddie, Sally and Tommy. "I'm going to do my part," he tells them, "things are going to be better not only here in New York but across the country."

It is a most unsatisfactory resolution to what had otherwise been a very realistic film. In the character of the judge the film invokes the paternalistic figure that Eddie's father and those like him were incapable of being. Eddie had left home because his own father had been economically emasculated. In the magistrate, Eddie, Tommy and those they represented found a sympathetic and understanding figure unshackled by traditional rules and regulations and concerned with finding more realistic solutions to the pressing problems of the day. The judge in fact is much more than a father figure. With the NRA eagle strategically located behind him and camera angles that fully render the authority of his position, he is an extension of the presidency of Franklin Roosevelt and he offers to the boys and girls who come before him nothing less than a new deal. The conclusion of *Wild Boys of the Road* requires that we abandon the social reality the film has so labored to create. In the end it promises all and provides nothing. Like Eddie and the others, the film audience is expected to accept the word of the judge and believe that better days are coming and work will be available. Like *Are These Our Children?*, *Wild Boys of the Road* delivered an end unsupported by the action throughout the rest of the film.

Eddie Brand died in the electric chair because crime had to be punished. Eddie Smith was provided with a job and returned to his family to no small extent because the studio that created him was firmly behind the Roosevelt administration. In 1933 the newly elected FDR had offered Jack Warner a diplomatic position overseas in gratitude for his help during the election. Declining the offer, Warner had told the President, "I think I can do more for foreign relations with a good picture about America now and then."[7] *Wild Boys of the Road*, with adolescents as its subjects and the Depression as its setting, was an affirmation of America in a time of crisis. It would not be the last time the industry abandoned reality in the name of patriotism.

Wild Boys of the Road and *Are These Our Children?* were significant films for several reasons. First, both films clearly grew out of the failure of school and family. Second, in seeking to replace parents and teachers as role models, the films turned first to the peer group and then to the magistrate and priest. If the judge proves to be Eddie Smith's salvation, then religion is Eddie Brand's salvation. As the time of execution approaches, he says the Lord's Prayer and the cell is flooded by the light referred to in the movie's prologue. In turning to religion and the courts as sources of authority these films clearly pointed the way to a trend that would be taken up later in the decade in *Boys Town*, *Angels with Dirty Faces*, and even the Hardy series, where the screen's most successful father was by no accident a judge. Third, both films surrounded themselves with the aura of realism, claiming to socially valuable, and to this extent were more than a little in debt to the gangster genre. Finally, both films suffered from a confused view of juvenile delinquency that rendered their conclusions illogical. This uncertainty was to be a hallmark of the thirties.

For the rest of the decade juvenile delinquency continued to be a prominent theme which was at least to some extent a reflection of the success of the gangster genre, most noticeably in films such as *G Men* (1935), *Bullets or Ballots* (1936), and *The Roaring Twenties* (1939). The depiction of juvenile delinquency throughout the 1930's reflects a division that existed in society in regard to adolescent lawlessness.

While the Depression had driven many unfortunate youngsters from their homes and many had subsequently embarked upon a life of crime, juvenile delinquency sprang from more than just one source. Writing in *Harpers* in February 1933, Zelda F. Popkin saw the increase in juvenile crime as a legacy inherited from an earlier time:

> Born after the War and the Volstead Act, these boys and girls were thrust into the custody of a generation which had taken to gin as if it were weaned on it. Drunkeness had ceased to be a reprehensible past-time of the 'lower classes' and had become almost a social asset. More than that, this post war world, which had flung off traditions and restraints, had become the golden age of the gangster and racketeer.[8]

Popkin's analysis clearly placed the blame for juvenile crime at the feet of parents and the adult criminals whose careers had been so glamorized.

In looking at Hollywood's response to the question of juvenile delinquency, it is apparent that the industry endorsed such a view to no small extent. The failure of school and family to adequately socialize the young was nowhere more obviously recognized than in *Boys Town* (1938). Hitting upon the idea of taking in the street kids, Father Flanagan spells it out when he says he wants to "give them a home" and "see to their schooling." Parental failure is also seen as a key contributor to delinquency in *The Devil Is a Sissy* (1936), *Boy of the Streets* (1937), and *Delinquent Parents* (1938). In 1933 studio publicity for *Mayor of Hell* said that the film "makes us wonder how much of what it shows parents are responsible for."

Later in the decade, in a rare image of both female and affluent delinquency, *Beloved Brat* (1938) similarly condemned parents. When a wayward teenage girl is brought before the courts, the judge announces that "my opinion of a reform school is that it should be for parents and not the children." The impact of glorified criminal activity that Popkins had targeted in her *Harpers* article was equally apparent in motion pictures. *Mayor of Hell*, *Boy of the Streets*, and *Hell's Kitchen* (1939) all depicted youngsters led astray by adult criminals. The most celebrated examples of this trend were *Dead End* (1937) and *Angels with Dirty Faces* (1939). In both cases, Billy Halop and the other Dead End Kids found themselves attracted to the lifestyle of Baby Face Martin in the earlier vehicle and Rocky in the latter film.

Halop, like Frankie Darro, was the thirties' epitome of the juvenile delinquent. Indeed, it was Darro's voice Disney used for the wayward Lampwick in *Pinocchio* (1940). Tough yet sensitive, both Halop and Darro struggle to survive in a brutal and degrading world. Loyal and true to their own code, they bring to their characters a vulnerability that always renders them more victim than criminal. In the urban squalor of the *Dead End* it is easy for Halop and those like him to seek escape by emulating the ways of hardened criminals and murderers like Martin. Society makes the rules but they are made by indifferent and callous authorities with no concern for the welfare of the poor and needy. If the kids are "cop haters," their view is endorsed. The police that harass them are the same police who attack and intimidate striking factory workers struggling for a better wage and working conditions. If the police turn a blind eye to the exploits of the young punks, it is not out of any pity or charity but simply because "there's no profit in chasing kids." While the newspapers look upon these delinquents as enemies of society, it is obvious that society has turned them into enemies. With no better example to follow they are thus abandoned to the pervasive influence

Opposite: *Angels with Dirty Faces* (1939): The Dead End Kids defined delinquency in the 1930's. The product of brutal environments and corrupt authorities, their waywardness was explained and excused.

of their own peer group and to the advice of men like Martin, who forsake all rules and conventions, advising only that the boys "kick the hell" out of whomever they happen to combat. In such an environment even the death of the gangster cannot dissuade the boys from following his example. Shot down in a hail of bullets, Martin is immediately elevated to the stature of martyr. "He must have been a pretty smart guy," the boys conclude.

It was just such a conclusion that was addressed in *Angels with Dirty Faces*. In the role of Rocky, James Cagney continued to portray the killer criminal whose lifestyle appeared attractive to city youth like Halop and the other Dead End Kids. Providing them with beer and scattering money like confetti, Rocky rapidly finds that the boys idolize and hero-worship him. His status as criminal is that of hero. Father Jerry pleads with him, "What earthly good is it for me to teach that honesty is the best policy when all around them they see that dishonesty is a better policy, the hood-lum is looked at with the same respect as the successful businessman."

Popkin may have been correct in pinpointing parents, family, and criminal influence as causes of juvenile delinquency, but many other factors were at work as well. A *Commonweal* article entitled "Salvaging Boys from the Dead End," published in January 1938, gave evidence of some of these other sources. Mayor LaGuardia, the article asserted, believed that juvenile crime sprang to a large degree from hopeless poverty. Commissioner of Correction MacCormick, on the other hand, felt that slum conditions were largely responsible for juvenile crime, and Superintendent of Schools Campbell believed that juvenile crime was encouraged by the inevitability of the life into which they were born, which promised few escapes from the tenements. In looking at Hollywood's depiction of juvenile delinquency throughout the 1930's, such views are also highly visible. *Mayor of Hell* saw its teenage criminals as "a product of the worst environment in the world, the city slums." The industry's uncertainty about the impact of the slums on delinquency was evident, however, just three years later when *The Devil Is a Sissy* told audiences that "the next generation is finding itself down there on the streets." *Boy of the Streets* introduced the unusual image of a benevo-lent policeman who understood the impact of environment upon crime. Watching Jackie Cooper and his gang members, the officer comments, "Sometimes I think we had better times than the kids have nowadays. We had the woods to tramp in, the fields to play in, a decent home to live in."

One other popular issue in the depiction of juvenile crime was the concept of punishment. The 1930's was a period marked by major debate about how best to deal with adolescent offenders. A Sub-Commission on Causes of New York State Crime Commission Report on Youthful Offenders early in the decade concluded that "the process of justice in New York City must have a bad psychological effect on the impressionable young offender."[9] The character of the reforming judge in *Wild Boys of the Road* can therefore be seen as an accurate reflection of changes taking place in the law at least insofar as it applied to the young.

In 1934 Sheldon and Eleanor T. Glueck, in their study "1000 Juvenile Delinquents," opened new vistas on crime prevention. Establishing a link between truancy in early school years with criminal activity in later life, they provided a new means of detecting potential delinquents. Progressive methods were also beginning to filter into police departments across the nation. In Berkeley, California, August Vollmer advocated that the role of police was not simply to apprehend criminals but to be seen as friends. In January 1930, Henrietta Addition was appointed Deputy Police Commissioner in New York. Under her guidance the Bureau of Crime Prevention sought to discover and alleviate community conditions that fostered juvenile delinquency. In 1938 the Federal Juvenile Delinquency Act became law.

Between 1933 and 1939 Hollywood motion pictures provide evidence of these developments. The most visible target, at least as far as Hollywood was concerned, was the institution of the reform school. Directing *Crime School* for Warner Brothers in 1938, Lewis Seiler said, "All too often reform schools don't reform. Politically controlled, they treat the boys as criminals and so criminals they become." When Billy Halop as the perennial juvenile delinquent, is brought before the court, the boy's sister pleads with the judge, "Maybe he's a little tough but a kid's got to be tough in our neighborhood to survive. If you send him away he'll come out hard and mean and bitter. If you want to do something for these boys, why don't you clean up the slums?" In condemning the reform schools, the girl spoke for the film industry which depicted these institutions as dominated by brutal, sadistic and callous individuals intent only on their own personal profit. Rather than acting as agents of reform, the schools were seen to actually foster crime. In *Mayor of Hell* a mother claims, "They sent my last boy there and he came out a murderer." While a bystander in *Dead End* suggests, "They'll at least take him (Halop) from the gutter and teach him a useful trade," we are more likely to believe the boys when they cunningly comment, "You learn a barrel of good things in reform school."

Having condemned reform schools and their administrators, the film industry openly advocated a new approach to treating juvenile offenders. In *Mayor of Hell* a character advocates startling changes in the treatment of the reform school inhabitants. "First of all I'd let the boys be human beings, and then I'd give them a chance of self government." She supports the principles of the juvenile republic and argues that responsibility fosters good citizenship. Such a view is also evident in *Boys Town* where Whitey Marsh and youngsters like him are introduced to democratic procedures and to responsible and worthwhile work. In *Crime School* Humphrey Bogart plays a crime commissioner intent on cleaning up the reform schools and their corrupt administrations. Giving the young inmates the right to paint and decorate their cells, he argues that "they'll take an interest in it and it'll teach them responsibility." Similar concerns are also present in *Beloved Brat*, *Boys Reformatory* (1939), and *Off the Record* (1939).

In looking at Hollywood's response to juvenile delinquency throughout the decade of the thirties, it is impossible to escape the conviction that the industry was genuinely concerned with the issue of adolescent crime. As such it was clearly a reflection of a widespread social concern. In March 1933, *American City* asked, "How Shall We Deal With Delinquent Adolescents and Wandering Youth?" In part Hollywood attempted to answer the question.

It would be erroneous, however, to suggest that their answer was either clearly thought out or altruistic. The dominant motivation, as always, was profit and the industry resorted to sensationalism and persuasive publicity campaigns to sell their products. *Girls on Probation* was one of the few films to address the issue of female delinquency and its publicity was lurid. "She lies, she steals, she cheats. She might be your kid sister!" "From rich homes and poor, from the Gold Coast and over the tracks come America's dangerous daughters." Pressbooks for *Angels with Dirty Faces* suggested a variety of ways of selling the film. "Local magistrates can be approached on a slant whereby juvenile offenders are reprimanded and sentenced to see *Angels with Dirty Faces* to learn a lesson in what can happen to a man who refuses to obey the law." "School teachers and principals should be enlisted for support in bringing this picture to the attention of all students since it shows the effects of unhealthy environment and improper association on the propagation of crime." But if the studio publicity machine recognized the function of the environment and bad influences on juvenile crime, the film itself seemed somehow to imply that delinquency was a matter of choice. The picture was "dedicated to the thousands of slum boys who next week or next year must choose between crime and honesty."

By 1938, therefore, it seemed that Hollywood had advanced little since *Are These Our Children?* That film had suggested that Eddie's criminal activity was a matter of free will, and while *Angels with Dirty Faces* paid lip service to the environment, it too succumbed to the notion that delinquency was somehow a matter of choice. Nowhere is this more apparent than when Father Jerry condemns Rocky's criminal acts. "If reform school did make a criminal out of him," he says, "then he chose to stay that way." *Boy of the Streets* similarly supported such a point of view. Though the police officer is sympathetic to the plight of the boys in his precinct, their delinquency is still considered to be a matter of choice. "Poor little devils; born without a chance. They're all trying to be hard and tough because they figure that's the way to get along in this world. I was born in this district myself. I liked the uniform so I became a cop but I could just as easily have gone the other way and become a crook."

It would be both unfair and unreasonable to expect the film industry to have articulated a logical and consistent viewpoint regarding juvenile delinquency during a period in which the attitude of the courts, law enforcement agencies, government, and society itself were being re-defined. Hollywood's uncertainty and confusion reflected these wider developments. But

Beloved Brat: **An unusual thirties image of both female and upper middle-class delinquency.**

Hollywood did more than simply attempt to address a social issue. It actively attempted to use a social issue as a source of profit. More than mere entertainment, it attempted to suggest that its products were useful social documents capable of playing a valuable role in the debate over juvenile delinquency. In attempting to sell these films Hollywood showed no hesitation in pressing itself upon the courts, the schools, and the police force. MGM delcared that *Boys Town* held up a mirror to society, but the image MGM and Hollywood as a whole reflected was more than a little distorted. With rare exceptions the films dealt only with boys. *Little Tough Guy* (1938) and *Beloved Brat* presented images of delinquency among the afflent, but overwhelmingly the industry concentrated on the working class delinquents of the New York tenements. Only rarely did Hollywood turn its gaze from the city. In 1937 Monogram, aided by the Civilian Conservation Corps, made *Blazing Barriers*, which celebrated communal spirit and depicted tough city youngsters transformed into "sons of the soil" promised "a place in the sun" in a rural environment.

While most of the films seemed to endorse Father Edward Flanagan's 1917 view that there was no such thing as a bad boy, only bad environments and bad example, they had a much more basic message. It was a message which once again clearly establishes the link between the early and late thirties. In *Beloved Brat*, the judge that Roberta is brought before declares, "We must build in this child a respect for law and order and above all a self respect that will guard her in the future from being a social outcast." His views are a direct extension of the notions of the juvenile republic expressed in *Mayor of Hell* and the attitude of the judge in *Wild Boys of the Road*. All three films were made by Warner Brothers, the studio that more than any other dealt with both the gangster genre and juvenile delinquency. In a perceptive comment, Gillian Klein sees such movies as the studio's appeal for law and order to its essentially working class audiences:

> Since the period was one of rank and file militancy, union activity, solidarity between black and white workers, and organizations of the unemployed, the film's (*Wild Boys of the Road*) deliberate arousal and subsequent destruction of the gang's alternatives was to carry a message, not to would-be child vagrants, but to the adult working-class audience of Warner Brothers movies.[10]

It is impossible to say conclusively what prompted the film industry at this particular point in time to depict juvenile dlinquency as it did. In part the films reflect the industry's awareness of social issues. In part, too, they can be read as Hollywood's attempt to endorse the new administration in Washington. Almost all of the films are concerned with the issue of law and order. While their villains are often corrupt and misguided administrators, these movies cannot be read as an attack on authority. While they pinpoint corrupt officials and make sometimes eloquent pleas for urban renewal and better relations between parents and children, they often have a much greater message. *Blazing Barriers*, *Mayor of Hell*, *Boys Town*, and others present articulate and forceful arguments for providing young people with the opportunity to experience responsible participation in the democratic process and to share in the goals of the American Dream. Such ideals seem strangely absent in the following decade, as though with the coming of the war Hollywood completely abandoned American youth and their role in society.

The earliest evidence of this trend appeared in 1939, the same year in which war broke out in Europe. The Dead End Kids had been the most prominent screen delinquents. Starring with Humphrey Bogart, James Cagney, Pat O'Brien, Ann Sheridan and others, they had achieved screen prominence in successful and popular films. Lifted from the Broadway version of *Dead End*, they had been transplanted to Hollywood and marketed as typical juvenile delinquents.

Leo Gorcey, the hard-bitten and most disagreeable of the boys, was described by studio publicity as "tough in the way any boy who has worked as a plumber's assistant would be tough. He drives too fast and is always getting arrested." But if Gorcey's personal life had anything in common with his screen persona, the other Dead End Kids were vastly different from

On Dress Parade: **Cleaning up the act for the war effort. The Dead End Kids in a very uncharacteristic role.**

the delinquents they portrayed. In 1939, eighteen-year-old Billy Halop began junior college, taking courses in sociology, psychology, and pan-Pacific relations. In show business since he was four, Halop was a long way removed from the characters he so successfully played. Gabriel Dell was the son of a Long Island physician, and Bernard Punsley's goal was to be a bacteriologist. The middle-class views and values of the young actors increasingly supplanted the working class nature of their screen characters.

The first movement toward this can be seen in 1939's *Angels Wash Their Faces*, the very title of which indicates the studio's desire to clean up the act. Further evidence can be found in Warner Brothers' publicity for the picture. "Sell it to the authorities," they said, "on the grounds that the uncertain world political conditions make it imperative that youth learn the workings of democracy." Such a statement suggests a continuation of the message found in early thirties films. What happened, however, was that screen juvenile delinquents were co-opted into society and almost vanished from the screen altogether.

From the outset, *Angels Wash Their Faces* demonstrated this change. As the film opens, Gabe Ryan (Frankie Thomas) is released from reform school. Unlike the schools of so many of the early thirties films, this reform school has had a positive influence on the boy. As his sister observes, it has not only taught him to wash behind the ears but has provided him with valuable experience and training in machine shop work. The view is further endorsed when Ronald Reagan, as the son of the district attorney, says, "If all the kids turn out as well as you, I'd send them all there." Gabe returns to life in the big city where, aided by Billy Halop and the others, he helps to clean up corrupt businessmen and demonstrates that youth can occupy a valuable and responsible role in society. In the same year Warners released *On Dress Parade*. Publicity for the film made the studio's new goal obvious. "In a complete reversal of form, the wise-cracking, long-haired, gutter-hardened denizens of the slums will become model American youths."

But if the Dead End Kids were now responsible young citizens, there were an increasing number of delinquents in the America that existed beyond the screen. Between 1940 and 1945 juvenile delinquency in New York City increased from 4,379 cases to 6,975, representing a fifty percent increase. On October 20, 1942, *Life* noted that "suddenly the country is aware of what war is doing to children.... American youth is on the same kind of lawless rampage that swept England during 1940."[11] Young offenders in the sixteen to twenty-one age group were responsible for 40 percent of all burglaries, 28 percent of the robberies, 22 percent of the larcenies, and 50 percent of auto thefts. In Toledo, Ohio, Judge Alexander, who served as president of the National Association of Juvenile Court Judges, argued that what was needed to alleviate the problem of juvenile delinquency was less sentencing and punishment and more diagnosis and treatment.

The increase in adolescent crime did not go unnoticed in the film industry; indeed, theaters became a setting for such crime. In a page one article in April 1942 *Variety* proclaimed, "Theater Vandalism Grows."[12] A wartime problem for the movie houses had emerged in the number of un-supervised youngsters who skipped school and destroyed property in the movie houses. In October of the same year theaters, particularly those that held late night screenings, were cited as a source of juvenile crime in an investigation in San Francisco. Indianapolis theater owners were asked by the local sheriff to refuse admittance to youngsters unaccompanied by an adult after the first evening show. New York City's license commissioner ordered curbs on the admittance of juveniles to theaters in the metropolitan area. In November *Variety* reported zoot-suited hoodlums running amuk and a 43 percent increase in female juvenile delinquency, "bringing a wartime headache to Detroit theaters."[13]

Aware of such developments, the industry saw the opportunity to cash in on the timely subject of delinquency, while once again claiming to be performing a community service. Warner Brothers seized upon the idea of re-releasing on a double bill *Girls on Probation* and *Crime School*. Studio publicity declared, "Making the front page along with the news of war from foreign fronts are the tragic casualties of the home front, the wrong-way girls and boys, warped and maimed by the feverish excitement of the war ... the menace and pathos of juvenile delinquency which the war has increased to a shocking degree are forcefully presented in the Warner Brothers pictures *Crime School* and *Girls on Probation*." But despite what the studio wished to claim, neither film did much to advance the understanding of delinquency within the context of a nation at war. The action of war in and of itself sanctioned violence. By removing parents from the home, sending them to the front or to war industry, it left many youngsters unattended and undisciplined, to go their own way and find their own amusements. None of these concerns and causes were addressed in the films that Hollywood produced at the time. Hell-bent on making a patriotic statement, the industry abandoned any resemblance of reality and in film after film delivered delinquents who miraculously became model citizens.

There is little doubt that if the war was responsible for the increase of juvenile delinquency in society, it was also responsible for the decline of juvenile delinquency on the screen. One of the first motion pictures to link delinquency and the war was *Junior G Men of the Air*, made by Universal in 1942. Set just prior to December 7, 1941, the film was a patriotic piece that attempted to demonstrate the role kids could play in the war effort. Studio publicity described it as "the story of how a group of boys did their part in helping their government and country to apprehend a group of saboteurs and foreign agents." Universal adovcated patriotic tie-ins with the Boy Scouts and advertising that reinforced government messages such as "keep your eyes open and your mouth closed" and "don't circulate rumors because Hitler likes a gossip."

Junior Army was a 1942 offering from Columbia which starred Freddie Bartholomew and Billy Halop in a story which demonstrated cooperation between a limey and a yank, and how anti-social youth could be brought into the mainstream of society. Universal's *Keep 'em Slugging* (1943) featured Bobby Jordan. Again the emphasis was on transforming street kids into patriots. Appealing to the other members of the gang, Jordan asks them if it's right to keep the police busy chasing them when they could be after "those Jap and German hooligans." *Boys of the City* (1940), *Mayor of 44th Street* (1942), and *Million Dollar Kid* (1944) also depicted redeemed delinquents.

But while the industry's heart was in the right place and its motive was admirable, as an attempt to depict juvenile delinquency it was a complete failure. Reviewing films for the Office of War Information, Barbara Deming noted the failure in assessing *Junior Army*:

> If the film really exhibited what it proposes to exhibit, the conversion of a boy from an anti-social to a social being ... it would be the best propaganda now possible, but it does not exhibit this. The plot makes the statement that he is converted but we never behold this really happening.[14]

Not until 1944, with the war in its last year, did Hollywood manage to come to terms with the impact of the war on delinquency. While few today remember *Youth Runs Wild*, it was a fine film, well received and by far the industry's best effort throughout the war years. In its review, *Time* magazine said that "for all its clumsiness [it] is remarkably full of warmth, of life and of real cinematic sensitiveness. A memorable amount of adolescent confusion and pain flickers on and off beam, illuminating its causes with an honesty, economy and piognancy which are rare on the U.S. screen."[15]

Set in the small community of Euclid Street, the theme of the film is the dislocation the war has brought not only to the young but to their parents and society as a whole. As the movie opens, newspaper headlines announce the spread of juvenile delinquency in the community. On Euclid Street the familiar rituals and routines have been shattered. A truck runs into a sign that reads "Drive slowly, we love our children." In these trying times new demands, pressures and roles have shattered the old securities and disrupted neighborhoods. Sarah Taylor (Bonita Granville) and her family are newcomers. The girl finds that she is an outsider isolated from the other children who taunt her. Next door to the Taylors lives the Hauser family, long-term residents whose routine has been disturbed by the war. Mary the daughter is expected home, having been away for three years. Her husband Danny, a purple heart recipient, has been injured and is also expected home soon. The Hauser parents like many in the neighborhood are preoccupied by their work in the munitions factory. As a result their adolescent son is left unattended and unsupervised. Lacking parental care and control the boy grows restless and wayward. Increasingly absent from school he is anxious to play some meaningful role in the war. "I'd sure like to wear one of them army uniforms." His situation is compounded by the feelings he finds awakening in himself for Sarah. While he tells his sister, "There's nothing mushy between us," he becomes increasingly enamored of the girl. With no role or status afforded him in the theater of war, his very masculinity and sense of self is undermined and he fears losing the girl to someone with a real role in life.

In 1952 *Member of the Wedding* showed Frankie's restlessness in wartime and her desire to fulfill a function. In 1971 *The Summer of '42* depicted Hermie and Oscie in similar conditions. Thwarted from asserting their masculinity within a military milieu the boys used their awakening sexuality for a similar purpose. *Youth Runs Wild* represented one of the very few films made during the war years to seriously address the nature of adolescents in wartime. As Frankie laments to his sister, "Danny's fighting and Mom and Dad work at the plant. Everybody's doing something but me." Next door, Sarah experiences her own difficulties. With her parents away at work all day the girl is forced to shoulder the burden and responsibility of housework. Relegated to the role of servant she is expected to fetch and clean for parents who forget that she is a child and their daughter.

Although Frankie's family disapprove of his association with the

Taylor girl their common needs serve simply to draw them closer together. Afraid of losing the girl to someone with money the boy succumbs to the suggestion of a friend that he commit a robbery. Yet like Dean and the confused rebels of the fifties, he is not altogether sure of what it is he is doing. "It's just that I don't know why I'm doing this," he says. Arrested for a traffic violation the boy is paroled into the custody of his brother-in-law Danny, who becomes to all intents and purposes the boy's father. Having fought in the war overseas, Danny returns to discover that there is a theater of war at home and that the casualties are most often the young. He and Mary set up a daycare center to look after neighborhood children whose parents are occupied in war industry work. "It's not so hard dealing with kids," Danny suggests, "you just got to find something for them to do, make them feel important, give them a place to stay, keep 'em away from joints and bad company." But Danny finds his most difficult case in the form of his own brother-in-law.

Obsessed with Sarah, Frankie becomes increasingly difficult to deal with. When the girl leaves home and gets a job in a sleazy nightclub the boy follows her and becomes inadvertently involved in a fight which leads to the death of a young woman. Death that so many American families lived with throughout the war years now affects Sarah and Frankie, who are no longer protected or immune. Seeking responsibility and trust they now find themselves embroiled in a situation which they cannot deal with. Taken before the juvenile court, they are treated as victims rather than criminals. "Kids may sometimes be guilty of crime," says the judge, "but it's rare when it's their own fault. Neglectful parents, modern life, the breaking up of the home; we've got so many reasons for trouble." Succumbing totally to propaganda, the film closes with a montage of young people involved in youth work and Danny's voice telling audiences, "We're not going to waste them anymore, we need them. After all, they're what we're fighting for."

Youth Runs Wild indicates that Hollywood was aware of the problems of young people in a time of war and conscious of the need for these youngsters to be given a valuable role to play. At the same time, however, in *Janie* and a host of other films, the industry sold out to the bobby soxer and a decidedly shallow depiction of American youth. Young people themselves were aware of the way in which Hollywood and the rest of society characterized them. In August 1944 the *New York Times Magazine*, in an article entitled "As the Youngsters See Juvenile Delinquency," the view of adolescents was featured. "We want to work," wrote one teenager. "We don't want to be interested only in jukeboxes and cokes. There's a lot of youth power in the country that can make up for the shortage in manpower. The adults must help us to organize it into a voluntary corps. Young people want a chance to do things and to have responsible jobs."[16] In the characters of Frankie and Sarah, *Youth Runs Wild* thus realistically served as a mouthpiece for many of the nation's young. In the character of their parents, however, they continued a trend that had been apparent in Hollywood since the thirties. While the juvenile court judge is aware of a range of problems leading to delinquency, the film overall holds the parents to blame.

In the same year such a point of view was abundantly clear in *I Accuse My Parents*. *Mildred Pierce* (1945) and *Boys Ranch* (1946) would continue to hold parents responsible for the behavior of the young. If Hollywood seemed intent on making parents scapegoats for juvenile delinquency, they were not alone. Not until after the war did the subject of juvenile delinquency come in for a better treatment. In the wake of successful problem films such as *Lost Weekend*, *Gentleman's Agreement*, and *Pinky*, juvenile delinquency was again considered to be both a controversial and profitable subject. Stars like Humphrey Bogart and directors like Nicholas Ray were again able to lend stature to the subject of adolescent crime.

Universal's *City Across the River*, for example, was based on Irving Shulman's novel, *The Amboy Dukes*. Employing the semi-documentary style reminiscent of some of the thirties' vehicles, the film begins by telling audiences that delinquency can happen anywhere. "For most of us the city where juvenile crime flourishes always seems to be the city across the river. But don't kid yourself, it could be your city, your street or your house." The action takes place in Brooklyn, where slum conditions undermine personal security. In such an environment a youngster begins life behind the eight ball, and the local pool room serves as the country club for confused kids on the road to gangsterdom.

The film concentrates on sixteen-year-old Frankie (Peter Fernandez). A basically decent kid, he is gradually warped by poverty, parental neglect, and peer pressure. Left alone too often by parents who need to work in order to make ends meet, he is abandoned to the influence of the Dukes. The boy denies that they're a gang. To him, "It's just a club, just a place to get together and have fun." What he has to learn, however, is "the Dukes are a pretty rugged outfit. You can't mess around with those boys without getting as tough as they are." Drifting closer to delinquency, the boy becomes involved in one incident after another. Aware of his son's problems and wanting to help him, Frankie's father asks him to bring his friends home to "play cards, listen to the radio." Frankie, however, is ashamed to bring his friends hom to "this dump." The impact of the environment on juvenile crime is made obvious when the boy's parents determine to move to the suburbs. Scraping together every dollar they can muster they attempt to get Frankie and his sister away from the influence of the slums. "We got to move. We got to get out of here. We've got to get the kids out of here. Someplace where they can grow up decent, where they can bring their friends and not be ashamed."

In recognizing the impact of the environment on crime, *City Across the River* reflected contemporary thought. A Duluth study conducted between 1928 and 1936 demonstrated a correlation between poor housing, low income, inadequate recreational facilities, and juvenile crime. In

February 1940, *American City* reported that, "When boys and girls go wrong, the chances are that the neighborhood's shortcomings are much more blameworthy than the child's shortcomings."[18]

When Frankie's mother is hospitalized, the money for their new home is needed for medical expenses, and the dream of escaping from the slum is shattered. Bitter and disappointed, the boy retreats further into the peer group and its aberrant ways. While his family have tried they have clearly failed. With their dreams dissipated, harmony gives way to disunity and bickering. The boy's behavior, his mother believes, is the result of his father's weakness. "A fine father you are! Never once in your life did you raise a finger to him!" Like the family, the school too fails to socialize the boy and creatively channel his energy. Teachers lack the ability to discipline and control. Frankie and the other boys operate in the school as they do on the streets, as a gang. They make zip guns and intimidate teachers with their hostile and threatening demeanor. Quarreling with a teacher, Frankie and another boy accidentally shoot him. The thefts and minor crimes that the thirties' delinquents engaged in gave way to more violent crime.

Seeking to avoid arrest, the boy becomes more and more deeply embroiled in crime. When he is finally arrested the movie closes with a narrator once more addressing the audience. "Perhaps with time he'll find hope, but what of all the other Frankies—that's the real challenge to us." Throughout the 1930's adolescent lawlessness was often seen by those in the industry as the product of the home, the slum, or indifferent and callous politicians, administrators and businessmen. *City Across the River*, while acknowledging the impact of the environment, extended the blame to society as a whole. If kids were corrupt, the film argued, society was responsible. Such a view was condemned by *The New Yorker*, which wrote:

> There seems to be an inclination in films like this one to excuse any kind of youthful depravity if the kiddies involved are poor. Can it be that Hollywood, having done so many sagas of gentlemen who started life with a nickel and wound up with satchels full of the necessary, have now lost faith in the American Dream?"[19]

In the post-war treatment of delinquency, one sees clear evidence of the dream turned nightmare. The hope of the thirties has been replaced by despair. The innocence of the young is replaced by their guilt and by the guilt of the society that raised them. *City Across the River* argued that delinquency could occur anywhere and held society responsible for it.

Produced in the same year, Columbia's *Knock on Any Door* repeated the message. Knock on any door, it said, and chances are you will find delinquency. The film introduced the character of Nick Romano (John Derek). A pretty boy, he is a pathological delinquent with a winning manner and a fixation with his hair that renders him a forerunner of Dean, Presley and Kookie. The film opens in the confined and shadowy environment of

the dead end. A cop is shot in a chase and the remainder of the film deals
with bringing his killer to trial. Using flashback sequences, the film sketches
Nick's background, the environment he grew up in, and his relationship with
his family. As the jury learns about Romano we also learn about him.
Equally as important, we learn about Andrew Morton (Humphrey Bogart),
the boy's lawyer and a man who himself managed to survive the squalor and
degradation of the city slums.

Knock on Any Door, while compelling, is at least initially familiar.
The themes and issues it raises, the nature and the causes of delinquency it
debates, had all been covered before. Nick's father had been jailed and died
in prison. To that extent the film followed a familiar theme in thirties films
like The Devil Is a Sissy. But while Mickey Rooney's father had been executed in that film, Nick's father died of illness while serving out a sentence
imposed upon him by bureaucratic incompetence and bungling. It was not,
the film implied, Nick's father that encouraged his crime but rather that his
crime was attributable to those who had irresponsibly allowed the man to
die in jail. This theme itself was not altogether new. Corrupt officials and
incompetent administrations had been the target for more than one film in
the previous decade.

In its attitude to the privileged, Knock on Any Door further revealed
its links with the past. While Bogart may not entirely trust Nick, his social
conscience and their common past motivate him to take the case. In
contrast, his business associates care nothing for the boy or justice. More
concerned with maintaining an image of confidence and dignity, they offer
him a partnership in the law firm if he will turn down the case. Bogart may
well have escaped the gutter and found a place for himself in the middle-
class metropolis, but his class and his basic instincts bind him umbilically to
Romano and those like him. In demonstrating no understanding of boys
like Nick, his associates align themselves with the indifferent and privileged
class of films like Dead End.

In its attitude toward the environment, Knock on Any Door was also
in debt to Dead End. "If only someone could get him off that street," a
social worker pleads. Bogart initially dismisses the impact of the
environment; after all he himself survived it and went on to succeed.
"According to my book," he tells the social worker, "if he was worth saving,
he'd get off the street by himself." In expressing such a view he appears to
locate the film clearly within the context of free will that was so prevalent in
the thirties films. But while Bogart asserts that the individual can pull
himself up by the boot straps, he is ultimately forced to recognize a more
brutal reality. "I wanted to believe that all the filth and fury and jungle of
this boy's past had not produced a killer," he tells the jury, but in the end he
acknowledges that Romano is the product of "the worst district that ever
disgraced a modern city."

Finally, in one last parallel with the thirties' depiction of juvenile
delinquency, Knock on Any Door raised the spectre of the reform school

Knock on Any Door (1949): While the Dead End Kids were redeemed in the previous decade, film noir and the bleaker mood of postwar America could not salvage John Derek.

and its role in shaping young criminals. Described as "an island of outrage," the reform school is a place where Nick was "degraded and demoralized." Punished excessively, treated with a savage brutality, the boy emerges worse than when he went in. Like *Mayor of Hell* and *Hells Kitchen*, the reform school in this movie is a place where boys not only are punished but a place where they die physically, emotionally, and spiritually.

Yet in spite of all these links with the past, Nicholas Ray presented audiences with much more than mere repetition. Nick Romano was a young thug like none we had ever seen before. Billy Halop, Frankie Darro, Mickey Rooney and the others, while at times impressive as delinquents, were always a little too close to lovable to be dangerous. Orphans of the storm, their vulnerability and aloneness rendered them as victims whose plight we could sympathise with. With the exception of the murder in *Are These Our Children?*, the crimes committed by these youngsters were usually minor offenses imposed upon them by circumstances and conditions beyond their control. The real criminals in most of these movies are the corrupt politicians and businessmen whose greed leads to misery and destitution for those less fortunate.

In 1949, however, John Derek introduced a new and more threatening delinquent. A violent youth capable of killing, he is at the same time strangely appealing. Bogart recognizes the fact when he fights to get seven women on the jury and tells the boy to "turn on the baby-face stare." Good looks and eloquent pleas cannot save him however. The boy of the streets has grown into a young man who must pay for his acts of violence. As the film closes Bogart farewells Nick on death row. Led from his cell the boy begins to walk the last mile. His back is to the camera as he walks away from us. Then in one remorseless gesture he combs his hair for the last time and turns to stare accusingly at Bogart and the audience. "This boy," Bogart had argued, "could have been exulted instead of degraded, student instead of savage.... Nick Romano is guilty but so are we and so is that precious thing called society."

In *Are These Our Children?* the execution of Eddie Brand promised salvation for the boy had repented his sins. *Knock on Any Door*, with its film noir style and statement presented a much bleaker vision of humanity. Nick Romano goes to his grave remorseless. The complete criminal, he is beyond redemption. "I drink, I gamble, I steal—that's how I live." If the thirties promised the delinquent hope, the late forties offered little prospect for reformation. Kids were sick, bitter, and twisted, and who could blame them, filmmakers seemed to be saying, after all, we live in a sick and twisted world. Nick, despite his crime, is thus able to assume the romantic mantle of a beautiful loser. While he is punished, he is able to move the guilt onto society. "Did I ask to be born?" he screams. His character, his mood and his temper would filter down into the following decade. Dying young, he achieved the role of romantic rebel. The code he lived by served as a fitting motto for Dean, Brando, and the adolescent legions of the Eisenhower years: "Live fast, die young, and have a goodlooking corpse."

9. Rebels With and Without Causes
1950-1980

"Where are they from?" "Beats me. I'm not
even sure they know where they're going."
Exchange in *The Wild One*; 1954.

Throughout the 1950's juvenile delinquency went from a social
reality to a national obsession and nothing or no one was more obsessed
than the media. Senator Kefauver's investigation into juvenile crime received national attention. The media, particularly motion pictures, represented in the fifties a site of, a source for, and a stimulus to juvenile delinquency.

With the decade just under way provocative headlines brought the
new menace sharply to the public's attention.

> When ten-year-olds carry guns; when youngsters 13 to 17 pummel inno-
> cent pedestrians with black jacks or lay open their cheeks with rings
> filed sharp as scalpels; when young wolf packs roam the streets for prey;
> when they flail their victims with chains and belts, smash at them with
> brass knuckles or fists weighted with lead; when kids who are still wet
> behind the ears worship a new god named violence, the city must sit
> up and take notice.[1]

Between 1945 and 1948 juvenile delinquency, which had grown to alarming
proportions during the war years, began to deline, reaching a low of
300,000 cases. By 1949 it was on the rise again. In 1953 the number of cases
had climbed to 435,000 and by 1955 it had hit the half million mark. The
cinema was not immune to the effects of this outburst of adolescent crime.
In November 1953, *Variety* reported:

> Vandalism in theaters, a serious problem since the end of World War
> II, continues unabated to the extent that theatermen in various sections
> of the country regard it as a greater menace than television.... While the
> degree of vandalism varies in different sections of the country, it is a

nationwide problem. Educators, civic authorities and social workers point out that it is not confined only to theaters but that vandalism extends to the streets, the parks, the schools and even the housing developments where the youngsters reside.[2]

Not only was the cinema the scene of juvenile crime, it was increasingly seen as a stimulus to such crime. In 1953 Dr. Hugh Flick, director of the motion picture division of the New York State Education Department, refused to license *Teenage Menace* on the grounds that it would incite crime. In September 1954 *Variety* reported that New York Police believed films depicting crooked cops fostered disrespect for the law, made the job of policemen more difficult, and served as a "juve crime aid."[3] Yet despite such comments, concerns and controversy, from 1954 on Hollywood embarked upon a deliberate policy of depicting juvenile delinquency. No period before and no period since has seen such a sustained and systematic attempt to court the adolescent audience by the sensationalized depiction of teenage crime and waywardness.

At a time when Frankie Lymon and the Teenagers sang "I'm Not a Juvenile Delinquent," the movies seemed to be going out of their way to suggest that among American youth, delinquency, rather than being the exception, was the rule. From the mid-fifties on, theaters were inundated by low budget B movies employing sensationalism and exploitation to capture the expanding teenage market. With their parents firmly ensconced at home with their eyes glued to the television set, adolescents escaped to the drive-ins and the movie theaters that fulfilled their fantasies.

At home on the small screen, the parents of middle America had their own fantasies fulfilled. While tabloids and Washington committees harangued them with tales of youthful excess and abandon, television served to placate their fears. Ozzie and Harriet never seemed to have trouble with David and Ricky. In *Father Knows Best* Jim and Margaret Anderson manged to raise Betty, Bud and Kathy without the intervention of the police and the courts. Wally and the Beaver, under the watchful eyes of Ward and June Cleaver, stuck to the straight and narrow. When delinquency did find its way to television, it was usually part of an anthology series such as Reg Rose's *Tragedy in a Temporary Town* or Robert Alan Arthur's *Man Is Ten Feet Tall*.

But on the big screens the silent generation increasingly encountered images of themselves as turbulent young people from dislocated homes. Roger Corman, American International Pictures, and others were not slow to realize the potential profit in catering to these kids. What followed was an avalanche of third-rate films which did nothing to further understanding between kids and their parents or between kids and the law.

In 1957 Warners offered *Teenage Thunder* and *Untamed Youth*. Allied Artists provided *Hot Rod Rumble*. From the AIP stable came *Motorcycle Gang* and *Dragstrip Girl*. 1958 saw Republic's *Juvenile Jungle*, Allied's

Hot Car Girl and *Joy Ride*. When AIP released *The Cool and the Crazy*, *Hollywood Reporter* was prompted to comment:

> A few weeks ago a Brooklyn school principal committed suicide because he could not suppress the rape and hooliganism in his institution. *The Cool and the Crazy* is a badly written, poorly directed, low-budget film that may well inspire more such tragedies.[4]

Sparta Productions released *High School Big Shot* and *T-Bird Gang* on a double bill with publicity that proclaimed that the films were "created from the point of view of today's youth, thrashing about a new and turbulent emotional world." *T-Bird Gang* concerned itself with "the one year out of high school crowd—fast cars, girls ... no place to go." In 1959 MGM made *Girl's Town*, which introduced itself as "a hard hitting drama of the mania of today's youth for kicks ... it is the story of girls and boys who have reached the turning point between adolescence and maturity and of young-sters who know too much too soon." What the industry seemed unaware of, however, was that if youngsters knew too much the movies were one of their major sources of information. While it is difficult to take any of these films seriously, it is equally difficult to ignore the new trend they represented. If their quality was poor, their style substandard, then their statements were decidedly familiar and echoed the decade's classier products from tinsel town.

In 1954 two major films emerged which were to have a profound impact on Hollywood's depiction of adolescence, not only for the rest of the decade but for years to come. Although Marlon Brando and the bike riders of *The Wild One* appear to be out of their teens, the film itself, by its anti-establishment, poor-misunderstood-kid stance, served the double function of attracting adolescents while appalling adults. As the inarticulate and mumbling Johnny, Brando etched a caricature of youth which long out-lived the era that created it. The Black Rebels Motorcycle Gang, like urban outlaws riding their chrome and steel stallions through the rural hamlets of middle America, proclaim that the times are changing. And yet though the gang has strength and power, a theme already seen in *City Across the River*, they have no idea how to channel it or use it. In 1944 the *Saturday Evening Post* had asked, "Are We Raising Another Lost Generation?"[5] In the character of Johnny and those like him the answer appears to be a decided yes. While the film was seen by many to be a glorification of violence and aggression, it was equally about alienation and a dreadful anger when generations collide but cannot communicate.

While the threat of violence creates tension which pervades the film, the story and the script also incessantly hammer away at the theme of aimlessness. *Variety* called Johnny "a hard-faced hero who never knew love as a boy."[6] His uncertainty and his search for kicks seems to stem uncon-sciously from his desire to be loved. His relationship with Mary bears out this awkward, wretched need. Wanting to reach out, he is at the same time intent upon appearing strong. In such a situation, feelings for a female render him vulnerable and the relationship becomes ambiguous.

Rather than being confined to this movie, the nature of the relationship between Johnny and Mary was repeated elsewhere throughout the decade. Brando and Eva Marie Saint depicted it in *On the Waterfront* the same year. *East of Eden*, also a product of 1954, found James Dean and Julie Harris in a not unsimilar role. The reaching out is always accompanied by a drawing away from and a profound sense of uncertainty and confusion. "I don't think you know what you're trying to do or how to go about getting it," the sheriff tells Johnny. "You're afraid of me," Mary tells him. "You're still fighting, aren't you? You're always fighting. Why do you hate everybody?" He is in fact the rebel without a cause, the angry young man in a hurry but with nowhere to go and life reduced to an endless search for kicks. Asked what he's rebelling against, his response is simple: "What have you got?"

In *Rebel Without a Cause*, Jim and Buzz stand overlooking the bluff before the chicken race. Locked into ritual and routine, neither boy understands why they must do this thing, only that there seems nothing else to do. Like Johnny's, theirs is a rebellion for rebellion's sake, because in the empty silence of post-war America, the mediocre and the mundane have become the order of the day. "What are they fighting about?" a character asks. The answer: "I don't know, they don't know themselves, probably." In the end, faced with Korea, the bomb, and the prospect of ultimate annihilation, these kids can think of no greater question than "what do you do around here for kicks?" When the answer is nothing, it's time to kick out and kick up. Like Nick Romano, they seem intent if not on dying young then at least on living fast.

The anger and anomie of *The Wild One* was forcibly repeated in both *East of Eden* and *Rebel Without a Cause*. Both films were important in the depiction of juvenile delinquency for they moved the problem and its cause from society as a whole to the family unit, from working class environments and inner city streets to the middle-class homes of American suburbia. *Rebel Without a Cause*, said *Time* magazine, is "a reasonably serious attempt within the limits of commercial melodrama to show that juvenile delinquency is not just a local outbreak of tenement terror but a general infection of modern U.S. society."[7] But in attempting to blame Jim, Judy and Plato's delinquency entirely on their parents, the film, according to *Nation*, went too far. "The trouble is," their reviewer wrote, that the picture burlesques the problem. It is easy to explain delinquency if you assume that parents are howling idiots; but the assumption is neither true nor very interesting."[8]

As Jim Stark and Cal Trask, James Dean delivered characters who echoed the sentiments of his screen contemporaries. If lack of love was the implied cause of Johnny's rebellion, there was no mistaking its role in

shaping the recalcitrant Cal Trask. Cal is neither the misunderstood teenager struggling against economic hardship nor the victimized working class
delinquent spawned by city squalor and political corruption. His rebellion
hinged on neither poverty nor oppression but upon the single fact that he
was not loved, or more importantly, that he believed that he was not loved.
While Roberta (*The Beloved Brat*) and James Wilson (*I Accuse My Parents*)
had claimed the same, their cries remained by and large unheard and
unheeded by film audiences. In the mid-fifties, however, the emotional and
psychological climate was ripe for a cry not only to be heard but to be taken
up as clarion call by a whole generation. When Cal cries to his father, "I've
been jealous all my life.... Tonight I even tried to buy your love, but now I
don't want it anymore," he struck a responsive note in audiences across the
country, across the years. Noting the long term appeal of the movie, Robin
Bean observed in *Films and Filming* that

> *East of Eden* made much of its money in re-runs when growing up and
> accepting responsibility had no appeal to youngsters; authority, whether
> parental or civil, was weak and uncertain in the fluctuating post war
> years—and Dean more than anybody else resembled a permanent em-
> bodiment and symbol of their frustrations and uncertainties in life, and
> like Peter Pan, never grew old.... Basically too it was a search for a
> simple love that had ceased to exist between generations; there was a
> barrier between that both wanted to penetrate but which society had
> made impregnable.[9]

One institution which was in no small way responsible for erecting
that barrier between parent and child was the mass media, particularly
movies. Increasingly aware of the box office power of the young, the
industry understood that parents were not going to the movies. American
International Picture emerged entirely as a response to this young audience.
In catering to them they constantly reinforced the attitude that the older and
younger generations were natural enemies. The cumulative effect of such an
era of movie making fueled fears among young and old alike.

Theories of adolescent development had long suggested the period as
a time of storm and stress with the young person given to sudden fluctua-
tions in mood and extremely volatile behavior. Such notions suddenly
found their way to the screen. In the mid-forties the terms adolescent and
delinquent were almost totally absent from the movies. In the space of ten
years American parents were suddenly told that the scatterbrained bobby-
soxers of the forties had been transformed into alien and hostile combat-
ants.

In the thirties Hollywood had suggested that delinquency grew out of
a combination of factors including economic conditions, the environment,
and family life. The forties, particularly in films like *Mildred Pierce* and
Knock on Any Door, raised the haunting possibility that such conditions

were too ingrained in the social fabric to be eradicated. If society was sick, and film noir seemed to suggest just that, then kids could be excused for just about anything. It was such a point of view that was increasingly evident throughout the 1950's. Unable to confront society as a whole, the film industry zeroed in on the family and on parents in particular as the source of juvenile delinquency. While parental scapegoats were hardly a new target for filmmakers, they were singled out for blame as they had been in no other period. *East of Eden, Rebel Without a Cause,* and *The Young Stranger* were among the best films to portray such a vision of life. The image they defined seemed to etch itself indelibly into Hollywood consciousness, pervading almost every film throughout the fifties that dealt with the topic of delinquency. Two interesting examples, which provide early evidence of the crossover effect between televisions and film, were *Crime in the Streets* (1955) and *Dino* (1957). Both films originated in television, which for the most part treated adolescents as the antiseptic occupants of some sit-com.

Crime in the Streets starred Sal Mineo as Angelo and John Cassavettes as Frankie. Confused, violent and hostile, they are extensions not only of Dean and Brando but of John Derek's Nick Romano as well. The pretty boy image of Romano is repeated in Mineo's character, who is nicknamed Baby. While the name serves to indicate his youth, it also carries the connotation of innocence. If thugs like Angelo and Frankie were twisted, such films suggested, they were somehow innocent of their acts of aggression because society and family had twisted them.

Like Cal Trask and Jim Stark, Angelo struggles with the reins of responsibility. His very nickname eats away at him, manacling him to a childhood he wishes to escape from. In his parents he finds shackles who want to bind him to the past. "Pop, let me grow up," he pleads. Like Adam Trask, Angelo's father finds himself unable to deal with the young stranger in his midst. In the past he believed discipline was the answer. "I tell you something. If they got their tails tanned once in a while they'd straighten out. Look to the parents I say, they're the ones who let 'em run the streets. Do you know all they understand? Boom, right across the face.... The only way they're gonna be good is if they're scared to be bad." But in attempting to discipline his son, he further alienates him. A barrier grows up between them and like Cal and Adam Trask, father and son confront each other as enemies unable to communicate. "Talk to me. I don't know you because we don't talk no more, just yell."

In *Dino,* Sal Mineo played a thirteen-year-old killer, "a kid who'll punch you in the mouth if you say hello to him." But the boy, argued the film, is not really to blame. His problems stemmed from his father who beat him even on his birthday and left him with a profound sense of worthlessness. Streetwise but desperately in need of love and understanding, Dino is

Opposite: *Crime in the Streets*: **An interesting and early example of the cross-over from television to the big screen.**

left asking, "How come nobody ever kissed me? He never took me nowhere. He never fooled around with me or gave me bearhugs."

Compulsion (1959) was based on the Leopold and Loeb case and concerned itself with two youths who coldbloodedly murder a young boy. But again the problem was clearly parental. Dean Stockwell, who had been memorable as the haunting nature boy in *The Boy With Green Hair* (1948) and the impish rascal in *Kim* (1950), made the transition to screen adolescence by playing a boy immensely disturbed by his family life. "I have very little in common with my father or my mother," he admits. Despite the disturbing nature of his crime, not to mention an attempted rape, the boy is sympathetically referred to as "a sick frightened child."

When the fifties did not place the burden of guilt at the feet of parents it argued, often eloquently, on behalf of young people. *The Blackboard Jungle* saw its angry adolescents as the products of a social process and a new age. A policeman tells us, "They were five or six years old in the last war. Father in the army, mother in a defense plant, no home life, no church life, no place to go. They formed street gangs. Maybe the kids of today are like the rest of the world—mixed up, suspicious, scared. I don't know; but I do know this, gang leaders are taking the place of parents."

Within twelve months of the release of *The Blackboard Jungle* similar feelings were in evidence in the popular press. Reporting on the Kefauver investigation into juvenile crime, *Atlantic Monthly* noted the link between social conditions, family life, and adolescent waywardness. "There is a direct relationship," they wrote, "between insecurity on the part of both parent and child and juvenile delinquency. Further, the insecurity is related to the general national feeling of insecurity during the cold war years and the hot Korean war."[10] In 1950, referring to new approaches to juvenile crime prevention being employed in San Francisco, *Colliers* spoke of a philosophy "which loves them without coddling them. It is firm without being cruel. For what it hands kids on a silver platter, it asks responsibility in return."[11] Both *Dino* and *Crime in the Streets* advocated such an approach. When family and school failed to socialize the young, the task was given to social workers, law enforcement agencies and other experts.

In *Knock on Any Door*, Bogart represented such a trend. *Rebel Without a Cause* handed James Dean over to the juvenile officer who was more useful to the boy than his parents had ever been. In *Dino* Brian Keith played the parole officer who managed to steer the boy back to the straight and narrow. In *Crime in the Streets* James Whitmore served as the voice of the new liberalism. "We're not talking about wild animals, we're talking about tough angry kids. You can beat 'em up—they just get tougher and angrier. Try to understand, try to remember, kids don't get tough without good reason. We listen, we sympathize, we talk; you can't tell a kid to be good. He's got too many reasons to be bad. So we're patient and every now and then we get to one of the really wild ones. But you know, everybody expects it to happen all at once."

But in the fifties, at least as Hollywood saw it, things did seem to happen all at once. The bobby-soxer boom surrendered to the decade of the delinquent. The pleasant middle-class families that were prevalent throughout the forties were suddenly dislocated by deep trauma. Crime and delinquency, which had been almost a working-class monopoly, suddenly engulfed middle America. Hollywood was certainly not alone in discovering delinquency or providing it with a public forum. In 1955 *Life* proclaimed "Teen-Age Terror in New York Streets."[12] In 1957 they headlined "Teenager Burst of Brutality."[13] In the following year *Look* asked, "Can Tough Cops Beat the Wild Kids?"[14] and in the same month reported on "Teen-Age Trouble."[15] Gangs like the Enchanters, the Dragons, and the Seminoles found their names and exploits splashed across the popular press with photographs that served to bring these frightening apparitions of adolescents gone awry forcibly to the attention of the American public.

And yet while Hollywood merely followed suit, expanding on a controversial theme and pocketing the profit, in the process they once again rendered disservice to the majority of American youth. As *Readers Digest* observed in August 1956, "lurid publicity about a tiny minority of teenaged delinquents has blinded us to the solid achievements and ideals of typical American youngsters."[16] The Camp Fire Girls, the 4-H clubs, and the Boy and Girl Scouts provided little in the way of dramatic format for either the film industry or the mass media as a whole. Bad news sold and throughout the decade Hollywood reveled in it. Even westerns like *The Left Handed Gun* succumbed to the image of the juvenile delinquent as Paul Newman played Billy the crazy mixed-up kid.

The problem was not that the industry seemed to have suddenly rediscovered that delinquency was a social problem so much as it was the way they went about depicting it. There were moments in many of these movies when Hollywood seemed to seriously address the issue of juvenile crime. There were scenes and speeches in which the industry articulated the need for a new approach to the problem. With dramatic consistency and well-developed plots, such films could have done much to further public debate. Inevitably, however, they succumbed to contrived endings and simplistic solutions. Cal Trask calms down when his father finally needs him. Jim Stark, having been saddled with an ineffectual father for 99 percent of the movie, seems to be headed for the quiet life because his father suddenly discovers parental responsibility. Dino's reformation is achieved through the ministrations of a parole officer and the love of a young woman. And in *Crime in the Streets*, Frankie is redeemed through the love of his young brother.

One of the superior films of the decade was John Frankenheimer's *The Young Stranger*, and even it promised an end it could not deliver. Despite the flawed nature of its happy ending, the movie was important for one major reason. Throughout much of the fifties, Hollywood had depicted young people as the victims of their misguided and misinformed parents.

The Young Stranger: **Still suffering from simplistic solutions, but with a decidedly more balanced view of family life.**

They had permitted their teenage characters and their adolescent audiences to perceive themselves as poor misunderstood kids. In *The Young Stranger* Hal Ditmar clearly inherits such a legacy. Not only does he see himself misunderstood by his parents, but he believes he is the victim of some adult conspiracy which is out to make him and all kids miserable. Rather than endorsing such a view, director Frankenheimer sees Hal as a product of a society and home that has its problems. Both the boy's mother and father have problems. They have as much difficulty communicating with each other as they do with their son. Rather than being the sole victim of an adult conspiracy, Frankenheimer suggests that Hal is caught up in a more complex situation and that if his parents need to understand him better, then he equally must try to understand them.

In providing such an image of upper middle-class life, *The Young Stranger* represented an improvement on *East of Eden* and *Rebel Without a Cause*, both of which had indulged the adolescent fantasy by having the parents conform to the demands of their son. It also clearly moved juvenile delinquency from the realms of the social problem that *The Blackboard Jungle* and its imitators saw it as, to the realms of a psychological problem. In the process it moved much closer to the world of the television sit-coms.

If Wally and the Beaver, Bud Anderson, and David and Ricky Nelson were non-delinquent, it was fairly obvious that they remained on the straight and narrow because within the confines of their families they found love and mutual support. *The Young Stranger* argued that while Hal Ditmar had the potential to become delinquent, the chances would be severely reduced within a happy and harmonious home environment. It was the last improvement the industry would make in response to juvenile delinquency.

As the sixties commenced the delinquency genre was dying. *Let No Man Write My Epitaph* (1960) explored the impact of parents and the environment on the adolescent as it watched Tony Romano maturely sidestepping winoes, skid-row bums and hopheads while looking for a few cc's of delerium. In 1961 John Frankenheimer directed *The Young Savages*, based upon a novel by Evan (*The Blackboard Jungle*) Hunter. Set in the teeming tenement of New York City, it concentrated on the rivalry between Italian and Puerto Rican street gangs. Three of the cast members actually had police records in the city. Members of local gangs were recruited to play feature and supporting roles. Police were so concerned at the possibility of violence during filming that the actual rumble scenes had to be shot in the less volatile climate of Hollywood.

Studio publicity described it as a story of "the young and the damned who grow in the cracks of the concrete jungle." It is a harsh, raw vision of life with teenage murderers and adolescent whores. But despite the attempts at authenticity the film fell flat and resorted to cliches. Burt Lancaster played the prosecutor who had himself struggled out of the slums. The role owed more than a little to Bogart's character in *Knock on Any Door*. Despite authentic locations and tough kids the film failed to deliver anything new or important. *Time* called the plot "make believe from the pasteboard jungle of Hollywood."[17]

In a graphic indication of the industry's failure to respond to the issue, *Variety* wrote:

> Juvenile crime is of course a very real, ticklish issue begging for attention.... It is rich ripe dramatic pasture for thoughtful creative minds and a source of some concern for all Americans, especially those in large cities who come into contact with the problem just by heading down the wrong street at the wrong time.
>
> (*The Young Savages*) fails to arrive at any novel insight into the environmental mess nor does it approach the subject with fully methodological logic or calculating objectivity required by the dramatic job it sets out to od. Instead it gets waylaid with a number of familiar stereotypes, cliches and convenient oversights, and eventually resolves the issue by pinning the blame for an unquestionalby heinous crime on that old reliable whipping boy, society itself.[18]

The urban ghetto was also the focus of another 1961 gang vehicle,

West Side Story. The film marked the death knoll of the delinquent films. Hugely successful, it marked the transition from reality to romance as violence became choreographed and stylized. The panorama of pain that had pushed these youngsters over the edge was submerged in a glamorized albeit bitingly satirical presentation. Many of the songs were themselves forceful. Mateship, camaraderie and communality were graphically celebrated by the Jets' proclaiming that acceptance by them into the group meant not only "You got brothers around" but, in fact, "you're a king."

In the song, "Officer Krupke," the kids make mock of the courts, parents, police and social workers. The concerns, issues and plots that had been part and parcel of Hollywood's depiction of the delinquent are reduced to cliches to be laughed at.

Writing in *The New Republic,* Stanley Kaufman suggested that in *West Side Story* audiences got to see for the first time street gangs as they really were. But there seems to be an enormous gap between the Jets and the Sharks and the gang members of *The Blackboard Jungle, The Young Savages,* or even the Dead End Kids. The characters in *West Side Story* are too allegorical, too one-dimensional and too contrived. Ultimately they function as cliches rather than characters. They are too neatly categorized under their little headings as the offspring of drunks, junkies and whores. Too much is taken for granted in their plea, "We ain't no delinquents, we're misunderstood, deep down inside us there is good."

Long plagued by contrived endings or characters who could not conform to the logic demanded by the plot, in *West Side Story* Hollywood encountered once again the dichotomy of romance and realism. Authentic locations could not disguise the industry's innate desire to glorify, glamorize and tone down the reality they claimed to depict. Looking at the initial drafts of the play, one sees basic changes that suggest the way in which the plot was watered down before it ever came to the screen. Based on *Romeo and Juliet* as it was, one would logically expect that the lovers Tony and Maria would die at the end. In earlier drafts a grief-stricken Maria returns to the dress shop where she takes a pair of shears and plunges it into her stomach.

Maria lives in the film and it is she who addresses the survivors. It is she who sees through the violence and hatred surrounding gang life and she who knows the way to peace. In *Romeo and Juliet* such observations fall to the parents, the priest, and the prince. *West Side Story,* however, as a product of the cinema of adolescence, had systematically destroyed or undermined the adult characters, leaving the young as always alienated from their elders.

Changes from the original draft also serve to indicate how the strength and vitality of the gang members was reduced. In one version Riff opens the action telling how he intends to avoid the draft, informing "dear sweet ass Uncle Sam, I am a hophead." Snowboy too talks about his drug habit: "I don't use no needle, Riff, I only take it up the nose." None of this dialogue found its way to the screen. What came instead was a weak, watery attempt to simulate reality. As a musical, *West Side Story* is great. As a depiction of delinquency it is a failure, caught of necessity in that fairytale realm of Oz, Brigadoon, or Camelot where one willingly suspends disbelief. In the end, as Pauline Kael so aptly noted, the film

> makes a strong appeal to youth by expressing the exuberant, frustrated desires of youth in the ugly constricted city life, but finally betrays this youth by representing the good characters as innocent and sweet and making the others seem rather comic and foolish. They're like Dead End Kids dancing—and without much improvement in the humor of the Dead End Kids. [19]

West Side Story, in romanticizing delinquency, made it commercially successful and palatable to the adult film goer's appetite. In the process it also served to alienate those young people who had looked upon such themes and subject matter as their own private property. In sweeping the Oscars, the film moved delinquency from the precincts of a subculture to popular culture, from a B movie cult to spectacular success in both the national and international markets. But it would be wrong to credit or blame this one film for the demise of the delinquency genre.

Between 1954 and 1959 Hollywood had saturated audiences with stories either totally or partially centered around delinquents. The life span of the cycle was coming to a natural conclusion by the time the sixties got under way. No period between 1930 and 1980 has been able to successfully cultivate a delinquency cycle that lasted longer than seven years; the longest period terminated with *West Side Story*. Social as well as cinematic factors also explain the end of the era. Peace and prosperity had provided the adolescents who grew out of the post-war baby boom with affluence and leisure time that had been denied their counterparts in the thirties and forties.

The twist, hoola hoops, and a host of other fads specifically geared for the teenage market began to spring up throughout the fifties and into the sixties. The movies were no longer the dominant medium they had been. Adolescents were increasingly able to turn to a diverse number of activities for their entertainment and leisure. Rock and roll provided them with a unique medium which was much more their own forum than the movies ever could be. In Elvis Presley they found an image as turbulent, erotic and youthful as anything the movies had ever offered. It was no accident that when the movies finally picked up Presley they packaged him and destroyed the very rawness that had initially attracted the young to him.

But the movies were not the only medium capable of packaging and processing the young for the young. *American Bandstand* emerged as a television institution. Week after week young people could tune in and watch other people their age dance to hits made by other young people. In the early days *Bandstand* served as a middle ground between Hollywood's wild ones and the cute kids of the sit-coms. It was a place where American teenagers could see kids just like themselves. Threatened by the sexual potency evident in the energy these kids danced with, the churches and other pillars of the establishment howled in protest. The kids just howled with pleasure. Said Dick Clark:

> People sat at home and fantasized about these kids. They wrote their own scenarios about Bob and Justine or Kenny and Arlene's love affairs. We gave the viewers just enough information without saying anything so they could do their own little mind trips.[20]

But as the years wore on the rawness was emasculated and *Bandstand*, like the rest of the media, succumbed to an artificial image of adolescence.

Frankie Avalon, Fabian, Bobby Rydell, Connie Francis, and others served to perfect an image of clean cut kids in a cleaned up America. "Where the Boys Are," "Swinging School," "Vacation," "Lipstick on Your Collar," "I'll Build a Dollhouse," "Venus," and other songs from the period bear ample testimony to this malt shop mentality that proliferated in the media.

Although songs like "He's a Rebel" still harked back to the days of *The Wild One* and *Rebel Without a Cause*, Dean and Brando were fading as icons of the age. When the Shangrilas sang "Leader of the Pack," they proclaimed the death of Brando's *The Wild One*, much as the beach movies' did in their parody, Eric Von Zipper.

If the New York slums had dominated the delinquent movies, then the teen screen in the sixties sought refuge in the waves out west. The Beachboys celebrated surfing for an entire generation. "Surfer Joe," "Pipeline," "Bombora," and others spread the sound. In the movies Frankie, Annette, and Gidget seemed intent on riding the wild surf. These young people had little in common with the troubled youngsters who had for so long dominated the nation's screens.

Off screen the media was beginning to more seriously consider American youth. The *Saturday Evening Post*, in a double issue in December 1961, reported the Gallup poll's findings on young people:

> No one can say that the American youth is going to hell. He's not. But he is a pampered hothouse plant and likes it that way. The beatnik is a rarity, the delinquent a minority. Our typical youth will settle for low success rather than risk high failure. He has little spirit of adventure. He wants to marry early—at twenty-three or twenty-four—after a college education. He wants two or three children and a spouse who is "affectionate, sympathetic, considerate, moral"; rarely does he want a mate with intelligence, curiosity, or ambition. He wants a little ranch house, an inexpensive new car, a job with a large company, and a chance to

watch TV each evening after the smiling children are asleep in bed. He is a reluctant patriot who expects nuclear war in his time and would rather compromise than risk all out war. He is highly religious yet winks at dishonesty. He wants very little because he has so much and is unwilling to risk what he has. Essentially he is quiet, conservative and cautious. He is old before his time; almost middle aged in his teens.... In general the typical American youth shows few symptoms of frustration and is most unlikely to rebel or involve himself in crusades of any kind. He likes himself the way he is and he likes things as they are. [21]

But like it or not, times change and people change with them. Within six years American society underwent a major transformation, and most striking of all was the change in American youth. Kennedy's youthful optimism and programs like the Peace Corps had given them a sense of purpose. The civil rights movement and the war in Vietnam began to form the young into a national coalition, more aware and articulate than at any time in the past. Rock music, as the medium exclusively of the young and Rock music, trusted as the medium exclusively of the young and for the young, created the anthems they marched to. In "My Generation," the Who forcefully proclaimed the sense of separation young people felt from their elders. Country Joe and the Fish, with songs like "Feel Like I'm Fixin' to Die Rag" and "Superbird" launched scathing assaults on American foreign policy and the President.

The year 1968 saw a fusion between reality, rock and roll, and Hollywood. The defunct delinquency genre emerged in the guise of the counter-revolution. In American International's *Wild in the Streets* Christopher Jones played Max Frost, a 22-year-old bisexual drug pusher who becomes a rock and roll messiah, courting the youth vote and ultimately becoming President.

Before the credits at the start of the movie, Frost writes obscenities on a mirror, says goodbye to the family dog, blows up the family car, and runs away from home. It is probably the greatest rebellious opening Hollywood had so far delivered.

But Frost is no agonized adolescent, desperately trying to be understood or tearfully running from the family home. He is a conniving clever young man with a plan and a purpose, and the ability to carry it out. That ability rests almost exclusively on his adolescent arsenal. Realizing that young people under 25 constitute 52 percent of the population, Frost employs rock and roll as an agency to enlist these young people in his assault on the status quo. In a remark that cannot help but remind us of John Lennon's infamous utterance we are told that Frost is "more famous than Jesus."

The films had other connections with the music industry. Campaigning for votes for fourteen-year-olds, Frost coins the phrase "fourteen or fight" and immediately turns it into a song. In "Five to One" Jim Morrison and the Doors had also done their arithmetic and counted on the strength of the younger generation. Frost declares, "We got the old tigers scared, Babe." Morrison seemed equally sure of the youth revolution as he sang, "They got the guns but we got the numbers, gonna win, yeah, we're taking over."

In Max Frost and the young people who followed him Hollywood moved delinquency to a state of demagoguery. In the movies that followed subculture became counterculture, and rebellion gave way to revolution as Hollywood's rebels suddenly discovered a cause. In England, Peter Watkins directed *Privilege*, which again linked rock and roll with the movies and featured former Manfred Mann lead singer, Paul Jones.

In 1969, in yet another link between rock, rebellion and film, United Artists released *Alice's Restaurant*, based on the Arlo Guthrie hit. Describing the film, director Arthur Penn articulated the attempt to define the change taking place in American youth. "We are witnessing something in which rebellion is not the essential characteristic. These kids are onto something much more genuine, much more tender.... I'm hoping that the film will be able to elucidate that part of their subculture in a way that I haven't seen done elsewhere yet."[22]

The kids of the counterculture, retreating from the harshness of urban reality to the romance of their rural restaurant, provided Penn with a means of looking at the manners and mores of the hippie movement. Rejecting the older order, challenging its traditional values and the assumptions underlying it, these filmic flower children were an extension of the wild boys of the road. No refugees from urban poverty and economic oppression, these traversers of the nation's highways were sons and daughters of affluent middle-class Americans. While the circumstances of their rebellion were different, they represented a similar search for a new solution. After years of agonizing and life in limbo Hollywood's young people came to the screen with a conscience, a cause, and a credo.

Like *Wild in the Streets*, which was released in the same year as the Democratic convention riots in Chicago, *Alice's Restaurant* merged with life in the real world beyond the darkened theaters. Fact and fiction blur, the line between the two becoming less and less distinct, the causal relationship less obvious.

Arlo Guthrie's tale was in fact based upon a real series of incidents in Stockbridge, Massachusetts, and Guthrie, Geoff Outlaw and Officer Obenaheim, three actual participants in the events, came to the screen portraying themselves. In the hospital scene in which Arlo visits his dying father, audiences watch Arlo and Pete Seeger reliving a moment which they had both experienced in real life. As a screen character Guthrie played a young hippie seeking educational deferment from the draft by enrolling at Rocky Mountain College in Montana. At the same time he represents a character from contemporary life who was becoming increasingly visible in everyday America where television news showed the growing legions of conscientious objectors and draft dodgers who refused to support the Vietnam war.

The young people of *Alice's Restaurant*, searching for their own meaning in life, represented a variation on the delinquency theme. The angry young men of the fifties had been transformed into the philosophers of the sixties.

While not as recognizably rebellious as the Brandos and the Deans, nor as obviously delinquent as the Dereks and Gorceys, these young people remain nonetheless teenagers apart from the adult mainstream, in revolt against a lifestyle they cannot embrace. Although the causes and manifestations of their revolt appear different, in their sense of alienation one finds a thematic thread that binds them closely and directly to their screen predecessors.

The Strawberry Statement (1970), *Bless the Beasts and Children* (1971) and the hugely successful *Billy Jack* (1971) continued such themes. Young people were depicted as alienated from a social system whose values they rejected. In a link with the past their delinquency or non-conformist behavior was largely attributable to the failure of school and the family to meaningfully relate to them.

In *Billy Jack*, Barbara is tormented by her insensitive and brutal father. In the same film Bernard is twisted into a teenage rapist and thug by the constant pressure to measure up and be a man that his father places on him. The failure of school to deal with these young people is vividly illustrated by the success of the Freedom School. Separated from the community not only by geography but philosophy, this school is startlingly different from those we traditionally encounter. Admitting anyone irrespective of race, religion, or troubled backgrounds, the school has only three rules: no drugs; carry your own load; and get turned on by creating something, preferably something that makes one proud of one's heritage and past.

In *Bless the Beasts and Children* Cotton, Goodenow and the others are the insecure and anti-social products of affluent homes that have neglected them. The school, or in this case summer camp, is seen by their parents as a dumping ground where the boys will be out of their way or as a means to cure them. "Send us a boy and we'll send you a cowboy," Box Canyon Boys Camp promises. What the boys learn there, however, is the same alienation and hostility they have found at home and in their regular schools. Unable to compete, they are humiliated as "bedwetters" and "dings."

But it is the sensitivity of these boys that binds them together in a bond of common need and concern. Horrified by the ritualized slaughter of the buffalo the boys set out to liberate the wild beasts. In the process they come to discover some fundamental truths about themselves and achieve self-esteem for the first time in their lives.

While the film was not without its flaws, its depiction of adolescence as a time of pain, adventure, struggle, embarrassment, and exhilaration was

Bless the Beasts and Children: **Rebels circa the counterculture; a rejection of rules and regulations coupled with a fierce desire to be free.**

one of the best the screen had managed. By raising issues such as gun control, conservation, and the whole notion of machismo it located the action against a relevant and timely backdrop. *Variety* called it "a most powerful, pervasive statement about social, political and environmental problems of today and tomorrow."[23]

But with few exceptions the time for such films was drawing to an end. Within one week of reviewing *Bless the Beasts and Children*, *Variety* reported "Youth Angles Can Drop Dead."[24] Failing to excite the box office interest of young audiences with current or controversial themes, Hollywood retreated into the past, and nostalgia became the dominant seller. With the exception of brief glimpses of gang members in *American Graffiti* or switchblade-carrying high schoolers in *Red Sky at Morning*, delinquency vanished from the screen.

Not until 1978 did delinquency re-emerge as a major box office presence. When John Travolta played Tony Manero in *Saturday Night Fever*, he did much more than catapult disco to the international stage. The film's success convinced Hollywood that delinquency was once again a viable prospect at the box office. Director Philip Kaufman had tried unsuccessfully for four years to get *The Wanderers* made. After *Saturday Night Fever* hit big Kaufman found his own project approved. "It's success," he said, "probably made it easier for *The Wanderers* to be made."[25]

Behind the bright lights and the dancing, *Saturday Night Fever* painted a bleaker picture of adolescence. Set in Brooklyn's Bay Ridge the film is about the adolescent search for identity and the need to belong. Tony's home life is empty and meaningless. His work is a boring routine. The only pleasure and escape he finds is on the dance floor, but within himself he knows that he's getting old and that the future holds little for him. With Bobby and the others he manages to form a sense of community, of family and friendship. But deprived of a positive model to draw upon the peer group must fail. When Bobby most needs Tony he's too caught up in his own world to respond to his friend. Bobby falls from the bridge and dies because he was trying to get attention in a "dog-eat-dog world" where kids are cliches, nobodies on their way to nowhere.

It was this pervasive sense of alienation and estrangement that became most noticeable in the successors to *Saturday Night Fever*. Set in East Los Angeles, *Boulevard Nights* explored the relationship between Raymond and Chuco, two brothers from the barrio. Like *Saturday Night Fever* the gang was seen as an alternative family which promised companionship and commitment. It also, however, made demands, and in dealing with these obligations the film looked again at the question of pain and vulnerability beneath a macho facade.

Walk Proud starred Robby Benson as a young man fiercely dedicated to his group. "We're his brothers, man, we're Chicano!" What Benson has to discover, however, is that belonging simply isn't enough. While a gang, a club, or a peer group can provide a sense of community, they can also completely subjugate the individual so that he no longer has an identity of his own. "I don't even know who I am," Benson laments in a universal utterance of adolescence.

The Wanderers, *The Warriors*, and *Over the Edge* all dealt with such issues. Gangs were seen as substitutes for failed families. They provided their teenage members with cameraderie in a world from which they were estranged. Whether in the working-class districts of Whittier Boulevard or in affluent New Granada, a town that proclaimed itself "tomorrow's city today," adolescents both rich and poor were united in their estrangement from society. Bored by the routine of life, the predictability of evening meals, and a lack of recreational facilities, these young people moved increasingly away from society as a whole. The fourteen- and fifteen-year-old white middle-class kids of *Over the Edge* attempt to lose themselves in sex, alcohol, pool, and staying stoned 24 hours a day. When their elders deny them these outlets their frustration turns to anger, their anger to aggression, and aggression into arson as they torch New Granada. Clubs, guns, and knives become the playthings of *The Wanderers*, *The Warriors*, and the street kids of *Boulevard Nights*.

While the violence in these films is frightening and extreme, the young people who live their lives in such a climate of hostility escape our condemnation. Faced with a brutal rite of passage they toughen because they are offered no alternative. Noble savages in a concrete jungle, these young people are depicted as romantic heroes. Misunderstood and deprived, they are pathetic victims. The delinquency movies of the late 1970's were full of pathos, stories of youthful strength and optimism snuffed out by the callous indifference of a society grown too large to care.

In attempting to define such issues as masculinity and responsibilty to the group, the films represented an advance on previous efforts. In dealing with minority groups, Hollywood also showed that it was aware of cultures beyond WASP America. While the danger existed of stereotyping racial groups, these films must be considered to be an attempt to recognize minorities and their cultures. As one East Los Angeles resident put it,

> Usually nobody outside the barrio cares anything about our culture. It's like we're invisible. But people pay attention to movies. [26]

If people paid attention to movies, then movies conversely paid attention to people. While *Saturday Night Fever*'s success and a new awareness of minorities were obviously factors in the new gang cycle, such films can also be seen as a response to an increase in juvenile crime. In January 1977, *Current* reported,

> Crime in America is increasingly a youth problem. Crimes by children — those under eighteen — have been growing at a higher rate than the juvenile population. According to FBI data, arrests of children for serious crimes — murder, assault, robbery, rape — have jumped about 200 percent in the past fifteen years, and arrests for less crimes — larceny, burglary, auto theft, forgery — have doubled. Arrests for juvenile prostitution have increased 286 percent; those for trafficking and use of drugs 460 percent. The increase of crime by children is three times that of adults over the same period. In 1973 1.7 million children were arrested for criminal actions — one-fourth of the total arrests in that year. At the present rate one out of every nine teenagers can be expected to appear in court before the age of eighteen. [27]

Yet despite some obvious improvement in the depiction of delinquency, and particularly in regard to the peer group, these films suffered

The Outsiders (1983): Devoid of positive adult role models, adolescents in S.E. Hinton's story, find themselves alienated from society, with only the peer group to comfort them. Young audiences were moved to tears by the depiction of these tough yet tender kids.

from the long legacy of Hollywood's traditional response to delinquency. Their teenagers exist in that place which Hollywood for years had led them to. With school and family failing to support them, they can only turn to each other for support. The gangs that dominated the films of the seventies are the logical conclusion to five decades of image making. With the eighties approaching there were no Father Flanagans to put these boys on the straight and narrow, no crusading district attorneys or social workers to give them new meaning in life, and no mothers and fathers to suddenly discover responsibility. Having systematically eliminated all adults as positive role models, Hollywood abandoned young people to their own custody and care. Aware of the manifold problems afflicting these youngsters and society, the industry seemed bankrupt of possible solutions.

The end of *Saturday Night Fever* finds John Travolta attempting to forge a new identity for himself. As *Walk Proud* concludes, Robby Benson has survived a savage beating from his own gang members and is preparing to break from their strangehold. As *The Warriors* closes, a softened Michael Beck surveys the bleakness of the Stillwell Avenue turfs and wonders sadly, "This is what we fought all night to get back to?" In each of these cases, Tony, Emilio and Swan are redeemed through the love of a woman. In the end it appeared, Hollywood responded to its own myths. Despite poverty, prejudice, parental failure and social injustice, delinquency, Hollywood seemed to suggest, could be cured by love. Like the students of the Freedom School, moviemakers seemed to believe, "There's no weapon can stop us, rainbow love is much too strong."

With the 1980's under way even that hope seemed to be fading. *The Outsiders* (1983) found Johnny Cade, Ponyboy and the others more alone than their screen counter parts of the seventies. So isolated were they, that they brought to the screen a new vulnerability. "There must be some place with plain ordinary people," Johnny cries, feeling himself trapped by the demands placed upon him by the greasers and the socs. Tulsa, Oklahoma provides a striking new location for this story of sixties delinquency and desperation. Yet a new environment cannot camouflage the familiar alienation and anger. "Get tough like me and you don't get hurt. Nothin' can touch you," Dallas (Matt Dillon) advises the boys. Yet even they can see through the bravado and know his life for the emptiness it is. It is an atmosphere of gloom that pervades *The Outsiders* for it has no answers. Sandwiched between the pain and misery the boys may find a moment of friendship and love if they can triumph over expectations and open up to each other. Beyond that, there is only more of the same.

It would be unreasonable to expect the motion picture industry to articulate answers to problems that have plagued society for decades. Yet in bringing such problems to the screen they have often perpetuated them by stereotyping adolescents and adults alike in negative roles, which do little to further our understanding of a complex social problem. Incapable of seriously exploring the issues they have repeatedly dealt only with images. It is not difficult to see why. In the make-believe world of the movies and those who make them, problems go away when one turns up the house lights. In real life, it is never so simple.

10. Coitus Interruptus or Endless Love

> I think it is highly unlikely that the movie, which has been rated R, will prompt any heretofore unknown lewd thoughts in the minds of any under-seventeen teenagers who might possibly see it, or that it will excite them to demand immediate sexual gratification of complete strangers.[1]

Thus wrote Vincent Canby of *The Blue Lagoon*. While Hollywood has made worse films, seldom if ever has the industry been so open in its self-praise. *The Blue Lagoon*, producers wanted us to believe, was the consummate depiction of adolescent sexuality. A full-page ad in the *New York Times* described the story in the following terms:

> Two children, a boy and a girl, are shipwrecked on a tropical island. The boy grows tall ... the girl beautiful. They swim naked over coral reefs. They run in a cathedral of trees. When their love happens, it is as natural as the sea itself and as powerful. Love as nature intended it to be.[2]

Yet in spite of such claims, the film is simply ludicrous. The dialogue is awkward and unrealistic. "I keep having these strange thoughts about you and me," Em tells Richard. When the girl experiences her first menstrual period she is repelled and tells the boy, "Go away, don't look at me!" "There's so many things I don't understand. Why are all these funny hairs growing on me?" Richard asks. Em spies on the boy as he masturbates and later threatens him, "I've seen you playing with it and I'll tell your father." It's not their reactions that seem difficult to accept so much as it is the heaping of one incident upon the other, all sandwiched in between naked romps, swims, and constant shots of the island wildlife procreating. After the youngsters experience intercourse and Em has a baby, neither of them seem capable of associating their acts of intercourse with the birth.

It is this excessive innocence and the unrealistic emphasis upon the ideal that makes *The Blue Lagoon* such a fraud. While publicity suggested that the film was a natural love story, one finds little in it that bears any resemblance to nature. The island itself is a peculiar paradise devoid of flies, mosquitoes, and other inhospitable creatures of the tropics. Despite what the filmmakers wished to claim, *The Blue Lagoon* was little more than an exercise in kiddie porn, specializing in titilation and attracting moist-palmed adolescents by the thousands. In the process it also served to once again raise the debate about the influence of the movies upon the young.

The debate is as old as the industry itself. From its inception the film industry has been keenly aware of the value of sex at the box office. In 1895 in Atlantic City, New Jersey, *Dolorita's Passion Dance* became one of the earliest subjects in this controversy. The following year *The Kiss* prompted complaints, as did *Courtship* in 1899. Nor was the cinema of adolescence immune to the influence and attraction of sex. "The Pickford teenager," wrote Alexander Walker, "is certainly not an obsessive flirt, but neither is she a passionless virgin."[3]

Perhaps in no other area is the potential impact of cinema on the young as great as it is in the matter of sex. Kracauer has argued that films reflect the mentality of the nation that makes them. In the case of what it reflects about a nation's sexuality, Schumach has suggested that "one can, by studying the exposure of the female anatomy in films of different periods, almost calibrate the attitudes of the average man and woman in the U.S. towards sex, vulgarity and pornography."[4] In the case of the impressionable adolescent, the depiction of sexuality in the movies has the potential to operate as a powerful influence. To a very large extent this depends more on the nature of adolescence itself than it does on the specific content of motion pictures. Havighurst, in establishing developmental tasks of adolescence, suggested that the first three tasks were fundamentally related to sexuality. The adolescent, he suggests is concerned with

> 1 achieving new and more mature relations with agemates of both sexes;
> 2 achieving a masculine or feminine role; and
> 3 accepting one's physique and using the body effectively.[5]

Erikson has also seen sexuality as a key aspect of adolescent development:

> the male at age fourteen begins to consolidate a sense of indentity around the biological nucleus of his maturing sexuality.... At the same time he is concerned with the question of what kind of man he might become.... To achieve a viable concept of the self, the boy chooses and conforms to a masculine style from among the options available in society.[6]

The movies and the mass media in general serve to create and disseminate these sexual options open to young people. Whether in the specific mechanics of copulation or in the more subtle but complex relationships between sexes, screen characters serve as readily observable behavior models for the young. In the process they become major signposts in the young person's passage to autonomy. In *Children and the Movies*, published in 1929, Mitchell quoted a sixteen-year-old girl who said,

Endless Love (1981): Succumbing to romantic images, the film failed to capture the novel's intensity, producing instead a tepid treatment of adolescent passion and sexuality.

> Those pictures with hot love-making in them, they make girls and boys sitting together want to get up and walk out, go off somewhere, you know. Once I walked out with a boy before the picture was even over.[7]

Herbert Blumer's *Movies and Conduct*, published four years later, documented the case of a nineteen-year-old girl who told researchers, "Ever since I saw Joan Crawford use her eyes to flirt with people, I caught that trick and used it to good advantage."[8] In Britain in 1950, Wall and Simson found evidence to support the contention that "the cinema stimulates and organizes the erotic impulses of young people,"[9] reporting that about one-third of the boys in their study claimed that the film they saw "made them feel more loving toward their girlfriends."

One of the major reasons for the potential influence of movies in the area of sex is the absence of other sources of information. Despite well documented increases in adolescent sexual encounters in recent times, today's adolescent is seldom better informed than his forebears. In 1977, responding to the need they perceived, a group of high school students in Madison, Wisconsin, prepared their own handbook on sexuality. In the introduction the teenagers wrote:

> The subjects covered were chosen because they were the things that

haunted us the most during puberty. Things like masturbation, getting horny and homosexuality were pretty scary to us. Most of the books about these mysteries were awful. They were either scientific play-by-play descriptions of how pigs produce, or church handouts that said what we had done so far was sinful and what we were thinking of doing was even worse. So we had to fake it and believe just about anything we heard until we learned the truth, and that we learned by braille and by hard core experience.[10]

Bandura and Walters[11] have argued that in the matter of sex, American youth are not only denied specific information they seek, but are denied an opportunity to observe and understand sexual behavior. Norms of privacy, they suggested, deny the adolescent exposure to all but the most peripheral forms of sexual exchange. The result, they felt, is that adolescents and children place added importance on the sexual behavior manifested by characters in the media. *The Hite Report on Male Sexuality*, published in 1981, gave further evidence of this. "Few men reported spending much meaningful time with their father—their male role models came from movies and television."[12] In the light of such observations, the movies emerge as a powerful potential force in contributing to adolescents' sexual knowledge and behavior. In its depiction of adolescent sexuality the cinema has moved, as we shall see, from coitus interruptus to endless love.

11. Good Girls Don't; Neither Should the Boys

"Well heck! A guy can't just neck around with a girl. It doesn't get us anywhere" — Marty in *Always in My Heart*; 1942.

In the first month of 1930, the *Christian Century* complained: The movies are so occupied with crime and sex stuff and are so saturating the minds of children the world over with social sewage that they have become a menace to the mental and moral life of the coming generation.[1]

The following Easter, Universal Studios released *All Quiet on the Western Front*. Ostensibly a war movie, it is also a story of a boy's coming of age in which the military milieu offers a forum within which the boy can explore the notion of masculinity. In the process the film linked sex and death in a pattern which prevailed for two decades.

As the movie opens, adolescent Paul (Lew Ayres) sits in a classroom with a group of fellow high school students. Beyond the confines of the classroom the wide warring world calls them. They are, their teacher tells them, brave soldiers "who shall defend the fatherland." Caught up in the patriotic fervor of the moment Paul and his companions declare themselves for the fatherland and enlist. Thus begins their odyssey to adulthood and their initiation into a brutal and frighteningly masculine world. "I'll kick the mother's milk out of you," an officer threatens them. It is a disturbingly realistic image of war and the youngsters' idealism soon gives way to harsh realities. The medals and dreamed-of glory are replaced by fear. death, and defecation induced by sheer terror. "When we get back I'll give you some nice clean underwear," an officer tells them as they encounter the enemy.

Set against the background of war and clearly associated with the encounter with death is Paul's growing awareness of his own sexuality. The first time it emerges follows quickly upon the death of a close friend. "I didn't know what it was like to die before," he says. But associated with his

207

first experience of death there is a sexual element that the young man does not yet recognize himself. "It felt like there was something electric running from the ground up through me," he tells his friends, recalling how his thoughts turned to young girls and green fields. The death of his friend has triggered in him a dim awareness of his own sexual energy. As he watches his comrade's life force slip from him, his own sexual energy awakens within him juxtoposing life and death, war and love.

Throughout the film food and hunger have served as dominant images. When the young troops arrive at the front they are disappointed not to find a canteen. Green and inexperienced, they are referred to as "fresh from the turnip patch." When food is provided it comes not from traditional sources but from the exigencies of war with its newly imposed morality and standards. A pig is stolen to feed the troops. When the young soldiers offer to pay for it they learn that their money is worthless. Their past habits are no longer applicable. At the front they discover they must forget who and what they were and learn new rules of survival. When they do finally get a decent meal, their hunger comes at quite a cost. The cook cynically complains that he prepared food for 150, but only 30 have survived the battle.

The physical hunger is related to the sexual hunger of the youthful troops. Later in the film Paul and his friends swim across a river for a rendezvous with three French girls. They gain their entry to the cottage by producing food. It is a world in which everything, even human affection, must be bartered for. And so in a cottage in the French countryside Paul is sexually initiated. It is the first on-screen adolescent sexual encounter of the 1930's. Like everything else in the film the encounter is depicted naturalistically. The boy moves off-screen to a bedroom with the woman. We do not see, but clearly understand, the action that takes place. The camera concentrates upon a record slowly turning on a phonograph. It is a device used by Robert Mulligan some forty years later for another sexual initiation, in *Summer of '42*.

Paul does not comment upon his encounter. It is a private act with a private meaning. His silence testifies to his disappointment with the encounter. Sex, an act of procreation and regeneration, becomes meaningless within the context of a war. A moment of love squeezed in between a lifetime of hate can be little more than a mockery. In the novel Paul refers to the soldiers' brothels he has attended with others. The movie, however, avoids such reference, so that the farm house becomes the scene for his first sexual encounter. That it remains for Paul a sad experience is evident from the book as well as the film. As he leaves the house the book has him comment, "I cannot trust myself to speak. I am not in the least happy."[2] As he has encountered war and death, so too he has now encountered passion and a fleeting moment of love. Both experiences have moved him physically and psychologically from his past.

When he returns home on leave, the world of his boyhood is foreign to him. His mother greets him with blackberries, a childhood favorite, but Paul is no longer a child. She is incapable of dealing with the young man who has returned to her. She offers him clean underwear and warns him to "be on your guard against the women out there." While she can continue to play mother, Paul finds it impossible to the play the role of son. Something in him cries out for the boy he once was and he laments that he can no longer place his head in his mother's lap. He has need for more than a mother now and in a war-torn world it is not the women he must be on guard against but the men who have promoted the war.

Paul has passed too rapidly from the family to the front. His encounters with death and sex have drained him. He exists in a world dominated by men and brutality because that seems easier. "At least we know what it's all about out here." Indeed the womanless world of the trenches and rat holes seems to exist as a sort of psychosexual environment. The bunkers seem to serve as wombs within which the men remain safe. Inside these confined surroundings the young soldiers remain safe. When they seek to stray beyond, to venture into the world outside, they encounter mutilation and death.

Paul's encounters have brutalized him. Deprived of an adolescence and sensitive human encounters, he has become like the others, a hollow man. "You can't live that way and keep anything inside you." In its depiction of men at war, *All Quiet on the Western Front* rejects the traditional image of masculinity achieved through conflict and combat. In the war zone there is no growth. His sexual initiation, rather than being a growth experience, has served only too fleetingly as a buffer to the brutality in the world beyond. It is in reaching for such a precarious and fragile moment of beauty that Paul ultimately dies. Alone in a trench, his best friend recently killed, Paul becomes distracted by a butterfly. Its beauty recalls to him the butterflies he had kept as a child. His hand reaches out as if in an attempt to recapture something of the innocence of his boyhood. A bullet sounds. Paul's faltering hand is shown in closeup as it twitches, then ceases to move. In reaching out to his past, the young soldier has lost his future.

Are These Our Children? continued the association between death and adolescent sexual activity. It might in fact be plausible to argue that Eddie's execution can be read as a punishment not simply for the murder he committed but for his fall from grace when he becomes sexually active. At the beginning of the film the boy and his girlfriend Mary are romantically and idealistically framed within a pulsating heart. There is little doubt that this is a wholesome relationship untainted by passion or physical consummation. But Eddie is a growing boy who becomes increasingly aware of his hormones. "He'll soon be a man," his grandmother observes. Initially his sexual awakening is suggested by his attraction to jazz. The beat gets to him. It makes him restless and stirs desires within him with which he is not yet acquainted. After losing the debating contest his restlessness is increased. At this point, when he is disenchanted with the world, he is most vulnerable to the attraction of the unknown. He encounters a group of girls who tell him to forget about the contest and have a good time. "Grow up! Be a man and forget it!" There is no mistaking the sexual overtones of the remark. Succumbing to the attraction the girls present, Eddie begins to frequent the nightclub with them.

One such evening presents the screen's frankest depcition of adolescent sexuality for the decade. Not until the 1950's would teenagers be permitted to express themselves in such earthy terms. The young people at the table drink alcohol and engage in telling dirty jokes. "Did the doctor tell you to watch your stomach?" Eddie asks a girl. On the dance floor the alluring jazz and the close body contact begin to take their toll on the boy. "Whew, I'm hot," one of the girls exclaims. "I'll say you're hot," the boy agrees. The girl than asks him if he wants to feel how hot she is and promptly takes his hand and runs it across her breasts. Continuing to assault his manhood, the girls belittle him for not drinking. "You don't know what you're missing, boy." But if Eddie appears to be a boy it is apparent that he is about to become a man. Strongly attracted to him, Flo attempts to seduce him. "You don't wear undershirts, do you?" "No, I'm the big outdoor type." "I'll say! You've got the stuff that get them, boy!" To the chagrin of her boyfriend it is obvious that Flo is "getting hot for the guy." Eddie too is getting hot. His grandmother worries, "You're all warm and perspiring." Eddie snaps at her angrily, "Don't baby me!"

One night after leaving the club, Eddie heads home with Flo. She asks him in for a drink, telling him that her mother is in the back room and will not hear. When the boy exits, it is 4:00 a.m. He is very drunk and music plays melodramatically as the screen turns into a swirling spiral. We are left with little doubt that Eddie and Flo have had intercourse. He has left behind forever the idyllic and innocent relationship he had known with Mary for a more violent and physical relationship with Flo.

In his own mind the act of intercourse has clearly made Eddie a man. While he continues to live at home, he is increasingly estranged from it. When his grandmother continues to fuss after him he condemns her angrily. "I want to live my own life. I don't want anyone waiting up for me and bothering about what I do. I don't want anybody babying me. You're making a sissy out of me! I'm a man now!"

When Eddie kills a man, he does so attempting to get alcohol to impress Flo. Not only does his crime stem from his relationship with her, but his death stems directly from his involvement with her. On the witness stand the peer group have stood together under rigorous examination and seem to stand a good chance of acquittal. Nick, however, has been jealous of Flo's relationship with Eddie. Stung by her rejection and frightened by the prosecutor, he cracks on the stand and tells how Eddie commited the murder. That his confession is attributable to Flo is made blatantly obvious when Eddie bitterly yells at him, "Jealous over a girl!" Flo is thus reduced to the role of Eve tempting her Adam, leading to his ultimate fall from grace.

Both *All Quiet on the Western Front* and *Are These Our Children?* established a link between adolescent sexual activity and death. They also both presented images of innocent young men seduced by more mature and experienced young women. This tends to confirm at least in part the contention of Peters, who reported in 1933 that with respect to the aggressiveness of a girl in lovemaking, "motion pictures are vigorously opposing present standards of value."[3]

It was such observations that led to increased demands for motion picture censorship. Particularly active in the campaign was the Roman Catholic Church. In October 1933 Monsigneur Cicognani, a newly appointed apostolic delegate, delivered an address in New York City that clearly indicated the intention of the Church in regard to motion pictures:

> What a massacre of innocent youth is taking place hour by hour! How shall the crimes that have their direct source in immoral motion pictures be measured? Catholics are called by God, the Pope, the bishops, and the priests to a united and vigorous campaign for the purification of the cinema, which has become a deadly menace to morals.[4]

The Catholic campaign was in no small way responsible for the creation of the Legion of Decency in 1934. In July of the same year the MPPDA agreed to the creation of the Production Code Administration headed by Joseph Breen. The result was that no company belonging to the MPPDA would distribute, release, or exhibit any film unless it received a certificate of approval from the PCA. The implementation of the code drove all overt displays of adolescent sexual activity from the screen. What was left was antiseptic, sexless adolescence, or an adolescence in which sexual activity inevitably resulted in death or mutilation.

In 1937's *Marked Woman*, virginal Betty plunges to her death when she draws too close to the world of prostitution. When Sally is raped in *Wild Boys of the Road* her assailant is killed by the boys. The same film also supported the view that girls were the active initiators of sex. At the opening of the movie Eddie and Tommy are heading to a dance at the high school. Tommy is in the back seat with his girlfriend. "I never saw such a woman; always wanting to kiss, kiss," he complains. It is by no means incidental that it is Tommy who later loses his legs in an accident. It was just such a theme that emerged in *King's Row* in the early forties. Drake (Ronald Reagan) is one of the few screen adolescents of the day to express any sexuality. A middle-class young man, he finds that middle-class girls are too virtuous for a red-blooded boy like himself. As a result he literally crosses the tracks and associates with Poppy Ross, a working-class girl who knows how to have a good time. While the townfolk condemn his behavior, Drake feels no guilt. "Just because I'm out in the open about such things, just because I don't sneak around," he says, dismissing their hypocrisy. The association between sexual activity and death or mutilation surfaces when Drake has both his legs amputated and is literally no longer able to sneak around. When one considers that his legs are amputated by the doctor/father of a middle-class girl to whom Drake is attracted, the amputation can be read as a castration that emasculates Drake in exactly the same way that Tommy's loss of his legs rendered him a child.

The forties abounded with similar links between sex, death, and violence. In *Mildred Pierce*, Veda's promiscuity leads to the murder of her stepfather. In *Always in My Heart*, young Marty finds himself attracted to the allure of Fish Town. Lolita is a fiery continental from the dock area. She represents a challenge to the traditional beliefs and values the boy has been raised with. In a clinging satin dress she is sensuous and sensual, the sexual aggressor who challenges Marty in the same way Flo had challenged Eddie. "What's the matter, afraid of your mother?" she teases him. Caught between his upbringing and his physical desires, the boy is ambivalent and confused in his response. "Well, heck! A guy can't just neck around with a girl. It doesn't get us anywhere." Such a viewpoint clearly represents the triumph of middle-class values over working-class values.

In the cinema of the 1940's the link between sexuality, class, and economics is abundantly evident. Middle-class life deals with appearances and clearly regulated patterns of behavior. When such patterns are disturbed, ruptures occur in the lifestyle. In *Mildred Pierce*, Veda's promiscuity was clearly related to her attempt to better herself socially. Her mother's attempt to improve her own lot economically emasculated her husband and dislocated the household. In *King's Row* the attempt to regulate life leads to repression, insanity and suicide. When Drake crosses the tracks for Poppy he rejects emotional and sexual constraints. In the process he rejects his class, its traditions and stability. The open association with Poppy threatens the power structure of the town, a power entrenched in sexual ideology. Poppy and Drake are threatening because rather than suppress their physical instincts and desires they succumb to them. Marty endorses middle-class values by rejecting Lolita. Her presence and passion are clearly threatening; he narrowly escapes being knifed by a jealous suitor.

Youth Runs Wild continued the association between sex, class, and violence. Frankie's attraction to Sarah is clearly frowned upon by his family. "You care too much about her. She has too much influence over you," his sister tells him. "You're too young to think about girls, you've got your education to think about," his mother tells him. Sarah threatens the boy both sexually and economically. Totally infatuated by her the boy confesses, "I can't get her off my mind. I can't stop thinking about her or worrying about her." In the process his school work suffers and his famly worries that he will not be able to carve for himself the place in the world they want him to aspire to. When the boy's infatuation turns to obession and he pursues the girl to the nightclub where she works, a fight breaks out. As a result a woman is killed and Frankie finds himself in court. His sexual desires and their excesses have led indirectly to the death of another.

It is impossible to view these films without coming to the conclusion that Hollywood regarded adolescent sexual activity as threatening. Even Joan Fontaine was cast in this mold. In *The Constant Nymph* (1943) she plays a love-struck adolescent infatuated with Charles Boyer. While one might expect Boyer to be more attracted to the sophisticated Alexis Smith, he succumbs to the girl, and only her death frees them from a traumatic *ménage à trois*.

Knock on Any Door elevated the sex/death metaphor to its zenith. Good looking Nick Romano marries a girl who wants to live in a big white house on top of the hill. But her dream is destroyed by his sexuality. Contemptuous of women, his love-'em-and-leave'-em style cannot easily be absorbed within the traditional bounds of matrimony. His sexual potency is in direct contrast to his economic impotency. Unable to find steady employment, he is reduced to a thief and killer. In the process he fails as both a husband and father. When his wife becomes pregnant he cannot stand the prospect of having a child, and in desperation his wife kills herself. The Romano household of *Knock on Any Door*, is a logical outgrowth of the film industry's attitude toward adolescent sexuality. It fails as a family because Nick has always placed pleasure and the immediate gratification of his desires above procreation. He fails to sustain himself and his family financially because he indulges himself sexually. This is the message that is repeated time and time again throughout the thirties and forties. Momentary pleasure must be rejected in favor of hard work. Such a view conforms to Cottrell's 1946 suggestion:

> If young people want good homes, good communities, good health, and good standards of human relationships, and if they want these things with sufficient patience, intelligence and courage, they can be had.[5]

Achievement in the future meant sacrifice in the present, and part of that sacrifice clearly entailed the regulation of one's sexual appetite. Active sexuality was equated with working-class existence and implied the inability to progress socially. Mickey Rooney, Jane Withers, Shirley Temple, Jackie Cooper, and others depicted the routines and rituals of middle-class adolescence. While some of these performances brought to the screen for the first time the notion of adolescence as a separate stage of life, in the matter of sexuality they were decidedly unreal.

In such films high school cuddlecats rub shoulders with young Lotharios intent on taking their woo wagons on small detours on love's highway. Yet such activities seldom went much beyond a kiss and a cuddle. Although Andy Hardy describes himself as "a born flirt and trifler," he is coy and inexperienced. In *You're Only Young Once* he accepts the advice of his father and stops seeing a girl the judge believes is too fast for him. In *Andy Hardy's Double Life* Esther Williams is more than a match for his boyish ways. Even after his army stint we still find him in 1946's *Love*

The Andy Hardy series: Hollywood defined the rites and rituals of juvenile romance, and a malt shop mentality proliferated for more than a decade.

Laughs at Andy Hardy turning Kay's photograph away from him as he undresses; this after we are told the army has "changed him from a boy to a grown man." If Andy wanted to grow up, his maturity was retarded by the studio head who believed, "If you let Andy get too crazy about girls you'll lose your audience."[6] It wasn't that Mayer and MGM were anti-sex, they were simply extremely careful when dealing with sex and adolescents. "Of course we shall have sex," said Mayer,

> as long as we have men and women in the world we shall have sex. And I approve of it. We'll have sex in moving pictures and I want it there. But it will be normal, real, beautiful sex that is common to the people in the audience, to me and you. A man and a woman are in love with one another. That's sex and it's beautiful in the movies and in life.[7]

Despite what Mayer wanted others to believe, sex would not always conform to his vision. The Hardy series succeeded most during the war, which had a profound impact on American society, including the young.

> A nation at war is a vast pathological museum in which every unspeakable vice is to be found in quantity; not one is lacking. Nor is the release of sexuality confined to adult ages; children are involved in all sorts of behavior. Because of the involvement of children the moral effects of war are more serious and lasting than they would otherwise be.[8]

In 1943, in "A Slum Sex Code," William Foote Whyte provided ample evidence of sexually knowing and active American adolescents:

> In Cornerville children ten years of age know most all the swear words and they have a pretty good idea what the word 'lay' means. Swearing and describing of sex relations by older people and by the boys that hang on the corner are overheard by little children, and their actions are noticed and remembered. Many of the children, when they are playing in the streets, doorways and cellars, actually go through the motions that pertain to the word 'lay.' I have seen them going through these motions, even children under ten years of age. Most all the boys that I know and my friends carry safes (condoms). Most boys start carrying safes when they are high school age. Safes are purchased from necktie salesmen as cheap as a dozen for fifty cents. Some boys buy them and make a profit by selling them to the boys at school.[9]

Yet despite such reports, one encounters little evidence of this aspect of adolescence on the screen. What one finds instead are movies depicting ritualized patterns of courtship. The teenage mating process is clearly designed, regulated, and articulated. Dating, tuxedoes, flowers, dinner dances, and the occasional good night kiss seem to be the major romantic preoccupations of these screen youngsters. If these screen characters were a long way removed from the street kids described by Whyte, the adult restrictions on them were evident on and off the screen. In 1943 the *National Parent Teacher*, in "Sex Guidance in Wartime," gave parents this advice:

> Forestall if possible too early a selection of a love object. To accomplish delay, a youth should be encouraged to form a large number of friendships, especially with members of the opposite sex. Freely acknowledge that desires for physical caresses are normal, but point out casually and without display of authority that serious consequences may result from getting into situations that encourage these desires. Admit that a brief kiss and a hug may be harmless, but tell the boy or girl that prolonged periods of love making cause a physical stimulation that creates greater and greater need for relief of mounting body tension, and that is how emotional control is lost.[10]

It would be convenient to explain this image simply by referring to the PCA, but it goes much deeper. The absence of realistic images of adolescent sexual behavior, like the absence of the Depression and adolescents, and the war and adolescents, represented an attempt on the part of the American film industry to portray an idealized vision of life. This vision was unmistakably wedded to an ideaology that espoused middle-class views and values. In such a social system, sex was threatening because it distracted from building for the future. While parents may have worried about their teenagers losing emotional control, the film industry seemed preoccupied with economic control. Sex, they seemed to imply, at least adolescent sex, endangered the financial future not only of the juvenile but of society itself. This view of life advocated abstinence and the acceptance of the philosophy that good girls don't and neither should the boys.

When sex did rear its ugly head the Bible was invoked and the boys weᵣ usually shown as victims of plotting and conniving women. *Seventeen* finds Jackie Cooper the victim of Lola, the femme fatale from Chicago. *Henry Aldrich Gets Glamor* found the love-struck adolescent as the unwitting dupe of a movie star. *Mildred Pierce* showed Veda trapping a boy into marriage. Women were seen as major threats to the boys.

It is ironic indeed that the industry which so carefully constructed this vision of adolescent sexuality provided the setting and opportunity for its own children to explore sex in a way denied their screen counterparts. While Andy Hardy got no further than a kiss and a cuddle, Mickey Rooney has admitted that "some of the most pleasant nights of my late boyhood were spent with ladies I did not know."[11] In *Seventeen* a romantic Jackie Cooper proclaims, "I'm sure I could never make love without feeling it. I think love is sacred." In reality, as his autobiography discloses, Cooper engaged in a loveless but very physical relationship with Joan Crawford. In sex, as in all else, Hollywood created a gap between illusion and reality.

12. The Family Way

"Your father never laid a hand on me until we were married and then I just gave in because a wife has to. A woman doesn't enjoy these things the way a man does. She just lets her husband come near her in order to have children" — Mother to daughter in *Splendor in the Grass*, 1961.

In the period between the end of the 1940's and the early years of the 1960's, major changes within society and the film industry led to a more liberal treatment of sex in both an adult and adolescent context. The Paramount Case, the Miracle Case, competition from television, and the success of Broadway plays with mature sexual themes all had their impact on Hollywood's treatment of sex.

Yet despite a more liberal attitude, such expression was always contained within familiar environments dominated by long established themes and concerns. The sexual fears of the forties came to fruition in the fifties and early sixties. If the castrating woman appeared as Mildred Pierce in the mid-forties, she reappeared as the nymph a decade later in *Baby Doll*. "There's no torture on earth to equal the torture which a cold woman inflicts on a man," Baby Doll's husband complains. Although she has denied him the pleasures of the marriage bed, it is not her act which emasculates him. Archie's failure as a husband is a reflection of his failure as a man, measured by his ineptitude in financial matters.

The economic fear of the forties thus emerges again in the fifties. Archie's sexual inadequacy stems directly out of his economic inadequacy. It is the failure which leads his teenage bride to reject him. "You told my daddy a mouthful of lies in order to get me." The wealth and success he had promised her is in reality "the biggest old wreck of a place in the whole delta." The relationship between sex and money remains a dominant theme in films of the period. In *East of Eden*, Adam's failure as a father and husband is matched by his unsuccessful business ventures. His wife has denied him the marriage bed and turned sex into a lucrative business. In *The*

217

Restless Years, Will Henderson's father is henpecked by a wife who wants him to aspire to be more than the manager of a supermarket. In *A Summer Place*, Helen Jorgensen uses money and her passion for social status as tools to achieve her own ends, ultimately losing both her husband and her daughter. Finally, in *Splendor in the Grass*, Wilma Deen's mother promotes her daughter's relationship with Bud, intent on having her marry into money. It was these film families that provided the forum within which the debate over sex and morality was waged.

As such, the screen served as a reflection of a trend noted in 1940 by Kingsley Davis in "The Sociology of Parent-Youth Conflict." Conflict within the family, he suggested, sprang from the rate of social change. Such change inevitably meant that youth were raised in an era different from that of their parents. In the value clash that resulted, sharp emotional conflicts were generated within the family. To this extent the troubled families of the fifties can be seen as a reflection of rapidly changing times in the post-war era.

On the screen, sex was a major battleground between the generations. *The Unguarded Moment* found John Saxon pressured to conform by his misogynistic father. Unable to break free to establish an identity for himself and develop healthy heterosexual relationships, the boy complains, "Can't even go to a dance by myself, he's got to tag along." In *Peyton Place*, adolescent Allison MacKenzie struggles with the question of her legitimacy. Selena Cross is raped by her stepfather. Rodney Harrington marries against his father's wishes and Norman Page tries to break free from the suffocating embrace of his mother. The fifties and sixties gave voice and vision to conditions that Davis saw an an inevitable part of family life:

> Our morality, for instance, demands both premarital chastity and post-ponement of marriage, thus creating a long period of desperate eagerness when young persons practically at their peak of sexual capacity are forbidden to enjoy it. Naturally tensions arise—tensions which adolescents try to relieve and adults hope they will relieve in some socially acceptable form. Such tensions not only make the adolescent intractable and capricious, but create a genuine conflict of interest between the two generations. The parent, with respect to the child's behavior, represents morality, while the offspring reflects morality plus his organic cravings. The stage is thereby set for conflict, evasion and deceit. For the mass of parents, toleration is never possible. For the mass of adolescents, sublimation is never sufficient. Given our system of morality, conflict seems well high inevitable.... As it is, rapid change has opposed the sex standards of different groups and generations, leaving impulses only chaotically controlled.[1]

Between 1959 and 1963, four major motion pictures significantly

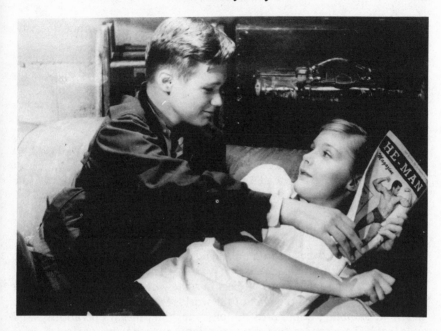

Blue Denim (1959): **The acknowledgment of adolescent sexuality activity but the failure to explore the post-coital situation.**

advanced the depiction of adolescent sexuality and brought a new maturity and sophistication to American films. All located sex within a family context. James Leo O'Herlihy's play *Blue Denim* was filmed by Fox in 1959. Directed by Philip Dunne, it starred Brandon deWilde and Carol Lynley as the high school lovers. Arthur Bartley is in his mid-teens and finding them tough going. His relationship with his father has deteriorated and they seem unable to communicate. When the boy's dog is ill, his father (McDonald Carey) has it put to sleep while the boy is at school to spare him pain. Arthur, however, is furious that he wasn't consulted. Frustrated by his son's reaction, Mr. Bartley confronts his wife:

> Mr. Bartley: A good officer looks after his men.
> Mrs. Bartley: But you're not an officer anymore and Arthur isn't one of your men, he's your son.

The film graphically locates the question of Arthur's awakening sexual urges against the backdrop of the family and in particular his relationship with his father. By introducing the military theme it establishes its link with the 1940's and develops a theme that would still be a subject for exploration in post-Vietnam America. Clearly for Arthur's father the notion of masculinity is umbilically wedded to the military. For Arthur, however, the question is not so simple and they face each other uneasily.

> Mr. Bartley: What's wrong with the boy, Jessie? Why won't he talk to me? When he was little we got along fine. Now if I so much as say hello, he hates me.
>
> Mrs. Bartley: Oh, Malcolm, he doesn't hate you, it's just a phase he's going through.
>
> Mr. Bartley: Now what does that mean, a phase?
>
> Mrs. Bartley: Oh, I don't know. It's just something you say about boys Arthur's age and everybody's supposed to understand.
>
> Mr. Bartley: Well all I understand is a few weeks in an Army camp wouldn't hurt that young man. Might shake him up a little.
>
> Mrs. Bartley: Malcolm, he's still a boy.
>
> Mr. Bartley: All right, he's still a boy, but he hasn't got much time left.

Trapped between childhood and adulthood, the boy retires nightly to the basement with his buddy Ernie (Warren Berlinger). The two of them play cards, talk tough, and drink beer in a show of what they think is adult and masculine. Playing the man of the world, Ernie tells Art, "This town is full of it, gamblin', dope, prostitution, smugglin', illegal operations," and adds that he had to steer the next door neighbor to a doctor for one of those operations. "Boy, from now on, I'm going to be really careful," Arthur tells him, implying that he has an active sex life.

Janet arrives and thinking it is the parents, the boys hurriedly stash the beer and cigarettes. When the girl settles in they amusingly put on their tough front to impress her.

> Ernie: What's your damn pleasure?
>
> Arthur: Well, give me some time to have a damn look, will you damn it?

But Janet is not impressed. "You boys kill me. This big act you put on down here, playing poker, drinking beer, talking tough." When she finds one of Arthur's magazines with an ad for body building in it she laughs at him. The boy jumps at her and wrestles her to the couch. As their eyes meet there's a sense of something between them. Sensing this, Ernie leaves and the two of them are left alone.

When the girl complains to him, "I just don't like to see you the way you are when Ernie's around," he abuses her. "Who do you think you are anyway, my mother?" Later he confides, "The poker and the beer — I don't really like it. I guess it's just easier to put on an act. Sometimes if you come out with what you're really thinking, people just laugh at you." Janet assures him she wouldn't laugh at him and tells him how much she likes him. The boy wants to kiss her but doesn't know how to go about it. He begins to ask her and she says, "It's no good if you ask." They kiss awkwardly, their noses getting in the way.

After a basketball game one evening, Arthur walks the girl home. "I don't want you to go around in the dark by yourself." They talk about going steady and their sexual feelings. "It's biologically normal, but whenever boys tried anything I always got scared or disgusted. Do you think I've got a sex blockade or something?" "No, you simply didn't like those guys, that's all." "I wish I was eighteen this minute and knew about everything," she tells him with the naive assumption that knowledge and understanding come magically to one at their eighteenth birthday.

Arthur's older sister Lillian is about to be married, and as Arthur and Janet stand in the front garden they watch Lillian and her fiance kissing in the car out front. The moment excites them. Arthur withdraws to the basement with the excuse of getting the compact Janet had left there. When Janet follows him down the two of them confront each other awkwardly in the silence, both feeling the physical urges rising within them, both unsure as to what to do about it.

> Janet: Arthur, have you been with lots of girls?
> Arthur: The regular amount for a guy my age, I guess.
> Janet: Is it ... was it like you thought it would be?
> Arthur: More or less.
> Janet: When it happened, did you like those other girls?
> Arthur: Nah, a man doesn't have to.

His old toughness is surfacing again. "I'm glad you know everything," she tells him and suddenly the boy breaks away, throwing himself face down on the couch. "Don't look at me," he tells her, explaining, "I never have either. I made it all up, about other girls. I don't know anything." "You big phoney," she chides him gently and they laugh, then kiss. For the late fifties this is as far as the cameras are allowed to go, but their awkwardness has been replaced by honesty and their relationship is now to be a physical one. Not shown on the screen, their sexual initiation is part of Hollywood's kiss and cut syndrome.

Some time later, at a high school dance, Janet sneaks off to the library and Arthur finds her with a biology book open at Chapter 42, Pregnancy, The First Stages. "But they don't tell you how to stop it," she tells him desperately. Terrified of their parents learning the truth, believing it would kill them, they try to get a marriage license, but they're both under eighteen and when they apply they simply become the butt of adult jokes ("Aren't they the cutest thing!").

Recalling his earlier conversation with Ernie, Arthur goes to him for help. In an intense scene in the basement of the house where the teenage games have quickly turned to tension and trauma, Arthur pleads with Ernie to tell him about the doctor. Pushing the other boy into the chair he screams at him urgently, "The one for girls, you know what I mean, don't act square. I know somebody who has to get hold of a doctor." When Ernie tells him it's a "crime ... murder!" Arthur knocks him down. "Always yakkin', always runnin' off at the mouth! Who is he, where does he live, tell me!" When Ernie tells him he doesn't know, that he lied, Arthur's eyes register horror as the last chance fades away. For Ernie it has been a moment of truth also, as his whole hotshot image has been shattered. Forced now to face each other honestly, Arthur tells the truth, that the doctor is for Janet who is three months along. Ernie takes him to a drugstore where they get a tip about an abortionist. The first inkling of what type of man they'll be dealing with comes when the tipoff tells Arthur, "Next time around the little lady gets a discount."

As the abortion begins to emerge as a reality rather than a kid's scheme, Ernie pleads with Arthur to forget it. Convinced and encouraged by Ernie, the boy goes to talk to his mother. Engaged in arrangements for his sister's wedding, she doesn't really hear what he's trying to say, and when she gets the general idea that it has something to do with sex she gives him a book. "This will clear everything up." The boy tries his father next, mixing a drink to prepare him for the shock. When he fills a glass with Scotch his father looks at him and then the glass, commenting, "You must have a real problem, boy!" and then gets lost in his ramblings about his own problems so that once more the boy is left without a solution and the truth still bottled up inside him. On the day of the wedding, the day that Janet is to leave for the abortionist, he tries once more to speak to his mother. "Mom, Mom, listen to me," but it's swept away in the search for his aunt's coat. As the happy bridal couple head off one way, Janet enters the black car that has been sent for her and is driven away blindfolded and alone. In a final desperate attempt to get the boy to tell his parents, Ernie turns on Arthur once more. Arthur hits him and orders him out, then retires to the kennel of his dead dog, crying, "Let it be all right!"

When his father discovers that the boy has taken one of his checks and cashed it, he confronts him. "Sit up straight! Look me in the eyes like a man! Now you talk or I'll ...." "What'll you do? Kill me? I wish you would," the boy cries. Realizing that something is awfully wrong, his father assures him, "Listen son, whatever it is, we'll back you up, even it it's the worst thing in the world." When the boy tells him, they rush to the drugstore, learn the abortionist's address and get to Janet in time.

> Because of censorship they could not use the central idea of the girl actually having an abortion. They had to save her from it at the last minute. By shirking that ugly situation they took out the truth, the guts, the intestines, the liver, all the vital organs of the story.[2]

Worried that marital responsibilities would ruin Arthur's life, Janet arranges with his parents for her to leave town without his knowing. When Ernie abuses the boy for letting her go off, Arthur is furious that once more his father has tried to protect him. "What are you doing, Dad, sparing me again like you did with my old dog—doing my job, running my life, sending my girl away?" Realizing that his son cares for Janet, that he's prepared to shoulder the responsibilities, they farewell him and the boy, armed with his mother's toast and his father's car, heads off after Janet, "Their childhood, their innocence, all those straight A's gone up the flue."

What the film promised was that the young lovers lived happily ever after. The compulsory happy ending failed to consider the post-coital situation. In marrying off the teenagers Hollywood returned them to the fold. Within the boundaries of the family, it was assumed that they would go on and prosper. Yet these youngsters had no preparation for marriage. If their parents had provided them with no guidance in matters of sex, they had equally failed to prepare them for marriage and the responsibilities that went with it. While Hollywood seemed content to suggest that a wedding ring brought domestic bliss, others were less convinced. In 1951, writing in *The Journal of Marriage and Family Living*, Judd Marmor described the failure of American society to adequately socialize the young and the sexual contradictions implicit in the culture:

> Our culture imposes stringent sexual taboos on children and adolescents—parents merely convey to their children what our cultural standards demand. Yet once people marry, in spite of the very more prolonged period of sexual repression which modern civilization imposes, they are expected to function with great sexual effectiveness and sexual inadequacy is regarded with contempt.[3]

Despite its flawed ending, however, *Blue Denim* was an important film and a significant advance in the depiction of adolescent sexuality. While it neither condoned nor endorsed pre-marital sex, it accepted it as a fact of life in a way the forties had refused to do. Equally important, it gave graphic indication of adolescence as a time in which youngsters struggle not only with their glands but with the whole notion of gender. Arthur and Ernie attempt to formulate for themselves a concept of masculinity and manhood which they can live with. Janet too is faced with defining her own sexuality. Neither she nor Arthur can be carbon copies of their parents but must seek to establish identities that they feel comfortable with.

While Janet and Arthur have been raised in ignorance, discovering what they know about sex from their peers and their own tentative explorations, the characters of *A Summer Place* experience adolescence and sexual awakening surrounded by scandal, sensationalism, and scare tactics. Written, produced, and directed for Warner Brothers by Delmer Daves, the film starred Sandra Dee as Molly Jorgensen, the daughter of a research chemist from Buffalo (Richard Egan) and a ferociously puritanical mother played by Constance Ford. As the film opens the wealthy Jorgensens are sailing to Pine Island, Maine, for their summer vacation. For Molly's father Ken it marks a return to the island where he worked as a lifeguard before he was successful. Unknown to him things on the island have changed. Sylvia (Dorothy McGuire) and Bart (Arthur Kennedy) Hunter are no longer well off. The island business has declined, Bart has become an alcoholic, and money is scarce at a time when their son Johnny (Troy Donahue) is approaching college age.

On board the yacht the divisions in the Jorgensen family are openly apparent. Helen insists on treating Molly as a child, forcing her to wear clothes that camouflage her developing body. Her father has a good relationship with the girl. She is able to confide in him in a way that is not possible with her mother. She tells him of the hot and cold flushes she has been experiencing, the naughty thoughts that have entered her mind, and how she undresses so the boy next door can see her. Rather than berating her, her father understands what the girl is going through and accepts it as natural. He rejects his wife's attempts to keep her a child, telling her, "Molly has a lovely, healthy figure, why do you insist on desexing her?"

When Johnny and Molly meet it is love at first sight. "I knew it would be like this. Who taught you to kiss so perfectly?" the boy asks her. He is a little surprised when she reveals that she spent lunchtime on the roof with a senior who taught her to kiss. But if Johnny is mildly shocked by the girl's behavior, Helen is outraged. "No decent girl lets a boy kiss and maul her the first night they meet," she complains. "I suppose it's your Swedish blood," she tells her husband, blaming the girl's behavior on him. An innocent kiss between a boy and girl in the garden becomes for Helen "that disgusting public display." The depth of her negative sexual attitude is revealed when she tries to explain men to her daughter: "You've got to play your cards right, you can't let him think your kisses come cheap ... you have to play a man like a fish ... that's what's cheap, wanting a man." Helen is cold, passionless, loveless; her marriage is hollow. In contrast, Ken believes "we've got only one great reason for living, to love and be loved."

He attempts to comfort the girl in a loveless, often hostile, environment. Molly has never heard her mother express love for her father. She is, as he says, "anti-people, anti-life." At a time in her life when the girl most needs an understanding mother to explain the changes taking place in her body, Molly finds little comfort from her mother. "She makes me ashamed of even having a body." Infuriated by the damage his wife is causing, Ken turns on her angrily. "Must you label young love-making as cheap, wanton and disgusting? Must you persist in making sex itself a filthy word?"

When Molly and Johnny are stranded on the beach all night following the capsizing of their yacht Helen overreacts and orders the doctor to examine the girl. "I want you to take off every stitch you've got on and let him examine you." Hysterically Molly begs to see her father. "I haven't done anything wrong. I'm a good girl." Johnny too finds that he has to deal with adults who don't understand how he feels. Deeply in love with the girl, he is hurt and offended by his father who looks upon her as "a pretty little wench," but "a common slut."

In the tradition of the fifties' film families, Johnny and Molly are forced to grow up and face adolescence in spite of their parents. When Ken becomes involved with Johnny's mother a major scandal erupts and the two youngsters find themselves separated and alone. Angry with their parents even after the wedding of Ken and Sylvia, they resort to furtive notes, secret phone calls, and clandestine meetings. "Let's face it, we're all alone on this earth." Reluctantly they agree to visit Ken and Sylvia, each attempting to adjust to their new step parent, and compensating their personal pain and anguish by the chance of seeing each other again.

In the romantic setting of blue skies, crashing waves, and golden sand, the two fall deeper in love and struggle to restrain their sexual desires. Johnny wants to get married but Molly tells him he has to finish college and go into the army. Life, it seems, conspires against them. Left alone with little adult supervision they find the salt spray, the hot sun, and their tanned bodies increasing temptations. Lying to their parents, they say they're going to a double feature and head off instead to a secluded and deserted hide-out on the beach. There, resorting to the cinematic cliche of waves crashing on a beach, the film has the young couple consummate their love. Molly becomes pregnant but their fear and embarrassment give way to love and understanding as Ken and Sylvia accept them, realizing that in looking at their children, they are looking at what they themselves were like in their youth.

A Summer Place, while showing that unbridled passion produced responsibilities, presented an interesting and appealing image of parent and child dealing with adolescent sexuality. It openly declared that sexual behavior among young people was not only to be expected but was natural. In the characters of Ken and Sylvia it provided sensitive and sympathetic voices and insights into the life of the young. "It's not so easy for them, they're so intense and in love." "So were we at their age and we didn't settle for a walk on the beach." Tired and hackneyed moralizing was shown as no longer applicable to the needs of modern youth. Waiting up for Molly and Johnny to return from their night on the beach, Ken struggles to find words that they will understand. "What honest advice can I give her? To be a half virgin? I can't tell her to be half good? I'd feel like a hypocrite."

Like *Blue Denim*, however, *A Summer Place* refused to consider the post-coital situation. Johnny and Molly married and the filmmakers seemed satisfied that as usual they would live happily ever after. The question of bringing up baby never seemed a subject worthy of address. The very issues that both films ignored were on the minds of American youngsters. In *The American Teenager*, published in 1957, Remmers and Radler found that problems with parents constituted a real problem for large numbers of teenagers. One of the biggest issues between parents and their teenage children was that of sex.

What things should I consider in choosing a husband or a wife? How long should we know each other before we get married? How can I prepare myself for marriage? What are the things that cause trouble between married people? Teenagers look for the answers from their parents, from older relatives, and from their teachers. Half the time they don't get answers.[4]

Yet despite this familiar failure, *A Summer Place* represented an advance on *Blue Denim*. In the characters of Ken and Sylvia it presented parents who existed as sexual beings with feelings and needs of their own. Though Johnny and Molly have difficulty dealing with their parents' sexuality, they were almost singularly alone in the American cinema as teenagers whose parents openly acknowledged their own sexuality. While we see little in Arthur's or Janet's parents to suggest they will be able to help them with the problems of married life, in Ken and Sylvia we find warm, considerate, and understanding adults who may well be able to do so.

If *Blue Denim* and *A Summer Place* seemed to wink at adolescent sexual activity, *Splendor in the Grass* (1961) actually seemed to endorse it. A controversial film, it produced strikingly different critical reactions. The *New York Times* greeted it as "one of the best films about children and parents that we have ever seen." The movie, said the paper, was an expression "of youthful tensions and repressions as a result of misguided, misplaced adult dominance and deceit ... showing the stark and sad effects of parental domineering and evasion in matters of sex."[5] But if the *Times* was lavish in its praise, *New Yorker* was scathing in its condemnation:

> *Splendor in the Grass* is as phony a picture as I can remember seeing. Not only that, it's phony in a particularly disgusting way. Although it purports to be a study of young love, what it amounts to is a prolonged act of voyeurism which we as adults are invited to become parties to on the pretext that it will provide us with fresh insights into the sexual anguish of the teenager.... William Inge and Elia Kazan must know perfectly well that the young people they cause to go trashing about in *Splendor in the Grass* bear practically no relation to young people in real life.[6]

In terms stronger than Hollywood had ever used, *Splendor in the Grass* located adolescent sexuality within the context of the family. The responsibility of the parent for securing a happy passage to adulthood for their offspring was dramatically presented. As the teenagers, Natalie Wood and Warren Beatty delivered appealing and understandable performances in which passion was balanced with pain. The sexually repressed mother was once again present. "Boys don't respect a girl they can go all the way with," Wilma Deen's mother tells her. Caught between her mother's views and her love for Bud, the girl experiences her sexual longings as a time of conflict, confusion, and shame.

Splendor in the Grass: **A rare happy moment for Bud and Deenie, anguished adolescents caught between biological drives and societal taboos.**

Wilma Deen: Mom, is it so terrible to have these feelings about a boy?
Mother: No nice girl does.
Wilma Deen: Doesn't she?
Mother: No. No nice girl.... You father never laid a hand on me until we were married and then I just gave in because a wife has to. A woman

doesn't enjoy these things the way a man does. She just lets her husband come near her in order to have children.

Set in southeast Kansas in 1928, the film opens with the two teenagers in the car and Wilma Deen resisting Bud's advances. Beside them a waterfall plunges and symbolizes the sexual torrent rising within them. The girl is a romantic who likes to listen to sea shells and imagine their secret whispering. But her dreams are constantly intruded upon by her mother's harping. "Bud Stanford could get you into a whole lot of trouble. You know what I mean. Wilma Deen, you and Bud haven't gone too far already, have you?"

Deenie may well resist Bud's advances but in the process, the film suggests, she seems to be making herself ill. She has a nervous mannerism of constantly stroking her hair. On the couch downstairs and later in bed she grinds her pelvis as though sexually frustrated. Her bedroom exists as a shrine to Bud, with her dresser and mirror plastered with pictures of the handsome high school football hero.

If Deenie's relationship with her mother is troubled, then Bud's relationship with his father is no better. "You're not doing anything you're gonna be ashamed of, are ya boy?" His one preoccupation and concern is with his son as a football player. "You're the captain of the team, son. The other boys look after you." Aggressively masculine, he slaps and punches at the boy, boisterously insisting, "Lay it on me; we got a future, boy!" But it remains a monologue and Bud is incapable of getting a word in edgewise. For his father, Bud exists as a extension of himself, an implement through which he may live himself. Lame, he uses Bud as a surrogate athlete. Bud will be the man his father is not. Man in this sense has no sexual connotation and his relationship with his wife is as cold and distant as Deenie's mother's relationship with her husband. Beyond the football field, the father is singlemindedly obsessed with his son going to Yale. Deenie thus appears as an intrusion and disruption. She is a sexual threat who promises to undermine Bud's success, a success that is traditionally measured in material terms.

In contrast to the girl's idealism, Bud is shown in conflict with his physical needs. The football game can only serve to sublimate so much of his drive. Later in the locker room the boys talk of Juanita, the town's easy girl. Bud remains silent as he stands in the shower and the water plunges down his face, recalling once again the waterfall that had been introduced earlier as a sexual symbol. "I don't know what's the matter with me lately, I'm always losing my temper," he tells Deenie later. In desperation he attempts to raise the matter with his father. "I feel like I'm going nuts sometimes." "What you need for the time being is a different kind of girl—get a little steam out of the system." "I love Deenie, Dad," the boy tries to explain. For his father there are only two types of girls—good and bad. If you love a woman you cannot expect to have sex with her. It is the same unnatural attitude held by Deenie's mother, and both children are finding their parents' values inadequate to their own needs.

Caught between their needs and their upbringing, both youngsters are increasingly miserable. Bud needs sex but finds his loyalties to Deenie prevent him from looking for it elsewhere. She knows his needs and fears they will drive him away from her. After a date one evening he takes the girl home and pushes her to her knees at his feet, forcing her to say she is his slave and will do anything for him. Crying, the girl does as he tells her. "I don't kid around about those things. I am nuts about you and I would go down on my knees to worship you." Her obsession and her compliance mirror the ways in which females have succumbed to Donahue. While Bud may hurt and ache and love, neither he nor his male counterparts are forced to subject themselves to such humiliation.

Unable to deal with his confusion, Bud tries to control his feelings. "We've got to stop all this kissing and fooling around," he tells Deenie, but his attempts to curtail his feelings result in even more tension. The coach berates him for lacking concentration in his game and his grades at school suffer. Sweaty, distracted, and nervous, he finally collapses during a basketball game. He turns to a doctor for help and guidance. "It's no fun to be in love. Every time that we're together I have to remember things, you know what I mean ... a guy can go nuts that way." The doctor, however, has no advice save to offer him iron shots.

If Bud's condition is cause of concern, then Deenie's is cause for alarm. Without Bud she is alone and a half person. The gossip in the school halls is that she has lost him by refusing to yield to him. Unable to satisfy himself with Deenie, Bud has turned to Juanita who seems radiant having been had by the school hero. Merely being at school is a humiliation for Deenie. Everywhere she turns she sees Bud and knows that she has lost him. Incapable of understanding their daughter's disturbed state of mind, her parents can simply advise a good meal and plenty of milk. Desperately the girl tries to explain to her mother, "I can't eat, I can't study. I can't even face my friends any more. I want to die!" In a violent and disturbing scene, Deenie bathes while her mother talks to her. The water once again serves as a sexual symbol. Afraid that the girl has given herself to Bud her mother harangues her, "Did he spoil you?" Tormented and terrified, Deenie submerges herself maniacally, screaming, "I'm a good little girl ... I hate you ... leave me alone ... I'm not spoiled! I hate you ... I hate you!" She rises from the bath and runs naked down the corridor. Although the sequence was filmed, censorship problems prevented her naked dash from ever coming to the screen.

Unable to have Bud on her terms, Deenie attempts to become like Juanita. She severely cuts her hair, dresses the part, and sings, "she's a tease, she's a flirt," as she prepares herself for her new image. Although she attempts to play the independent young woman, she finds it impossible to keep away from Bud. At the school dance they are magnetically drawn

together. Cigarettes and alcohol have now entered their lives as means by which they suppress their sexual urges. "Every night after dinner I have to force myself from going to the telephone and calling you," he tells her. Desperately wanting him back, Deenie tries to maneuver him into a car, determined to give herself to him. But now that she is ready for sex she finds herself trapped by Bud's conception of her as a good girl. "Cut it out, you're a nice girl." "I'm not ... I haven't any pride," she screams at him.

Rejected, she turns to another boy for companionship, but when he attempts to make love to her it is Bud's name she calls. Ashamed and humiliated, she runs from the car and rushes to the waterfall. It is at the same time an image of her attempt to cleanse herself of her shame and a symbol, like the bath, of her desire to submerge herself sexually. "Oh Bud," she whispers almost orgasmically as the water washes over her. On a more literal level, Deenie's rush to the falls is an attempt to kill herself. Unable to control the conflicting emotions rising within her, she has crossed the line from santiy and reason and is institutionalized.

While the girl's mother blames Bud entirely, believing "he's the cause of it," it remains apparent that both Deenie and Bud are victims of social attitudes toward sex. That this is meant to be seen as a general condition and not simply one peculiar to the youngsters is indicated by the setting of the film. Like Dorothy (*The Wizard of Oz*), Bud and Deenie live in Kansas. Bud says it's "right in the middle of America ... very friendly, everybody knows your name and they know who you are." While such a situation makes for community and commitment, it also is the source of Bud and Deenie's problem. In such a social setting it is impossible for them to find the space and privacy needed for their search for self. It is such a claustrophobic environment that limits personal growth and produces the loveless, passionless liaisons represented by Bud's and Deenie's families.

In 1963, *Hud* addressed itself to the question of personal growth and adolescent sexuality. As Lon, Brandon deWilde represented a more mature version of Arthur, Johnny, and Bud. All three boys had suffered in part from the inadequacy of their family life and all three had rushed rather ill-prepared into starting their own families. *Blue Denim*, *A Summer Place*, and *Splendor in the Grass* had helped bring to the screen a healthier and more honest vision of adolescence in which sex was seen as a natural part of growing up. But all of their characters experienced sex before they had grown, and there is little in any of the films to suggest that intercourse functioned for them as a growth experience. Instead it plunged them into marriage and parenthood before they had time to fully develop and enjoy their youth. In *Hud* we encounter a teenager who, while longing for sexual fulfillment, postpones the moment and addresses himself to the more crucial concern of establishing his own identity. Lon looks at the lifestyles of the two main men in his life (his grandfather and his uncle) in order to

Opposite: *Hud* (1963): A rejection of the western myth of manhood.

determine what type of man he wants to become. Like Clinton in *All Fall Down*, he finds himself initially attracted to the drinking, womanizing, free-wheeling spirit as exemplified by his uncle Hud (Paul Newman).

As the film opens it is dawn in a small Texas town. Lon is out looking for his uncle. Piece by piece we are presented with an impression of the sort of man he is. "If I find a pink Cadillac he'll be around here somewhere." "I had Hud in here last night is what I had," a bartender tells him, cleaning up the mess. The screen is almost a repetition of Clinton search through the bars and alleys of Key Bonita, Florida, for his brother in *All Fall Down*. When the boy at last comes across Hud, he has been drawn by the sexual symbolism. The pink Cadillac is parked outside a house and a woman's shoe lies on the sidewalk. Nervously he calls for his uncle. "You got trouble right here, bub, I'm just getting nicely tucked in," Hud berates him. Roused from his bed, Hud wanders towards the car. When he sees the husband of the woman he slept with arriving home, he quickly moves the blame to his nephew, promising to "lower his temperature some." Embarrassed, Lon complains, only to be told, "Relax, you'll be able to charge a stud fee by the time that story gets around."

Attracted by the devil-may-care attitude of his uncle, the boy asks to come along with him in the future only to be told, "The pace would kill you, sonny." Hud obviously has little place in his life for him. The boy remains alone with neither father nor mother, and with his best friends his grand-father and Elma (Patricia Neale), the cook and cleaning woman.

It is through Elma that Lon encounters a tender and compassionate side to women that his uncle's stories and exploits never reveal. It is through her also that he comes to view sex as something healthy and natural. Play-fully aware of his growing pains and new yearnings, she teases him. When he asks for peach ice cream, telling her he's been busting for it all winter, he leaves himself open for her gentle gibes. "Is that what you been waitin' for all winter, sugar? How about those peachy pinups you keep hidin' with your socks and shorts?"

In contrast to her chiding, Hud seems meaner in his responses to the boy. When Lon asks to accompany his uncle to town, Hud takes the oppor-tunity to belittle him. "What big deal you got lined up, sport, a snow cone or something?" When they get to town, Hud tells him to get lost and chase a couple of Dr. Peppers. He loses himself in the drugstore flicking through paperbacks. Looking at *From Here to Eternity* he tells the store owner, "The people in it seem a lot like the ones I see." When he sees his uncle go by, Lon chases after him. Hud is on his way to the local whorehouse. "I don't think that's a house you're likely to have heard much about." "Yeah, I've heard some. I'm out of my three-cornered pants, you know, have been for some time." Momentarily amused by the boy, Hud recognizes in him something of his lost youth. "When I was your age I couldn't get enough of anything. I dunno which we ran the hardest, them cars or the country girls we do-si-doed and chased a lot of girlish butts around that summer." "I wouldn't mind going that route myself," Lon tells him, but when his uncle invites him along he declines.

Not yet ready for sex, he nonetheless has it on his mind. When Elma asks him if he's sleeping in the raw again he turns the question back on her. "You ever wear any of those little shorty things?" "What kind of question is that?" "I just wondered.' "Does your mind usually run in that direction?" "Yeah, it seems to." "Boys with impure minds come out in acne, you know." "That's all bull, Elma!"

While candidly dealing with the boy's encounter with puberty, the film deviates from the novel on two important sexual matters. In the Larry McMurtry novel (*Horsemen Pass By*), Lon actually loses his virginity. At the conclusion of the film he is still a virgin. Additionally, in the book the character of Elma is Halmea and she is black. Hud actually rapes her in the novel (he attempts to in the film) but the film changed the character, rejecting in the process the suggestion that a white man would want to have sexual relations with a black woman. Finally and perhaps most understandably, *Hud* ignores the reference to bestiality present in the book, wherein McMurtry writes, "Half the boys in the town had had a wild soiree with a blind heifer."[7]

Lon's relationship with Elma, like Clinton's feelings for Echo, is more puppy love than anything serious. Although both boys physically desire the women, they are both mature enough to realize that the question of age makes it impossible. The women function as mothers, older sisters, and distant love objects to them. They are women who can be admired and worshipped; the boys can be close to them without any feelings of threat in either direction. Lon's feelings for the woman are quite obvious. "You're really beautiful, you're one of the best people that ever was. You're good to me, Elma, in fact you're good, period."

As Berry-Berry's treatment of Echo led his brother to reject him as a role model for masculinity, so Hud's behavior with Elma alienates Lon. When Hud drunkenly attempts to rape her, Lon comes to the woman's defense. Hud accuses him of wanting to do it himself but the boy knows the difference. "Yeah, I've been wanting to do it, but not mean like you." When Elma leaves and his grandfather dies, Lon knows that life with Hud is impossible. While Hud "can get more woman company than anyone around," the encounters are all meaningless. Lon has grown from a kid attracted to the lifestyle and the women and the booze to a young man who can see through it all. Hud is a thoroughly disreputable character and one who must be rejected. The danger for Lon, as his grandfather saw, was that he might succumb to the image and embrace the nihilistic ideology. His grandfather, talking to Hud, had told him, "You've got all the charm going for you and it makes the youngsters want to be like you and that's the shame of it, because you don't value nothin', you don't respect nothin'. You keep no restraints on your appetites at all ... you live just for yourself and that makes you not fit to live with."

Initially attracted by the potency and sexual prowess of the god-figure Hud, Lon comes to discover that his lifestyle is devoid of warmth, compassion, understanding, and love. At the film's conclusion the boy packs his bags and turns his back on his uncle, his Cadillac, and the beer with which he blots out his feelings. Rejecting the overtly masculine life-style of Hud, he replaces it negativism with an optimism and faith in the future and himself. Hollywood had moved its adolescents from the question of sex to gender, from the issue of simply having sex to the question of what it meant to be sexual.

13. What a Difference a Gay Made

"Why isn't he a regular fella?"—Father speaking of his son in *Tea and Sympathy*, 1956.

In turning his back on Hud, Lon liberated himself from long-cherished notions of manhood. Like Jim Stark he was concerned with what it meant to be a man. If he had not yet discovered the answer to Dean's impassioned plea, he at least had seen enough to know what he did not want to be. This preoccupation with masculinity played an important role in the screen's depiction not only of heterosexuality, but also of homosexuality. Sal Mineo was killed off at the end of *Rebel Without a Cause* because his needs were suspect. Ostensibly he asked no more than Jim Stark. Both boys desperately needed fathers, positive symbols of masculinity and manhood on whom they could model themselves. Jim was salvaged through the intervention of the juvenile officer, the miraculous personality change of his father, and his relationship with Judy. Plato had no one to turn to for help but Jim. While he plainly admitted he wanted him to be his father, there is a lingering suspicion that on an unconscious level at least, Plato looks to Jim for that speical friendship which the American cinema has always had trouble acknowledging.

The year after Dean's death, MGM brought to the screen *Tea and Sympathy*, the story of seventeen-year-old boy whose behavior and mannerisms raised suspicions about his sexuality. Based on the controversial stage play by Robert Anderson, the story concerned Tom Lee (John Kerr), a loner and misfit in an east coast college, and Laura Reynolds (Deborah Kerr), the wife of a college coach who sees the boy through troubled times. Isolated at the school, the boy feels most comfortable in the presence of faculty wives, particularly Laura. While the coach and most of the young men are at the beach training and involved in overtly masculine pursuits, Tom prefers to remain behind with Laura in the garden. He tells her of his unhappy childhood and his belief that he was born to try and keep his parents together. When that failed, he was bounced from summer camp to boarding school, seldom spending time with either parent. Like Plato he has

Tea and Sympathy (1956): **The sexual suspect ostracized in the era that demanded conformity.**

been deprived of the presence of a father figure for most of his life. The result, the film suggests, is that he is not quite sure how men act. While he eschews sports in general, he plays tennis very well. Unfortunately he does not play like the other young men. "Why doesn't he hit the ball like a man?" they complain.

When the boy's father visits the college to watch his son play tennis, he is dismayed and embarrassed by the silent antagonism of the gallery and deserts the boy for the baseball diamond. In the locker room he later hears students refer to his son's match as a "mixed singles final" and in alarm asks the coach, "Why isn't he a regular fella?" Coming to the boy's defense, Laura tries to explain the pain and pressures of adolescence. "It's a heartbreaking time. They're no longer a boy and not yet a man, wondering what's going to be expected of them as men and how they'll measure up."

His father insists that the boy stand up to the other students. "You're going to have to show them." That means that Tom must give up his own interests and become like the others. His father forces him to give up his role in the school play and badgers him to give up the dance and go mountain climbing. There is an ironic twist to the father's demands, for in trying to prove that his son is a healthy, red-blooded heterosexual, he removes him from the mixed company of a dance and seeks to cast him into the all masculine world of Bill Reynolds and his jocks.

The viciousness of adolescence and the terrifying pressures produced by the demand to conform surface at the traditional bonfire held each year after the first victory over Hanover. Each year, ritual has it, the freshmen are brought out to the bonfire in their pajamas while the other students attempt to tear them off. For Laura it is a degrading spectacle, but her husband assures her, "No one ever gets hurt in this thing." While the other boys are dragged into the fracas, Tom is encircled, protected and ostracized. Once again he is forced to face the public proclamation of his difference. When things finally erupt and it appears that the boy will be hurt, Laura calls out in his defense and thus intrudes upon the masculine ritual and rite of passage.

Tom's ostracism is broken by his roommate Al (Darryl Hickman), but he quickly finds retribution in the form of his own father who demands that he get a new roommate. Tom's difference and his refusal to be the same as others disturbs Al, who looks to Laura Reynolds for advice. "Why doesn't he talk about the things the other fellers do? Why does he walk so ... so...? He's never had a girl up for any of the dances." Laura, however, will not let gossip and innuendo dissuade her from Tom's defense. It's very easy to smear someone, she tells Al, explaining how manly vistas can be changed into suspicious characteristics.

Afraid of losing his chance to be captain of the ball team, Al nonetheless attempts to help Tom. He suggests a crew cut and a more masculine way of walking. While Tom is grateful, Al's comments make him more self-conscious than ever. "The terrible thing is I find myself self-conscious about things I've been doing for years." As a last resort, Al tells Tom to visit Ellie Martin, the easiest girl in town. Such an encounter, he assures him, is bound to help his reputation. The other boys all do it, no one ever gets caught, and on Sunday mornings, Ellie "tells and tells and tells." When Tom confesses to never having been with a girl before, Al admits that he too is a virgin. Angered, Tom demands to know why it isn't necessary for him to visit the girl, but he answers his own question, for he knows that "you don't have to prove it."

Goaded by the suspicions of a father who insists that he has to "learn to run with the rest of the horses," and the homosexual accusations leveled at him by the students, Tom determines to visit Ellie in an attempt to prove his manhood. Laura overhears his phone call to the girl and as he prepares to leave, she invites him inside. The boy has had some whiskey to fortify his courage, but at the same time it has also rendered him more susceptible to Laura's comfort. Tomorrow will be his eighteenth birthday, he tells her. In Tom Lee, Laura sees something of her first husband. "He was kind and gentle and lonely." He was killed in the war being conspicuously brave. "In trying to be a man," she tells Tom, "he died a boy."

Each time Tom rises to leave, the woman engages him further in conversation as they reminisce over their lives. But while Tom likes her, he will not tolerate having her sorry for him. "Why are you so kind to me?" he demands. "Is it because no one else likes me? Is it just pity?" Finally convinced of her care and concern, he yields to the fear and frustration welling up within him and gives way to tears. "There's so much I don't understand." Holding the boy close to her, Laura unwittingly encourages him to respond. Given that she had earlier told her husband, "We so rarely touch any more," her closeness to Tom fulfills not only his need but hers, while at the same time raising questions about her husband's own masculinity. Tom attempts to kiss her and when she prevents it, he flees from her, confused and hurt.

Tom's encounter with Ellie is a nightmare. Shy and sensitive, he is incapable of communicating with her. She for her part senses that he is a misfit and a loner. Racking her mind, she struggles to remember what the other students call him. When at last she does remember, the words "sister boy" set him off in a rage and he grabs a knife in a frantic effort to kill himself. When first word reaches the campus, nothing is known of his suicide attempt. All that is known is that the police came to Ellie's place and Tom was with her. A smug and self-satisfied father tells Laura, "A boy can't keep in bounds all of his life." For Laura, it is outrageous that such an event should, for the first time in his son's life, inspire pride in his father. As Mr. Lee sees it, the incident is "one of the calculated risks of being a man ... just another amusing smoking-car story."

Mr. Lee's moment of pride is rapidly deflated when he learns the truth. What strikes him most is not that his tormented son has been nearly driven to suicide, but that he has failed to prove his manhood. For Laura, Tom's desperate plight proves a breaking point. She turns angrily on her husband: "Manliness is not all swagger and swearing and mountain climbing." In looking at Tom she discovers the love she had known with her first husband and knows her marriage for the half-love it is. "Why won't you let me love you?" she demands of him, confessing that she wished Tom had proven his manhood with her.

When she finds a note in Tom's room, she fears the boy may make another attempt on his life. Searching for him, she discovers him in a secluded wood. Ashamed, he tells her, "Kissing me last night must have made you sick." Although Laura tries to assure him that one day he'll meet a girl and things will work out, his encounter with Ellie haunts him. "Do you think after last night I could ever...." The woman rises to leave. She pauses, turns, looks down at where he is lying and moves toward him, holding out her hand. He raises his hand to her. Gently she holds his face in her hand. "Years from now, when you talk of this, and you will," she tells him, "think kindly of me." In giving herself to Tom, Laura grants him manhood by functioning as both mother and lover.

Had the film ended on such a note, it would have been truer to the original, and a more authentic and honest statement. A prologue was added, however, in which Tom, now an adult, returns to the school and encounters Bill Reynolds. Laura has left him, but she has written a letter for Tom, a letter that tells him the book he has written is not altogether accurate. "You have romanticized the wrong we did and not seen it clearly."

Like *Rebel Without a Cause, Tea and Sympathy* is forced to a false closure. That the screen necessitated a new treatment of the original theme is made clear by Murray Schumach in *The Face on the Cutting Room Floor*:

> In the play, the heroine makes it clear to her husband that their marriage is finished. At the climax of the play she is about to sleep with the youth, Tom, to prove to him that he must not consider himself homosexual because he was unable to have intercourse with a whore. But in the movie, her adultery with the youth had to be the cause of her marriage breakup.[1]

Deborah Kerr, commenting on the changes necessitated by the transfer from stage to screen, said:

> They should have waited a few years to make the film. They had to obscure the idea that Tom Lee was homosexual by making the basis of gossip about him the fact that he was somewhat effeminate. Now that homosexuality is a topic of conversation, the film could be made more honestly. It was not, afer all, about homosexuality so much as it was about prejudice and gossip in a small college town.[2]

Kerr was right. In a sense it didn't matter whether Tom Lee was homosexual or not; the suspicion was enough. It is hardly surprising that

Five Finger Exercise (1962): Rosalind Russell as the smothering mother who suffocates her son's sexuality.

Tom became a victim of rumor and innuendo in a period so dominated by McCarthyism and in an industry that had betrayed its own during the HUAC investigations. It would, however, be misleading to dismiss the suggestion that the film dealt with homosexuality. Whether it existed or not, the real point was that the boy came to doubt himself, doubt himself so deeply that in the end he wanted to die. His vulnerability in the area of his sexuality, rather than being a new image on the screen, is directly related to Jim Stark's search for self, and to the new notions of masculinity that he, Brando, and others had helped to create.

More importantly, his pain and predicament grows directly out of the film industry's traditional depiction of adolescence. The product of a fractured family and an unsupportive school system, Tom Lee is abandoned to the pressure and dictates of the peer group where so many screen adolescents found themselves. Sexuality happened to be his Achilles heel; the causes, however, were the traditional villains. These villains were equally evident in the adult cinema, where homosexuality was ushered in through the same back door.

Unable to confront the issue head on, Hollywood skirted the issue with vague dialogue or by continuing to kill off characters. Mineo's death at the end of *Rebel Without a Cause* became Hollywood's standard response to homosexual characters. *Cat on a Hot Tin Roof* (1958) finds Paul Newman agonizing over the death of his buddy Skipper, who leapt from a hotel window under sexually suspicious circumstances. *Suddenly Last Summer*, made in the following year, has Sebastian Venables cannibalized for his abnormal sexual appetites. *Advise and Consent* (1962) sent Senator Don Murray along the road to suicide following a scandal about his homosexual past. *The Best Man* (1964) featured Shelley Berman as a weak, cowering, and nerve-wracked homosexual.

Given the inability of Hollywood to maturely depict adult homosexuality, it is hardly any wonder that the topic was so stifled in the cinema of adolescence. In 1962 Columbia released *The Five Finger Exercise*. The screenplay was written by Frances Goodrich and Albert Hackett, who had won the Pulitzer Prize for *The Diary of Anne Frank*. The story concerns the Harrington family and how son Philip (Richard Beymer) is torn between his mother (Rosalind Rusell) and his father (Jack Hawkins). "We're not a family," the boy declares, "we're a tribe of cannibals.... We eat people!" Clearly a product of the early sixties, Philip's character is a continuation of Norman Bates, Berry-Berry, Clinton, and the other young men struggling to break free from the suffocating embrace of their mothers.

He is also an extension of the troubled teens of the fifties. When his father says he does not understand him and wonders what he's going to do with his life, the boy answers in familiar phrases: "Did it ever occur to you that I don't understand you? You think of me as a child, as some kind of extension of yourself, but I'm me, Dad, myself. What am I gonna do? What am I gonna be? I'm gonna be me, Dad!" While Dean had asked "Who am I?" Beymer seems to have discovered himself and established an identity. Rejecting the pseudo-intellectualism of his mother and the philistine manners of his father, he appears to have arrived at an identity with which he is comfortable.

But his independence is merely an illusion. He remains drunk throughout much of the film, twisted and tormented by a side of his nature that can never be fully revealed. His homosexuality is hinted at and buried in obscure dialogue. He likes his best friend, he tells his father, because "he understand birds, he loves Ella Fitzgerald, and he makes the best shrimp curry in the world." While such lines may not be conclusive evidence of Philip's homosexuality, production notes from the film clearly demonstrate that the character was homosexual and that pressures forced the producers to obscure that aspect of the boy's personality. In the early stages of script preparation, correspondence between Geoffrey Shurlock and Samuel Briskin at Columbia Pictures pinpointed such objections. A letter dated 8 November 1969 contains the following passage:

> While this basic story seems acceptable under the provisions of the Production Code, the present version contains one element which would be unacceptable, so that a picture based on it could not be issued a Code Certificate. We refer to the inference of homosexuality which occurs on

pages 129 and 130. At this point it appears quite clear that the mother is
telling her son Philip that he is jealous of her because he has an affection
for Walter. As you know, the Code forbids homosexuality or any in-
ference of it. It seems that Philip's problem could quite easily be changed
so as to avoid the suggestion that he suffers from a distorted and unnatural sex drive.[3]

In contrast to the conservative approach of the American film industry, British filmmakers tackled homosexuality with a much more honest
approach. *A Taste of Honey* (1962) introduced audiences to Geoff, whose
homosexuality was openly acknowledged even if it was presented in cliched
terms which reduced him to the effeminate and harmless level of house-
wife.

Reach for Glory (1963) dealt with early adolescents and examined peer
pressure and sexual hostility in wartime England. *The Leather Boys* (1966)
starred Colin Campbell, Rita Tushingham, and Dudley Sutton in a curious
ménage à trois. *If* (1969) accepted homosexuality in a boy's school as a
natural part of adolescence.

While all of these films dealt with early and late adolescents, it would
be more than ten years before such concerns could find their way to American screens. In 1972 Scott Jacoby starred as the teenage son of Hal Hol-
brook in *That Certain Summer*, a story which dealt with a boy coming to
terms with his father's homosexuality. A sensitive and moving story, it
remained one of the few to deal with adolescence. *The Fox, Staircase, The
Killing of Sister George, Norman Is That You*, and *Boys in the Band*, while
representing a franker depiction of homosexuality, still tended to deal with
it as something to either laugh or cry about.

Ode to Billy Joe, made in 1976, while dealing well with adolescent
heterosexuality, conformed to the old formula when it came to homosexuality. Robby Benson starred as the ill-fated Billy Joe. With his hormones in
full bud, the boy agonizes with his unfulfilled sex drive while girlfriend
Bobbie Lee struggles to reconcile her body's needs with her social training.
When Billy Joe gets drunk at the county fair he becomes involved in a
homosexual encounter. Distraught, he confesses to the girl that it was "a sin
against nature ... a sin against God." Although the girl is sympathetic and
understanding, filmmakers were no more able to deal with the subject than
they had been a decade before. Billy Joe commits suicide by drowning himself. *Fame* (1980) introduced a homosexual character that the film treated
sympathetically, mainly by implying that he was doomed to a loveless life of
unhappiness.

In the same year *Happy Birthday Gemini* took a quantum leap
forward in Hollywood's treatment of adolescent homosexuality. Twenty-
year-old Francis (Alan Roxenberg) is plagued by self-doubts about his own
sexuality. His father (Robert Viharo), a charming lady's man alwyas on the
make, responds to his son and his problem in a way that we may not have

Ode to Billy Joe: **One drunken encounter was still enough for Hollywood to condemn its adolescent star to death.**

expected. As the boy attempts to unburden himself of his doubts, his father tells him, "It doesn't matter. It doesn't matter what you are and what you aren't or what you think you might be." The important thing, he tells the boy, is to face it and find out and then be man enough to be himself. "No matter what, I love you. I got to, you're the best thing I've ever done, you know," he exclaims effusively. It represented a dramatic moment in the American cinema, one which clearly fused together the issues of sexuality and family life. Rather than squelching his child or wanting him to be a mirror image, a chip off the old block, as had been demanded by many film fathers, Viharo's character and his response to his son opens the way for the boy to assume adulthood on his own terms.

In the past the spectre of homosexuality had always been enough to condemn characters to death or despair. The absence of supportive friends and family had clearly contributed to this. Thus in *Rebel Without a Cause*, *Tea and Sympathy*, *Ode to Billy Joe*, *Fame* and others, the sexually suspect were abandoned by parents and peers alike. Those who did not die seemed doomed to a life of emptiness. *Happy Birthday Gemini* not only allowed Francis to live, but it permitted him the prospect of a happy and whole future. The role of his father in this was crucial. "Without the father," said director Richard Benner, "the son would probably have killed himself".[4] The survival of the son and his father's support represented a startling new attitude in Hollywood's response to adolescent homosexuality.

In part, this attitude was a response to a more tolerant mood in society toward homosexuality. In part it was also a reflection of changing attitudes in society to men's and women's roles and behavior. These changes had manifested themselves in films such as *Norma Rae*, *An Unmarried Woman*, *Alice Doesn't Live Here Anymore*, *Blood Brothers* and others. Such films had done a great deal to re-define traditional sex roles and family relationships. For years Hollywood had relentlessly articulated a mystique of manhood which set standards that few could live up to. Whether on the battlefield or in the bedroom, the film industry depicted behavior and values, which, while often admirable, were beyond the reach of many who made up the movie audience.

The death of John Wayne symbolized the passing of the last great bastion of movie machismo. In the late 1970's and early 1980's Hollywood began to re-examine its notion of sexuality. In the first few months of 1982, American film audiences were confronted with a series of films that gave dramatic evidence of this new version of sexuality. In particular, *Making Love*, *Victor Victoria*, *Partners* and *Personal Best* presented more liberal and tolerant images of homosexuality. Perhaps nowhere was the social and cinematic change of attitude more evident than in *Death Trap*. In the 1960's Michael Cain had played *Alfie*, a cocksman par excellence. In the 1970's, Christopher Reeve starred as *Superman*. In *Death Trap* when these two lovers kissed, film audiences were confronted with a startling new indication of the increased tolerance the industry had towards homosexuality.

On the night of Monday, April 11, 1983, the Academy Award ceremony provided further evidence of the pervasiveness of the trend. Among the nominations were *Victor Victoria*, *The World According to Garp* and the astonishingly successful *Tootsie*, all of which had helped to change the notions we had long held about masculinity and feminity.

Almost thirty years had elapsed since James Dean had asked what to do when you have to be a man. Social and cinematic taboos regarding homosexuality, coupled with Hollywood's traditional macho stance had denied him an answer for too long. *Happy Birthday Gemini* and these new films at last responded: "Be yourself," Francis is told by his father, "Be yourself."

14. Daring to Do It

*"You a virgin?" "Yes I am." "Too bad." "I
don't want to be, though." "I don't blame you.
Come back and see me when you're not"*—
(Conversation between girl and boy in *The
Last Picture Show*, 1971)

The growing maturity of the industry as evidenced by its more sophisticated interpretation of homosexuality was equally in evidence in its
depiction of heterosexual relationships. *Splendor in the Grass* and *Hud*
were early signposts on the road to his new maturity. Throughout the sixties
major developments in both society and the film industry contributed to a
franker and more honest interpretation of adolescent sexuality. The introduction of the pill had a major effect on American attitudes toward sex and
upon sexual behavior. There is little doubt that the decade of the sixties saw
fundamental changes in the way in which Americans regarded sex. In 1968
Smigel and Seiden, in "The Decline and Fall of the Double Standard,"[1]
reported that the sixties had been transitional in terms of sexual attitudes.
Such a view was confirmed in 1970 by Bell and Chasker,[2] who saw the
double standard being replaced by permissiveness with less affection.

The Graduate (1967), *The Sterile Cuckoo* (1969), *Me Natalie* (1969),
and *The Heart Is a Lonely Hunter* (1968) among others, reflected these
changing attitudes. Teenage characters were no longer confined to monog-
amous relationships that led automatically to the altar. This more adult
approach to the subject of adolescent sexuality resulted not only from
changes in society but from developments within the film industry. In-
fluential figures inside the industry campaigned for more freedom and
maturity in filmmaking. Joseph E. Levine declared that "the things that
make money are sex, violence, and action."[3] In the mid-sixties Jack Valenti,
the new president of the MPAA, designed a new rating code which introduced a "suggested-for-mature-audiences" classification. In constructing the
code, Valenti said he wanted to "keep in closer harmony with the mores, the
culture, the moral sense and expectations of our society."[4]

The British cinema, with their franker and more realistic depiction of

246

sex, may also have contributed to Hollywood's new response. *Saturday Night and Sunday Morning, A Taste of Honey, The Loneliness of the Long Distance Runner*, and *The Leather Boys* all dealt with sex in a much more realistic manner than Hollywood. When *Tom Jones* won the Academy Award for best picture in 1963 the American film industry came a long way to comprehending how sex could be dealt with in an adult manner. There is little doubt that there was a spillover effect between the liberalization of the adult cinema and the depiction of adolescence. Franco Zeffirelli brought *Romeo and Juliet* to the screen and provided a cultural cover for nude scenes featuring strikingly beautiful adolescents. Having introduced the bare-bottomed Leonard Whiting as Romeo, it was possible to extend the image. Advertising for his next film read, "Leonard Whiting — from Romeo to Cassanova. Youth and adolescence — splendor, libertinism, and permissiveness of eighteenth century Venice."

The sixties also saw an explosion in the record industry, buoyed by the expansion in the teenage population. Less subject to the rigid controls imposed upon the film industry, rock music often dealt with sex in a frank and startlingly honest manner. Songs such as "Satisfaction," "Let's Spend the Night Together," "Give It to Me," and "I Can't Control Myself" clearly reflected changing attitudes among the young. Such attitudes inevitably found their way to the screen where the long-acknowledged relationship between rock and sex was given visual expression. Films such as *Blowup* and *Here We Go Round the Mulberry Bush* were quick to link the two aspects together.

But the changes in film were neither sudden nor continuous. In 1960 *Where the Boys Are* still reflected the double standard and the notion of good and bad girls. "Some girls were innocent, some wise. They were kissed, caressed, double dated and double crossed. It was fun, fun, fun, but just so easy to go one step too far." The adolescents of the early sixties appear more sex wise than their parents. "Now Dad, don't give me any of that malarkey about cold showers and things," a boy complains in *Because They're Young. Take Her She's Mine* (1963) found James Stewart as the hapless father of two teenage daughters whose burgeoning sexuality clearly intimidates him. *With Six You Get Egg Roll* (1968) found a teenage daughter who reversed roles with her father, demanding, "Are you having an affair?" "Dad, I'm not a baby anymore. I understand about sex. I've known about it for years." On the other side of the Atlantic the same message was repeated loud and clear. *Prudence and the Pill* found Geraldine announcing, "Mother, I'm not a child. I take my precautions." Even Tammy (*Tammy Tell Me True*; 1961) is capable of declaring, "I ain't a child! I'm a woman fully growed. I know about livin' and I know about dyin' and I know about begettin' and bein' in love." Films such as *Susan Slade* (1961) *Parrish* (1961), *Too Young to Love* (1961), and *Claudelle Inglish* (1961) all reflected changing attitudes in the industry's response to the young.

With it inevitably came opposition. In 1962 Arthur Mayer observed in the *Saturday Review* that "today any teenager who attends movies has supped well on the abnormal,"[5] and *Readers Digest* had asked the previous year, "How to Stop the Sickening Exploitation of Sex?" But despite these concerns, changes on the screen represented a growth process even if exploitation went hand in hand with it.

Screen females were liberated and permitted to be both knowledgeable and sexual rather than simply passively submitting to handsome leading men as they had done in the fifties. Troy Donahue had epitomized the screen male of the late fifties and early sixties. Handsome and virile, his good looks, muscular body, and sensitivity proved too much to resist for girls like Sandra Dee. By the early sixties, Donahue's relationship with female adolescents was being re-defined. In *Parrish*, while he is still virile, he is less experienced than Connie Stevens. The Sandra Dee image of the good girl who surrenders to the right boy was being replaced with an image of a young woman who existed as an independent sexual being, capable of enjoying sex without necessarily wanting to fall in love or get married.

In altering the image of the screen female, Hollywood re-defined its notion of the adolescent male. While good looks and virility were still dominant traits, sexual vulnerability and uncertainty surfaced as features of the teenaged male's path to manhood. *You're a Big Boy Now* (1966) touched on the subject of impotency and dealt with sexual initiation as neither conquest nor consummation but as humiliating failure. *The Graduate* and *The Sterile Cuckoo* repeated images of young males intimidated by the overt sexuality of the women in their lives.

The sixties in both cinema and society represented a questioning of traditional values and an experimentation with new ideas and behaviors. 1966 found Daisy Clover rejecting love outright. Who needs it, she asks. While she may not have been in step with the love generation and the hippie movement that flowered in San Francisco the following summer, she was significantly different from the fifties females who seemed to live for love. *Winning* (1969) found sixteen-year-old Charlie asking his stepfather, "What do people get married for?" In terms of specific sexual acts and attitudes, the sixties also represented a growth process. *Up the Down Staircase* depicted an "erotic teenager" who attempts suicide when a teacher fails to reciprocate her affection. *Wild in the Streets* featured a fifteen-year-old bisexual wondering if he could "make it" with a United States senator.

Yet despite this the decade abounded with indications of a more conservative nature. *Looking for Love* (1964) found Connie Francis proclaiming, "Now I can concentrate on my big ambition in life, to get married and have babies. I'm selling myself as a wife and potential mother." *Billie* (1965) starred Patty Duke as a high school student who wanted to compete on the boy's track team. Seemingly an image of a new and more independent female, the character is returned to the traditional fold and becomes a gushing female the first time a boy holds her hand. The year 1965 found Rick

Nelson in *Love and Kisses*. On the surface the film seemed aware of the nature of adolescence. "Those children are groping for an identity ... they're seeking refuge from anxiety." But when it comes to the matter of sex, the film retreats to the early fifties with Rick and his new bride revealing themselves as virgins.

The movement toward a more mature and realistic depiction of adolescent sexuality was slow. While films often appeared different, many remained different in style but not substance. Progress was often accompanied by a clinging to the past. *The Graduate*, for one example, despite the startling nature of its subject matter, was no further advanced in its resolution then *Blue Denim*. Both films ended with the young lovers being carried along who knows where on public transportation, ETA unknown. The failure to consider the post-coital situation remained as real in the American cinema of the sixties as it had been in the fifties. Only the British seemed capable of addressing the problem, and films such as *The Leather Boys* and *The Family Way* both attempted to explain events after love steps in and takes you for a fling. Hollywood for its part still found it difficult to deal with adolescents as whole people. Although screenagers were now permitted to acknowledge and employ their genitalia, such acts often did little to further our understanding of the characters. As Pauline Kael noted, "so now Andy Hardy fornicates, but he still isn't a person."[7]

The sixties were almost over before this imbalance was seriously addressed. *Last Summer* was based on the novel by Evan Hunter. While exploring sex as its central theme, the movie also did much to counter the media hype that persisted in categorizing and classifying adolescence. Assessing the film, Judith Crist commented that it

> certainly painted the most realistic portrait of upper-middle-class fifteen-and sixteen-year-olds to have come to the screen; in addition, they have made a scathing commentary on what lies beneath the youth and beauty that are our contemporary fetishes."[8]

While spending their summer on New York's Fire Island, Peter (Richard Thomas) and Dan (Bruce Davison) meet Sandy (Barbara Hershey), a young girl about their own age who has found an injured seagull on the beach. In removing a fish hook from the bird's beak, the youngsters form a communal bond and establish a friendship. Beer serves as truth serum, a potion that forces one to reveal his middle name. As they open more to each other, they play "major truth" and cautiously reveal more and more of themselves. Dan tells them his mother has a boyfriend and Sandy asks curiously, "Were they doing it?" Wishing to show her maturity, she offers to take the top of her swimsuit off. "I mean, after all, we're not kids." But if they are not kids, equally they are not yet adults. As Roger Ebert noted in the *Chicago Sun Times*, "They are not men and yet must be concerned with manhood."[9] The boys are embarrassed but by the

Last Summer: **Shattered the cliche of the love-generation and presented a frightening image of peer pressure and the ugle side of adolescent sexuality.**

same token intrigued. When she removes her top it serves as a further bond to seal their friendship. "You know, we're really got to be like this all the time."

Yet what appears to be freedom and liberation proves to be deceptive. Although Sandy has saved the bird, rather than freeing it she creates a harness for it and dominates it. The bird, removed from it natural environment, is traumatized and cannot fly. The girl, in restraining it, emulates her mother's treatment of her father. "She says she's going to make my father pay until he dies."

One afternoon they are joined on the beach by Rhoda (Cathy Burns), a plain and plump fifteen-year-old. Critical of their treatment of the bird, she nonetheless wishes to become friends with them and reaches out tentatively. Her opportunity for securing the relationship come when Sandy kills the bird. Although Rhoda is physically the odd one out, it becomes evident that being overweight does not mean that she is without inner beauty. Peter, disenchanted with Sandy as anything more than a body, begins to shift his attention to Rhoda. He teaches her to swim and wonders aloud what it would be like to kiss a girl with braces. "I don't think you'd hurt yourself," she assures him.

Sandy meanwhile has arranged a computer date with a Puerto Rican. She convinces Peter and Dan to come along and the three of them take Rhoda to the mainland where they set her up with a date while they proceed to get drunk. The man is attacked by thugs and the youngsters flee. Once again the vicious and callous side of their natures has surfaced. "You know we didn't mean any harm, we just wanted to have a little bit of fun," Peter tells an outraged Rhoda. "You three treat people like they were made of plastic," she berates them. While Rhoda is not like them, at the same time she wants to be part of them. To that extent she is caught in the pressure of the peer group. Neither Peter nor Dan approved of Sandy's treatment of the bird, yet they could not break from her. Nor can Rhoda sever her connection to them, particularly to Peter. A perpetual outsider, she functions always on the periphery of the clique.

When she interrupts a picnic the other three are having, Sandy is irritated by the intrusion and challenges her. Removing her bikini top, she dares Rhoda to do the same. "What's wrong, Rhoda, you look as though you're going to choke." When the girl tries to leave, Sandy goads the boys into restraining her. Frightened, she appeals to Peter for help, but rather than aiding her he joins Sandy in holding her down while Dan rapes her. She has become like the gull and the Puerto Rican, a plaything to be toyed with and tormented. The wooded glade on the island serves as a form of Eden; their act becomes that of expulsion from their island paradise. Like the youngsters in *Lord of the Flies*, these young people find themselves reduced to herd instincts and savagery on an island. "Share and share alike," as they put it, comes to function as the group dynamics of savagery. Their island serves as a symbol of modern society. The absence of their parents and the scorn they feel for them establish them as youngsters with no adult role models to follow.

The strength of *Last Summer* was not simply that it offered an alternative, albeit a frightening one, to the image of the love generation, but that it rejected the cliche of the generation gap and presented an image of youth confronted by an enemy within. In the hostility and aggression that accompanies the adolescent peer group's awesome insistence upon conformity, sex is reduced to just another weapon in the arsenal. Until *Last Summer*, Hollywood had dealt with adolescent sex by ignoring it or by permitting it and then punishing it with pregnancy. The implications and aftermaths of the encounters were seldom considered. Love seemingly conquered all. In removing sex from its idyllic plateau, *Last Summer* located it in a much more realistic plain. Erikson has noted that for young people sex is often far from idyllic:

> Much of sexual life is of the self-seeking, identity-hungry kind; each partner is really trying only to reach himself. Or it remains a kind of genital combat in which each tries to defeat the other."[10]

Last Summer also made some tentative advances toward breaking other stereotypes. In finding himself attracted to Rhoda, Peter not only acknowledges inner beauty but turns his back on traditional notions of beauty as represented by Sandy. In depicting these clean-cut, middle-class kids as capable of a violent act such as rape, the film also moved away from traditional images of violence and aggression as acts of only working-class delinquents.

If *Last Summer* provided a new, more dramatic and adult version of adolescence, it was a view that only adults were permitted. The classification the film received severely limited its exposure. Commenting on that point, *Christian Century* complained,

> The best film I have ever seen about mid-adolescence could not be viewed by youngsters whose life and problems are portrayed ... it is ironical to say the least that the same young people who are acutely conscious of their own sexuality and are expected to meet rather mature academic standards by their high schools are banned from the very films which are today's morality plays. These late adolescents are being taught not to distinguish between art and exploitation films — are being taught that sexuality is dirty (and all the more attractive therefore), that the inanity of G and GP films and TV programs is more normal than sex. So they are forced to seek understanding of their own bursting sexuality in locker rooms, from leering sophisticates, or the always available pornography."[11]

Two years later Hollywood produced an even bleaker vision of sexuality in both an adolescent and adult context. *The Last Picture Show* was directed by Peter Bogdanovich and based on the novel by Larry Mc-Murtry (*Hud*). Set in the small Texas town of Anarene in the early 1950's, it traces the late adolescence of Sonny Crawford (Timothy Bottoms) and his best friend Duane Jackson (Jeff Bridges). Outside of school, where they participate in the spectacularly unsuccessful football team, most of the boys' time is spent at the pool hall, cafe, and movie house, owned by Sam the Lion (Ben Johnson) who serves as a sort of father figure for the boys.

On Saturday night at the movie house Sonny sits in the back row with his girlfriend, Charlene Duggs (Sharon Taggart). On the screen, *Father of the Bride* is screening and the contrast between the romantic vision of Elizabeth Taylor and Charlene is apparent. When she tells Sonny it's their first anniversary of going steady, he mumbles, "It seems a lot longer." Clearly for Sonny love is not all that it's cracked up to be. Later, as they sit necking in the pickup, the girl rather mechanically removes her bra, hanging it on the rearview mirror, and berates Sonny, "What's the matter with you, you act just plain bored." When he responds by trying to go further with her, she back off, telling him, "We'll have plenty of time for that when we're married." But Sonny isn't looking for marriage, particularly with her, and they split up.

At training one day Coach Popper asks Sonny to do him a favor and drive his wife to the doctor's office. "You know women, there's always

The Last Picture Show (1971): A brilliant story of sexuality in a small town society. It was one of many films to deal with the relationship between a young man and an older woman.

something wrong with them," and the boy, only too delighted to get out of civics class, agrees. "It beats sittin' through civics, Ma'm," he explains to Ruth Popper (Cloris Leachman). After he drives her home, the desperately lonely woman asks him in. "Wouldn't you like to come in and have a soda if you can stand me a few more minutes?" While the boy is drinking his Dr. Pepper, the woman's emotions get the better of her as she begins to cry in front of him.

Later, as he helps her put out the garbage, she tells him, "I don't think Charlene's near nice enough for you." Responding to her kindness and loneliness, the boy kisses her and when she asks if he'll drive her to the doctor's again he responds a little too eagerly, "You bet!" When Sonny next visits the Popper house, she leads him to the bedroom. Shyly they remove their underclothes beneath the bed covers. "It's all right," she assures him and the camera closes in on Sonny's face recording his tentative, uncertain exploration as they begin to make love and the bed squeaks. "How can you like me?" Ruth asks him, crying with emotion because after years of unhappiness with her husband, love has returned to her life. In a reversal of screen tradition, it is the older woman who now becomes the more enamored partner, lavishing attention on the boy. She feeds him, wall-papers her bedroom in his favorite color and buys him a wallet for a gradu-ation gift. And yet, although she lives for her relationship with the boy, she will not leave for it. "I wasn't brought up to leave a husband," she tells him.

The Last Picture Show is a wonderful film, worthy of consideration because so much of what happens in it is concerned with sex not simply as an act between two people, but as an image one tries to project. When Duanne and Sonny begin their initial sexual explorations, they are not simply fulfilling their biological needs, but are living out what is expected of them. The expectations of the town sit high with them. A loss at football means that they become the subjects for ridicule and harassment from townsfolk who expect not only competition, but victory. "You're never going to have the chance to get stomped for your high school again," Sonny is told, as though it's an honor to be driven into the ground. The movie house is not simply somewhere to see films, but like the football field serves as the site for spectator sport. In *Hud* Lon's grandfather sat with him at the movies watching the necking couples. "You'd think they'd do it in the hay-loft" he muses. But he has missed the point, for the movie house is the place where one publicly proclaims that they are making out, particularly when they are not. The beautiful image of Elizabeth Taylor as the bride contrast sharply for Sonny with that of the girl he finds himself with. Plainly he is with Charlene not because he wants to be, but because there is nothing else to do and somehow it is expected. Later when he breaks up with her, she turns on him saying, "you ain't good lookin' enough, you ain't even got a ducktail." It is not enough that a boy be a nice person. For Charlene and those like her, he must conform to an image of acceptability, an image created in no small way by the movies.

At school, a teacher tries to interest the teenagers in the poetry of John Keats' "Ode to a Nightingale," telling them," all you have to do to be immortal is to lead a good Christian life." Sonny however is much more concerned with the present than the future and finds him attention diverted by a mare and a stallion in a field outside the classroom window. Every-where it seems, sex is the emphasized goal. "What kind of female you ever goin' to get." Coach Popper berates the team, telling them they're out of shape and jack off too much.

Sex preoccupies the adults and the girls of the movie as much as it does the young male leads. A conversation between Jacy Farrow (Cybill Shepherd) and her mother (Ellen Burstyn) is a striking indication of this. Aware that her daughter is infatuated with Duanne, Loise advises her to sleep with him to get it, and him out of her system. "there's nothing magical about sex and you'll find that out. Everything gets old if you do it often enough, so if you want to find out about monotony real quick, marry Duanne." In a strange reversal of screen tradition, it is the mother who advocates sexual experimentation while the daughter believes that sex before marriage is a sin. Lois however continues the screen tradition of mothers who take the magic and joy from life for their children. "Everything is flat and empty here, there's nothin' to do" she complains. Yet if her life is a misery, she has made it so. As she tells her daughter she scared her husband into getting rich, the radio plays "A Fool Such As I", an incisive commentary upon her lifestyle. She has known love and looks upon her time with Sam the Lion as the romantic peak of her life, yet she still fills Jacy with cynicism. When the girl becomes harsh, cruel and calculating there is only one place we need to look in assigning the blame.

When Lester asks the girl to go to a party with him at Billy Sheen's, she is attracted by the prospect of mixing with the country club kids and the titillation of skinny dipping. Although she has a date with Duanne that night, the prospect of something better lures her away. In a cruel display of sexual salesmanship she uses her body to break the news to the frustrated boy. As they neck in the car outside the dance, she maneuvers his hand between her legs. The expression on the boy's face is enough to indicate that she is allowing him more than ever before. He smiles awkwardly, a sense of pleasure and surprise registering on his face, and begins to make more advances. As his passion increases he pushes her down on the seat only to have the girl sit up and leave, telling him she's going with Lester.

Later at the party, she stands alone on the diving board and strips as the other kids already naked in or beside the pool, watch her. When she dives, it is not simply into the water but into a social set that she cannot have with Duanne. Her shallow indifference to all but her whims is clearly indicated when she realizes she's still wearing the watch he gave her. Previously she had made much of the gift. Now, she glances at it casually and dismisses it without another thought. Plainly manipulative and at the same time awkward, she seeks to lose her virginity to Billy Sheen. "You a virgin?" he asks. "Yes I am." "Too bad." "I don't want to be though." "I don't blame you. Come back and see me when you're not," he tells her.

Rebuffed, she has to look elsewhere and turns once again to Duanne. She arranges a motel room for the two of them in a mercenary attempt to qualify for Billy Sheen's favor. It is Jacy, not Duanne who is in control of the situation. He is unaware that he is even being manipulated. The girl lies on the bed waiting for him, telling him to hurry up and get undressed, while he, anxious and excited, gapes at her in open mouthed awe. As if to frustrate her scheme the inexperienced Duanne is unable to make love. "Well get off me. You might fall and mash me," she tells him angrily. Outside in the parking lot of the Cactus Motel, other students have gathered for a ringside seat at the girl's deflowering. Again, sex is reduced to the level of a spectator sport. When the main event fails to get under way it is necessary for Jacy and Duanne to go through the charade of pretending to their peers that everything went according to plan. "I just can't describe it in words," Jacy tells her excited girlfriends.

Later at the graduation ceremony, while the students sing the school song, Duanne assures Jacy, "I can do it now, I know I can." Back at the motel they successfully make love and Duanne emerges, his face a picture of puffed up pride and accomplishment. "Oh quit prissing," the girl deflates him, "I don't think you did it right anyway." As her mother had predicted, for Jacy, sex holds little magic. She has used it as a process to attract Billy Sheen and she is interested in him not as a person, but as a position, a social status that she aspires to.

While we may feel sorry for Duanne, he is as capable as Jacy of committing a callous and insensitive act. On the night she went to the party at Billy Sheen's, Duanne sat outside the dance hall getting drunk with his friends. "Let's all go out and get a fuck" one of the boys suggests while another adds that he knows where there's a good heifer. None of the boys react to the suggestion as though in their rural farmbelt environment, the experience is not unknown. Rather than getting action for themselves, the boys settle for the more accessible act of getting a piece of action none of them want, for the mute boy Billy. They take the boy to Billie Sue, the monstrous town whore. Although Sonny is opposed to the idea he does little to protest it and goes along with the others. The boys put the helpless Billy in the back seat of a car with the woman and sit back to enjoy the proceedings. Billy ejaculates prematurely, angering the woman who bloodies his nose. Later when the others take Billy home to Sam the Lion, they find themselves condemned for their behavior. "Scaring a poor unfortunate kid like Billy just so you could have a few laughs; I've been around that kind of trashy behavior all my life," he tells them angrily. Though Sonny has not actively participated in the prank, he faces Sam the Lion's wrath like the others and finds himself banned from the pool hall, the cafe and the movie house. Duanne on the other hand, has hidden from Sam, unwilling to accept responsibility for his actions and to be punished for them.

Finally, Sonny himself succumbs to the behavior that surrounds him. Despite his involvement with Ruth Popper, he is lured away by younger flesh in the mistaken belief that he can have Jacy for himself. In the process it is a double act of betrayal, for he pursues the girl his best friend wants, and he deserts Ruth without explanation.

It is a cruel and thoughtless act, based on little more than physical desire. In the end he finds himself the victim of a teenage temptress who desires nothing more than to string men along for her own amusement. A pathetic pawn he is an easy dupe for the wilful girl who manipulates him into a marriage knowing full well her parents will have it annulled. Completely caught up with her own ego, Jacy proceeds through life with little regard for anyone or anything, save that she always be the center of attention in the town so that she might rival the stories of the picture show.

Sonny's weakness has left Ruth a shattered and lonely woman, more empty and insecure than she had been before he had come into her life. Like Duanne with Billy, Sonny is unable to face the consequences of his actions of his responsibility for her condition. The only thing that he can face is forced upon him when Duanne angrily confronts him about his involvement with Jacy. For the girl, it is everything that she has dreamed of; a romantic image plucked from the silver screen and come to life in Anarene. That the two friends do battle with each other and Sonny almost loses an eye, seems somehow insignificant to her.

In the end, Duanne leaves Anarene for the Korean war. Jacy is well on her way to becoming as bitter as her mother. Sonny returns to Ruth, the two of them bound together out of common misery and need, victims of a town without pity, where sex is reduced to little more than the competitive sports that obsess the town, and the act of two animals in the field.

The Last Picture Show was about much more than the coming of age of two boys, or the involvement of one with an older woman. It painted a picture of a people and their social and sexual environment. Anarene, Texas is a small town in the process of dying. The West and the cattle empire that grew with it have left it behind. When the picture show closes there is no more ribbon of dreams. The illusions are over and only an ugly reality and an empty street remain; a street that for its final act, claims another victim when a car hits and kills Billy, What kills Billy is the same senseless indifference to life that has blinded Sonny, driven Duanne away, made marriage a misery for Ruth, turned it into a cheating game for Lois Farrow and made Jacy into a cruel and self seeking young hedonist. Masquerading as masculinity the values of the townsfolk of Anarene are shallower than the two dimensional images of the silver screen that bring momentary magic to their lives.

The Last Picture Show represented a triumph for the Huds of the world. In 1963 Lon had been able to break free from his uncle's influence and establish a new life for himself. His escape reflected the more optimistic climate of the Kennedy and Camelot years. In the early seventies with the war in Vietnam dragging on interminably, and the generation gap a constant topic of the mass media, such a resolution was impossible. Lon had escaped because in Elma and in his grandfather he was afforded positive role models to follow. For Sonny, Duanne and Jacy, the townsfolk of Anarene offer little encouragement or guidance. With school and family providing little support and the death of Sam the Lion depriving them of the last vestige of decency, they are abandoned to the culture and customs of Anarene.

The film was an important one because it clearly located sex within a cultural context and attempted to demystify it. It also clearly acknowledged the role which media and movies themselves play in perpetuating romantic and sexual stereotypes. Sonny is disappointed because Charlene does not live up the screen image of romantic love. In the same year *The Summer of '42* located Hermie and his friends at a screening of *Now Voyager*, by which standards they too seek to measure their lives. On a more fundamental level, the picture show served not only to create romantic ideals but to define a notion of manhood. When John Wayne says, "Let's take 'em to Missouri!" no one doubts that he will get there. The myth of manhood he created makes the boys' failures, whether on the football field or in the bedroom, even more painful. In recognizing these fears and failures, *The Last Picture Show* moved audiences toward a more realistic image of both gender and sex.

Duanne's inability to make love to Jacy was an important step forward for Hollywood. Certainly he was not the first screen adolescent to know such failure. In *Tea and Sympathy* Tom Lee had failed, but his suspect sexuality undermined the strength of that image. In *You're a Big Boy Now* Bernard had been unable to make it, but he was weak and motherdominated which served to reduce the impact of that scene. Duanne, however, was a good-looking, hot-blooded jock. The image suggested virility. Cast in the fifties he would have proven every bit Troy Donahue's equal. By 1971, however, sterotypes were beginning to be questioned. For the first time the American screen presented an image of adolescent sexual awakening and arousal in which sexual skill and accomplishment were not assumed. For the first time adolescents were able to see reflections of themselves with doubts, fears, and failures every bit as strong as the optimism and romance that had so long characterized them. For almost the first time the sexual image that adolescents were asked to measure up to was an image that recognized vulnerability as well as potency, failure as well as success.

In the life of the adolescent, the loss of virginity is an important psychological step.

> The importance of the event does not simply lie in the physical act of sexual intercourse. The range and intensity of emotions reflect the effects on self-image which are generated by the experience."[12]

In a culture where the young are given little formal instruction of sex and led to believe that sexual skill is innate rather than acquired, adolescents are hesitant to admit either fear or failure. In such situations the peer group, rather than providing comfort, serves as an agency of contempt and condemnation. Rather than admit their uncertainty and ignorance, many adolescents put on a brave front. As a fifteen-year-old boy told a researcher,

> I don't know for sure how I felt. It was like not knowing what to do. That was the whole overtone of the thing. It wasn't a beautiful or relaxing thing, but I told everybody it was great."[13]

The Last Picture Show, despite a bleak vision of life, went a long way to filling in a gap in these kids' lives and letting them know that they weren't alone; that sexual reality often fails to measure up to cinematic dreams. The image was repeated in *Summer of '42* (1971), *The Go Between* (1971), *Pretty Maids All in a Row* (1971), *Cactus in the Snow* (1972), *Our Time* (1974), and *Corvette Summer* (1978), in which eager but gauche youngsters stumble through their initial sexual encounters.

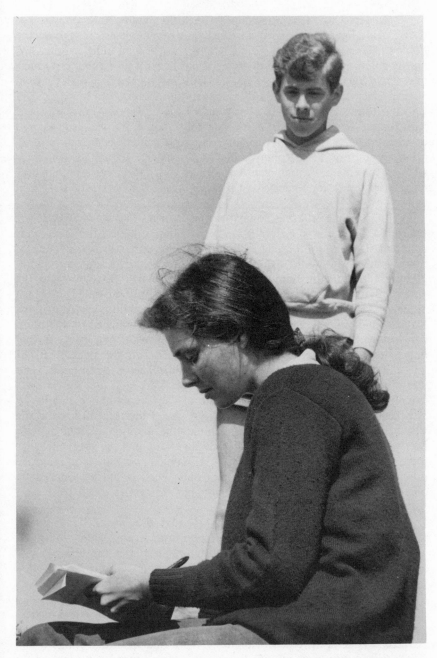

Summer of '42 (1971): A tender, touching and humorous account of three boys and their awakening sexuality, it was marred by an ambiguous advertising campaign.

In depicting the relationship between Sonny and Ruth Popper, the movie also aligned itself with an important development throughout the decade. The relationship between a young man and an older woman was hardly a new discovery for Hollywood. Tom Lee lost his virginity to Laura in *Tea and Sympathy*. In *King Creole* Elvis Presley had a fling with Carolyn Jones. Given the dictates of fifties conventions, Laura was banished and Carolyn Jones was killed. The early sixties found Richard Beymer in bed with Joanne Woodward in *The Stripper*. Miss Woodward was also required to depart, leaving the boy free to find some more suitable companion. After his encounter with Mrs. Robinson in *The Graduate*, although the woman is allowed to remain, Benjamin leaves. While these examples represent isolated cases over a long period of time, the seventies elevated the issue to a cult.

In the same year that Sonny became involved with Ruth, *Summer of '42* found Hermie involved with Dorothy. Comparing the two films, it is apparent that Hollywood had not entirely relinquished its sexual conventions. While Sonny and Ruth find each other out of a common bond, Hermie and Dorothy cannot remain together. When Dorothy takes the young boy to bed it is a beautiful moment, sensitively presented, in which audiences clearly understand her need and her vulnerability, having just lost her husband. But the maturity of that scene is not matched by the film's conclusion. Like Laura Reynolds, she abandons her young lover, leaving only a note. "I will not try to explain what happened last night because I know that in time you will find a proper way in which to remember it." But it is a little too trite and much too convenient to suggest that this impressionable boy will understand her motivation. The film assumes the ability of a fifteen-year-old boy to comprehend and understand that in leaving she was neither deserting nor punishing him. One additional problem with *Summer of '42* was the publicity which suggested that "in everyone's life there's a summer of '42." Whether the filmmakers meant that everyone experienced sexual awakening or that young boys would be seduced by older women was not clear. Impressionable youngsters could have been forgiven for believing the latter.

In England *Deep End* (1971) and *The Go-Between* (1971) also dealt with impressionable youngsters and their infatuation with older women. It was a theme taken up in popular music. In "Summer the First Time," accompanied by the sound effects of waves crashing on a beach, Bobby Goldsboro sang of the seduction of a seventeen-year-old boy by a 31-year-old woman. In "Desiré," Neil Diamond told of a similar encounter in which he became a man at the hand of a girl almost twice his age. Nor was television slow in picking up on the theme. An episode of *Family* found Buddy attracted to one of her teachers already having an affair with a student. *The White Shadow* gave an episode to an encounter between a student and a teacher, as did *Eight Is Enough*, which found Tommy in pursuit of an older woman. *Anatomy of a Seduction* was a 1979 made-for-TV movies which

Rich Kids: In the late seventies, movies depicted sexual encounters between increasingly younger teenagers.

ran the following advertisement in *TV Guide*: "She's 40 and in love again. He's twenty and her best friend's son." Back on the big screen John Travolta teamed with Lily Tomlin in *Moment by Moment*, which dealt with the relationship between a young man and an older woman. Despite the popularity of the image throughout the mass media, however, researchers have found little evidence in real life for such a theme. Schofield reported that "the proselytizing older woman in search of virgin boys is either a myth or very unsuccessful ... the number of adult females who have introduced boys to intercourse is very small."[14]

In contrast to the adolescent's involvement with the adult came the increasingly youthful depiction of sexual activity between the young. In 1979 United Artists released *Rich Kids*, the story of two youngsters barely into puberty who comfort each other in and out of bed against a backdrop of domestic discord. Jamie and Franny make love, bathe together, and deal with their sexuality as an uncomplicated and natural act. In contrast their parents seem unable to respond maturely in any relationship. "I don't understand why they have problems, being married is easy," the children comment.

Rich Kids was by no means the start of the trend. Films emerging from England and Europe early in the decade no doubt had an influence on American filmmakers. *Melody* (1971) was about a lonely eleven-year-old boy and his misunderstood schoolmate who fall in love and are harassed by

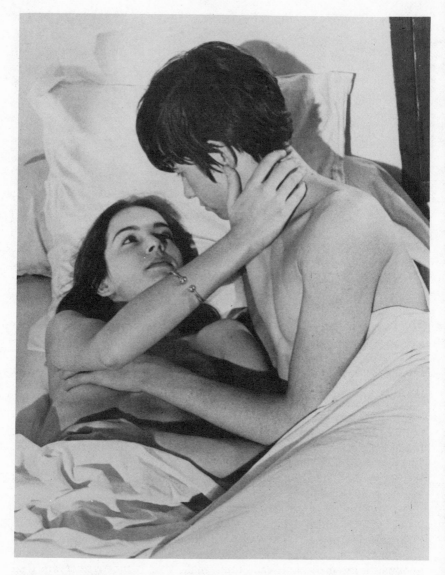

Friends (1972): **An English film, it encouraged the franker depiction of sexuality in American motion pictures.**

parents, teachers, and peers. Married by a friend in an unofficial ceremony, they flee from their parents and the adult world they represent. In 1972 Paramount introduced us to the screen's youngest lovers. Directed by Lewis Gilbert, with music by Elton John and Bernie Taupin, *Friends* was an adolescent love story full of cuteness and cliches. Aimed at the young set it lost them when it was awarded an "R" certificate due to the nudity in it. Judith Crist condemned it as "this latest entry in the youth cycle complete with the usual copout freeze frame finale in which life is a medley of love and suns rising and setting and slow motion cavorting and kissing."[15]

Fourteen-year-old Michelle LaTour (Anicee Alvina) goes to live with her cousin in Paris after the death of her father. When she feels unwanted she wanders through the local zoo where she encounters fifteen-year-old Paul Harrison, equally unhappy at the prospect of his father's impending marriage. Paul takes his father's car and they head off through the country-side until the boy drives straight into a pool. Scared to go home, the boy decides to go with Michelle to a cottage in remote Camargue owned by her late father. In this idyllic environment they make a new life for themselves and tentatively explore their feelings toward each other. The movie moves through bath scene and bed scene with a level of offensiveness that very much depends on the individual viewer. The *Chicago Times* thought it was aimed at readers of *Teenage Nudist*, while the *Los Angeles Times* said the movie was a poignant love story and a drama of teenage struggle for survival. When Michelle becomes pregnant they decide to deliver the baby themselves. At the village church they exchange marriage vows during the wedding ceremony of another couple. Paul reads up on childbirth and manages to deliver the baby successfully. The romance of their rural re-treat, however, is shortly to be lost, the bubble burst as those in the tub scene. As Paul heads off to work one morning we know what he does not, that detectives have tracked him down and are waiting for him. The story was picked up some time later in a sequel titled simply *Paul and Michelle*.

Jeremy (1973), which found success at Cannes, featured Robby Benson and Glynnis O'Connor in a Manhattan love story. A bittersweet teenage romance, it concerned the relationship between an awkward music student and his dancer girlfriend. Jeremy's home life subjects him to harass-ment, the spectacle of incompatible parents, and the constant pressure to succeed. When he meets Susan he conquers his initial awkwardness and a relationship develops between them. Feeling like half-people they discover a fullness and a wholeness in their relationship. Their off-screen sexual initia-tion is confirmed when the girl tells him, "I could still feel your lips on mine .... I could still feel you all over my body. I thought to myself, 'I'm a woman and he loves me'."

But like Jamie and Franny, the youngsters find that adults intrude upon their world. When Susan's father moves to Detroit, the relationship is terminated. What they feel can never be known to an adult; their pain and their pleasure are private things. For the girl's father, there is nothing to say but the hollow assurance, "There'll be a hundred other boys in your life before you're married." For Susan and Jeremy it is a meaningless utterance.

Alice Doesn't Live Here Anymore (1974) featured a precocious youngster of twelve who demanded of his mother, "Did you sleep with him?" A boy with "the foulest mouth of any kid his age," Tommy has his

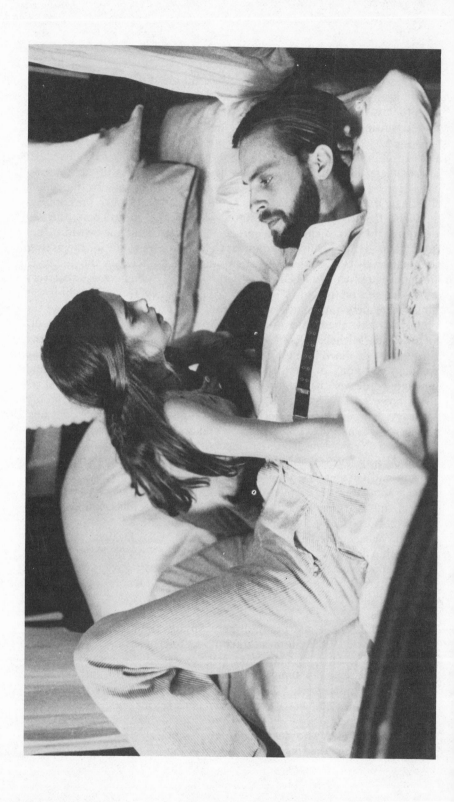

female counterpart in Audrey, who seems nonchalant about the fact that her mother is a hooker. In 1977 Brooke Shields (at age eleven) starred in *Pretty Baby*, a Louis Malle film, in which she played a child prostitute. Surprisingly enough it was not the first such image of the adolescent to come to the screen. In *Taxi Driver* Jodie Foster had played a similar role. *Madame Rosa*, the Best Foreign Film of 1977, introduced the character of Momo, a sensitive young Arab boy living with an aging whore. "You're a good-looking boy, you know that, and that's dangerous. Never sell your body," he is advised.

An Unmarried Woman (1978) featured a teenage daughter who asks her mother, "Did the earth move?" and tells her father, "You're just feeling the loss of separation. I'm not your little girl anymore." In *The End* (1977), Burt Reynolds finds his teenage daughter forthrightly telling him how well she did in her class paper on menstruation. *The Little Girl Who Lived Down the Lane* (1977) furthered the image of the sophisticated adolescent. Jodie Foster starred as thirteen-year-old Rynn Jacobs, while Scott Jacoby played her somewhat older boyfriend. When the girl's father dies, she covers up his death and determines to live independently without the intervention of the authorities. Fiercely determined to live as she pleases, she defends her privacy aggressively. When she accidentally kills a do-gooder she covers up the killing and later is forced to defend herself against a would-be rapist.

Set as a backdrop to the intrigue and mystery her relationship with Mario appears to be remarkably normal. In an adolescent bathroom scene she is shown fully clothed as she bathes the boy. It is a peculiar moment for it precedes their sexual initiation and yet neither one seems at all embarrassed. The actual act of sex itself, grows out of a moment of comfort. When Mario is sick, Rynn puts him to bed, offering to get in with him if he is cold. The boy lies half-heartedly about his sexual experiences, telling her he's done it "hundreds of times," but it is apparent, that like Rynn, he is a virgin.

Everywhere teenagers seemed to be depicted as more knowledgeable, sexually sophisticated and honest than adults. In *Manhattan* (1979) alongside the complex maneuverings and intrigues of the adults, seventeen year old Tracy seems more mature and open. While forty-two year old Isaac seems plagued by indecision and guilt because "I'm older than her father," the girl deals much more easily with the relationship. The problem as she perceived it, is not her age, but his unwillingness to deal with her as an individual. He seems determined to classify and categorize her. "You're seventeen years old. You were brought up on drugs, television and the pill.... You can't be in love with me. You're a kid, you don't know what love means." But as the film demonstrates, Tracy is fully aware of both love and sex. When Isaac's anxiety bothers him she tries to take his mind off it and suggests they make love. Not only does she initiate the invitation but she

Opposite: *Pretty Baby* (1976): A franker treatment of adolescent cinema was to have a major impact on American film throughout the seventies.

suggests they do it in some strange way that he's always wanted to. Unable to deal with her frankness he once again retreats into his preconceptions of adolescents. "I'm shocked. What kind of language is that from a kid your age?" Yet by the end of the film he has been forced to recognize the girl's maturity and his need for her. "You're not such a kid," he concedes. As she flies off to London to study for six months, it is she who assumes the role of adult, counseling and advising him; "six months isn't so long. Not everybody gets corrupted. You have to have a little faith in people."

Television picked up on the increasingly youthful depiction of sexuality. With her mama away in the hospital, Elizabeth Walton embarked upon puberty and a real case of the in-betweens, with only her father to steer her through. A 1979 episode of *Little House on the Prairie* was accompanied by an advertisment in *TV Guide* that told readers;

> Her Pa still calls her 'Half-Pint' but Laura's in love with an older man and discovers that becoming a woman means more than shedding pig-tails.

"Disco Queen," a 1979 episode of *Family* pitted eleven year old Annie Lawrence against the amorous advances of an equally youthful Brock. "I'll lose my status among my peers if I don't kiss him," she tells her brother. The boy, however, seems to have more than a kiss in mind, but Annie stands her ground as the young football star experience his "first incomplete pass" and is "penalized fifteen yards for illegal use of hands." *Mork and Mindy* found young Eugene referring to a girl as "a cute chick, a fox, real hot stuff," and *Eight Is Enough* found Nicholas Bradford, not yet in his teens, chased by a girl his own age. "She's warm for my form," the boy observes. In several epissdoes of *Family*, viewers pondered the age-old question of will she or won't she as Buddy came under increasing pressure to surrender to her boyfriend Zack. The successful series, *James at Fifteen*, found its young hero experiencing sexual initiation. One writer commented:

> James' television plunge planted the anxiety-producing notion in the mind of the adolescent viewer that he was sexually lagging behind not only the precocious kid down the block, but the Average American Boy character of James.[16]

In 1980 publicity for one movie almost seemed to challenge youngsters to have sex. *Foxes*, which starred Jodie Foster and television's Scott Baio, appeared under the provocative slogan, "Daring to do it!" *The Last American Virgin* (1982) was released under the slogan "See It, or Be It." In part these films reflected changing sexual patterns in the United States. In 1979, for example, the same year in which *Rich Kids* was released, a provision was made in the New Jersey criminal code lowering the age of consent among juveniles from sixteen to thirteen. It also legalized sex between younger

Top: *The Little Girl Who Lived Down the Lane* (1977): Jodie Foster treats her boy-friend to a bath. The director hoped his own children would experience sex the way it was depicted in the film. **Bottom:** *Manhattan* (1979): A typical example of adoles-cent sensitivity and sophistication pitted against adult cynicism.

children provided there was less than four years age difference. A Congressional survey reported that "20 percent of thirteen- and fourteen-year-olds in the United States have sexual intercourse."

But there is a vast difference between the cinema acknowledging such activity and endorsing it, between depicting it and over-representing it, between observing it and idealizing it. Manhattan psychoanalyst Peter Bloss believes that while a child may be physically capable of having sexual relations, emotional maturity is often lacking. "If a child tries to grow up too fast ... he may never grow up at all."[17] Claudette Kunkes, clinical psychologist at The Door, a New York adolescent treatment center, has seen evidence of such unhappiness among sexually active youngsters:

> Sex before sixteen or seventeen is counterproductive emotionally.... Younger kids haven't developed the ego functions which are crucial in making their own choices about sex. The younger girls I've interviewed never really enjoyed it."[18]

As Jade tells David in *Endless Love*, "It came at a time when we were both too young to handle it."

Discussing the sexual relationship between the characters in *The Little Girl Who Lived Down the Lane*, a director Nicholas Gessner said that when his own children experience sex, "I would like it to happen under these circumstances or in the way it happens in our film."[19] Gessner's wish is understandable. We often wish life was really the way it seems to be in the movies. Unfortunately, however, life is not always as romantic, as glamorous, or as full of happy endings as Hollywood might have us believe. It is in the area of sex more than any other that the film industry must be keenly conscious of its responsibility in realistically representing life.

It is impossible not to notice the increased sophistication with which the movies have dealt with the subject of sex. Throughout the 1970's and early 1980's the cinema of adolescence has reflected this maturity. Masturbation was mentioned in *Bless the Beasts and Children*, *Pretty Maids All in a Row*, *Ordinary People*, and *The Blue Lagoon*. Menstruation was mentioned in *Carrie*, *The End*, and *The Blue Lagoon*, Bathroom as well as bedroom scenes became common place.

But more significant was the changing relationship between the sexes. Adolescent females were becoming more liberated and more libidinal. If they had acknowledged their sexuality in the fifties and sixties, they had usually passively succumbed to the advances of the male. By the seventies adolescent women were in hot pursuit of the young men they desired. *First Love* (1978) found Elgin rather taken aback when a casual date asks him if he wants to make love. "You been reading *Cosmopolitan* or something?" he asks. The same film provided evidence of the increasingly franker depiction of intercourse. Having made love to Caroline, he asks the young woman if he satisfied her. "Do you come? Do you have orgasm?"

"I'm sorry, next time I'll send up flares. It's just that with a guy there's an obvious progression of events. First you're hard and then ... white sticky stuff, and then ... and then you're soft and no good to me anymore." What is significant about this exchange is not simply the frank dialogue but the concern of the adolescent male for his sexual technique. In the past the female was a sex object, the passive recipient of her screen lover's organ. The important thing was that he was satisfied. By the late seventies relationships between adolescents were more equal.

When *Saturday Night Fever* acknowledged Tony's sensitivity this trend was strengthened. The young man who believed there were only two types of women, good girls and cunts, finally recognized women as whole people rather than receptacles for the penis. Friendship comes to be valued more than meaningless sexual encounters in a world where "even the humpin's dumpin'" most of the time. *Little Darlings*, despite the trite and tasteless theme of two teenage girls hell-bent on losing their virginity, also provided evidence of the film industry's improved depiction of adolescent sexuality. Both Randy (Matt Dillon) and Angel (Kristy McNichol) manage to strip away the tough exteriors the peer group expects of them and find in their vulnerability a sense of sharing neither of them have known before. After the couple make love, Hollywood, in what was still a rare post-coital scene, revealed a moment of rare adolescent uncertainty and ambiguity. Embarrassed and somewhat ashamed, the girl tells Randy, "Don't look at me!" Fearing that he has in some way failed to live up to her expectations, the boy blames himself, wondering, "What did I do wrong?" But it had very little to do with Randy and a great deal to do with Angel and the expectations society had given her about sex. "It wasn't what I thought it would be.... It was so personal, like you could see right through me. Making love was different than what I thought it was gonna be."

Ode to Billy Joe provided additional evidence of the film industry's more sophisticated response to adolescent sexuality. Glynnis O'Connor and Robby Benson played two southern teenagers confronting society's contradictory demands that they remain pure while being able to "perform." In the character of fifteen-year-old Bobbie Lee, the movie presented audiences with the image of a young girl trapped between biological imperatives and societal demands. "Mama," she complains, "things are out of whack. You dress me up real pretty. You like for me to be attractive ... and Brother Taylor says don't and Papa says can't.... You parade me and show me off and then you tie me to a fence post when I'm all primed up to be a woman." Margaret Mead acknowledged just such a condition when she wrote:

> We bring up girls to be free and unafraid without the protection given by shyness and fear to girls of many other societies. We bring our boys up to just as free and easy, used to girls, demanding to girls. We actually place our young people in a virtually intolerable position, giving them the entire setting for behavior which we then punish when it occurs."[20]

Grease: **A big step backward. A return to the double standard; the movie indulged Danny's fantasy of being able to both play around and marry a virgin.**

Yet for all obvious advances, the seventies and early eighties still showed Hollywood's hesitancy and uncertainty in dealing with teenage sexuality. While *Saturday Night Fever* was undoubtedly a step forward, *Grease*, which was made in the following year, was a step backwards. The relationship between Danny and Sandy is a throwback to the fifties. While it might be argued that their relationship accurately reflected the times, it must also be acknowledged that in repeating the image, the film served to perpetuate sexual stereotypes. The film closes with Danny and Sandy flying off in their car to some Disneyesque fantasyland. In the process the boy seems to have rejected "the pussy wagon" so celebrated in the song "Greased Lightning." The attempt to pass him off as rehabilitated, however, is a film fraud. While we may sympathize with Danny and understand the peer pressures that have shaped him, it is apparent that he has not only been sexually active with girls less wholesome than Sandy but that he has also treated them shabbily. If we are meant to smile upon Danny and Sandy's commitment to each other, we must realize that in the act we are also meant to indulge Danny's behavior and his perpetuation of the double standard. In settling for Sandy he has fulfilled the traditional role of the sexually active adolescent male who expects to be able to both sleep around himself and still marry a virgin. While *Saturday Night Fever* asked Tony to grow up and reconsider his opinion of women, *Grease* demands nothing of Danny. *Ode to Billy Joe*, while breaking new ground in its depiction of heterosexuality, revealed itself still tied to Hollywood tradition in the case of homosexuality. Though *Endless Love* ultimately acknowledged that David and Jade were too young to deal with their passion, the film itself emasculated their passion. Unable to realistically depict the physical power of young love or blunt dialogue between teenagers, the film destroyed the whole guts of the book. A self-indulgent Franco Zeffirelli tried to do for Brooke Shields and Martin Hewitt what he had done for Leonard Whiting and Olivia Hussey. The result was romantic nonsense that detracted from the power of the story and left adolescents in the audience tittering.

The same inability to let go of the past was apparent in 1974's *Our Time*. A rare example of coming of age seen from the girl's point of view, the film concentrated on the ugly duckling character of Muffy, who desperately wants to lose her virginity. On the one occasion she has sex it is a disappointing experience and one complicated by the resultant pregnancy. In permitting her to have an abortion the film showed that Hollywood and society had matured since *Blue Denim*, but as if wanting to have it both ways, the plot had the girl die as a result of the operation. It was a perfect example of Hollywood's own adolescence, attempting to grow up but at the same time restrained by the trappings of its past.

15. Conclusion

"You can't stay seventeen forever." Steve to
Curt in *American Graffiti*, 1973).

In financial terms there is no doubt that the young continue to be a major source of profit for Hollywood. *Grease* became the biggest musical of all time. *Animal House* grossed more than $240 million world wide and in its first few weeks of release in 1982, *Porky's* grossed more than $40 million. In 1984 *Purple Rain* provided evidence of the powerful link between film and folk music. Some 50 years after the Payne studies, the subject of film and adolescence still remains controversial.

The media's response to adolescence remains a source of concern and conflict both within the entertainment industry and in society itself. In April 1982, talking on the *John Davidson Show*, Marion Ross of television's *Happy Days* confessed that current movies about adolescents sent her scurrying to her teenage daughter with the plea, tell me it isn't true. Later that spring, public television's *Middletown* series withdrew a program in which real life adolescents in their own language frankly discussed sex and drugs. On the one hand we are confronted with an industry that tends to stereotype adolescents while on the other, it seems apparent that many adults simply do not wish to accept adolescents for who and what they are.

While it has often been suggested that films need to be censored in order to protect impressionable adolescents, the *Middletown* experience suggests that in television at least it is adults, not teenagers, who want protection. Raised on *Father Knows Best, Bachelor Father, The Donna Reed Show, The Waltons, The Brady Bunch*, and others, it may well be that many of today's parents find the real ty of parenthood too much to deal with. Unable to respond to the changing nature of society and the nature and needs of the young, they seek instead to retreat into television's fantasy land. Neither the Hardy family nor the Nelsons can provide solutions to today's problems, nor the issues that will confront families and society tomorrow. If the cinema has tended to present a negative image of the young, television has failed us by glamorizing and idealizing the young. Neither response has done justice to adolescents or to their families. There

272

is, however, some evidence of a growing maturation in the media's response to the young. It is difficult to look at American films made in the last ten years and not be optimistic. Probably at no time in its history has Hollywood responded so maturely to adolescents and their environment. Enormous strides have been made since 1968 when *Variety* complained that there was "a great deal more to youth appeal than boy gangs or girl gangs or beach parties or psychedelic optical and sound effects."[1]

While I have been critical of the industry for its excessive dependence upon formula and format, I have not been reluctant to praise it nor to acknowledge a growing maturation in its response to the young, the family and sexuality. *Breaking Away*, *Bloodbrothers*, *Personal Best*, *The Great Santini*, and *Ordinary People* are among a growing number of films produced in the last few years in which the depiction of adolescence has achieved a new depth and maturity. The optimism, however, may not be totally warranted.

At the same time these fine films have developed a new image of adolescents and their social environment, other movies have shown a noticeable lack of taste and sensitivity in dealing with the subject. As both an art form and an industry Hollywood is faced with the problem of reconciling artistic merit with the desire for profit. *Animal House*, *The Blue Lagoon*, and *Porky's*, in chalking up enormous grosses, threaten audiences with a plethora of sequels. It may well be that such lighthearted fare can exist side by side with the better products coming out of Hollywood. It may also be that the industry, in its understandable desire for profit, opts to cash in on what has proven successful. If that is the case, the years ahead may find the film industry replacing gangs, beach parties, and psychedelic effects with peer groups and toga parties in which only the music, the amount of beer consumed, and the degree of physical contact seen will separate these teenagers from those Hollywood foisted upon audiences throughout so much of its past.

There is little doubt that motion pictures have the potential to influence adolescent audiences. The ability of a medium of communication to influence its audience depends upon a complex set of factors, including the nature of the medium itself, the strength and pervasiveness of the message transmitted, and the nature and needs of the audience receiving the message. The adolescent, as has been stated, is neither child nor adult. Caught in transition the young person is the stage of formulating a new identity. In this process film and the mass media in general have the opportunity to function as a valuable source of information. Excessive reliance upon stereotypes in the past has limited the honesty and the variety of the information imparted to the young.

As a highly selective medium the film industry has been too preoccupied with the dramatic, the tragic, the delinquent, and the aberrant. In the process it has not only stereotyped the young but the institutions such as the family and the school through which they are socialized. These stereotypes run the risk not only of misinforming the young as to the nature of the world about them, but of misinforming parents, teachers, police, and the adult community in general as to what they can expect from the young. Joseph Adelson has referred to this process of dwelling upon the delinquent and offbeat as "the tyranny of the visible."[2] Harvard psychiatrist Robert Coles sees the trend as part of a widespread prejudice, not only in the media but in society as a whole.

Not only do we concentrate on the offbeat and way-out, but we seem more interested in certain racial groups and geographic regions than others. Coles complains of scholars of the alienated "who never analyzed Mexican-Americans, kids from Montana, black kids or those from Appalachia."[3] If the academic world is guilty of such a jaundiced view, it may well be that Hollywood has played some role in determining its interests and preoccupations. In the cinema of adolescence, whites outnumber blacks, WASPs outnumber other racial and religious groups, big city stories depicting life in Los Angeles, New York, or Chicago by far outweigh images of small towns or rural life, and stories about boys outnumber those about girls. Yet despite these failings, progress is being made; the Hollywood-made motion picture is dealing with adolescents more sensitively and less sensationally than at any time in its past.

It has been impossible in the scope of this book to deal with every film made about young people, or even with every good film made about them. Readers may feel that I have glossed over some of their favorite films, or given undue attention to obscure movies that few have ever heard of. In attempting to assemble this material I have tried to weave together themes and issues that not only have preoccupied the film industry but that remain relevant to growing adolescents. In the process I have been forced to ignore films that have been personal favorites, as well as good films about adolescents that simply could not be dealt with adequately. *Promises in the Dark* (1979), *The Trial* (1955), *The Diary of Anne Frank* (1959), and *Intruder in the Dust* (1949) are among valuable and worthwhile films that did not find their way into print.

This work is not intended to be the definitive study of the cinema of adolescence. It has raised questions, many of which still remain unanswered. In the process I have attempted to map out a cinematic terrain, the geography of which must now be thrown open for further exploration. In looking at the way in which film depicts adolescence, it has been possible to learn something of the way in which the film industry and the society it serves view themselves. Adelson has suggested a reason for the pervasiveness of the cinema of adolescence. "The young," he says,

> have always haunted the American imagination.... They reflect and stand for some otherwise silent currents in American fantasy. In these images and in our tendency to identify ourselves with them, we can discover the alienation within us all, old and young. We use the young to re-

East of Eden (1954): The mirror metaphor so often applied to movies. In the case of the cinema of adolescence, the images revealed distort our vision of young people.

present our despair, our violence, our often forlorn hopes for a better world. Thus these images of adolescence tell us something, something true and false about the young; they may even tell us more about ourselves."[4]

The cinema of adolescence then can be read, understood and evaluated not only as a commentary upon the young and the film industry, but upon the society of which they are both a part. In a culture in which film is often used as a guide to reality, viewed as a mirror image of the physical world, the potential of such a medium is heightened. Because of the nature of adolescents and film alike, the motion picture industry has the potential to function as an influence in the life of the young. Films may function as a source of socialization; they may provide a cathartic experience, permitting emotional release; they may fill a knowledge vacuum providing the young with information they cannot learn elsewhere. While there is growing evidence of a greater diversity and sophistication in the images of adolescence, Hollywood's past suggests that movies have seldom lived up to their potential to serve as a positive influence in the life of the young. Stereotyping and a persistent portrayal of conflict between parent and child, teenager and teacher, youth and the law, have served to perpetuate an image of hostility between young people and society. When criticized and challenged, the industry has been quick to claim that its films are realistic depictions of life, drawn from actual events. There is, however, a significant difference between a film being realistic and a group of films being representative. The cinema of adolescence, rather than being concerned with a particular film, is concerned with a group of films and the overall statement and impression they make. Taken as a whole, these films provide audiences, young and old alike, with a peculiarly jaundiced view of American society and the role of adolescents within it.

If the familiar mirror metaphor is to continue to be employed when discussing film, the cinema of adolescence demands a clearer definition. For if film functions as a mirror, the nature of that mirror must be understood. In its depiction of adolescents, the motion picture does not serve as a normal mirror. It functions rather as a distorting mirror such as that encountered in an amusement park or penny arcade. The images it reflects distort the real world—at times enlarging, at times diminishing—but always producing an image that is out of proportion to physical reality. It is possible too to suggest the film functions as a two-way mirror, capable at the same time of both concealing and revealing.

In looking at the images in these films, it is necessary to consider, therefore, not only what we see and are told, but what we do not see and are not told. The adolescent, still in the process of establishing his or her own self-image, may well fall prey to mistaking the screen image for the self he or she is to become. Adolescence itself is a time of role play and identity experimentation. Standing in the wings of life, waiting to be cued, the young person may well mistake the cues Hollywood sends. This work rejects the notion of the movies as deliberately manipulative equally as much as it rejects the belief that young people are passive pawns surrendering to the images and ideology of the screen. What it does believe, however, is that for some adolescents, the film industry's repetitive images and stereotypes offer the opportunity for a pre-packaged identity that subverts the natural emergence of an authentic self. Touching upon such vital issues as sex, family, marriage, schooling, and the law, the cinema of adolescence serves as a potentially powerful source of information providing young people with a vision of society and what they can expect from it. In impacting upon today's young, the film image has the capacity to actively intervene in tomorrow. Edgar Friedenberg has said that "adolescents and adolescent groups respond as they do in very large part because of the way adults and adult institutions respond to them."[5] If that is the case it may well be that in perpetuating stereotypes of adolescence, the film industry, rather than merely mirroring reality, helps to create it.

Chapter Notes

Chapter 1

1 Henry James Forman, *Our Movie-Made Children*. New York, 1933, p. 121.
2 Paul F. Lazarsfeld, "Audience Research in the Movie Field." *Annals of the American Academy of Political and Social Science*, 254, Nov. 1947, p. 163.
3 W.D. Wall and W.A. Simson, "The Effect of Cinema Attendance on the Behavior of Adolescents as Seen by Their Contemporaries." *British Journal of Educational Psychology*, 19, 1949, p. 57.
4 Peter Hopkinson, *The Role of Film in Development*. Paris, UNESCO, 1971, p. 19.
5 *Variety*, 26, July 1939, p. 9.
6 *Variety*, 4, January 1939, p. 5.
7 *Variety*, 19 April 1935, p. 9.
8 *Variety*, 30 September 1939, p. 1.
9 *Variety*, 23 August 1939, p. 5.
10 *Variety*, 27 January 1937, p. 12.
11 *Variety*, 8 September 1937, p. 18.
12 *Variety*, 31 August 1949, p. 5.
13 *Variety*, 9 March 1955, p. 1.
14 *Variety*, 22 August 1956, p. 3.
15 *Variety*, 13 November 1968, p. 1.
16 *Variety*, 19 November 1969, p. 5.
17 *Variety*, 26 August 1970.
18 H. Keith Evans, "The Adolescent and the Screen." *Screen Education,* May-June 1967.
19 Siegfried Kracauer, *From Caligari to Hitler*. Princeton, NJ, 1947, p. 7.
20 Marjorie Rosen, *Popcorn Venus*. Avon Books, New York, 1937, p. 9.
21 Carnegie Council on Policy Studies in Higher Education, *Giving Youth a Better Chance: Options for Education, Work and Service*. Jossey-Bass, pub., San Francisco, 1979, p. 5.

Chapter 2

1 *Variety*, 30 September 1939, p. 27.
2 J.M. Mogey, "A Century of Declining Parental Authority," in *The Family and Change*. Edited by John N. Edwards, New York, 1969, p. 255.

3 Sydney Jackman, *A Diary in America*. Knopf, New York, 1962, p. 351.

4 Robert S. and Helen Merrell Lynd, *Middletown in Transition*. Harcourt, Brace, World, 1937, p. 152.

5 Marjorie Boggs, "Family Social Work in Relation to Family Life," in *The Family*, vol. 15, July 1934, pp. 146–148.

6 Andrew Bergman, *We're in the Money*. Harper and Row, New York, 1971.

7 Winona L. Morgan, *The Family Meets the Depression*. University of Minnesota, Minneapolis, 1939, p. 68.

8 Lynd, *Middletown in Transition*, p. 146.

9 Morgan, *The Family Meets the Depression*, p. 68.

10 *New York Times*, 28 July 1936, p. 16.

11 Marjorie Rosen, *Popcorn Venus*. Avon Books, New York, 1973, p. 184.

12 Paul Popenoe, "Should a Family Have Two Heads?" *Parents Magazine*, Feb. 1939, p. 20.

13 Helen Ellwanger Hanford, "Parents Need to Stand Together." *Parents Magazine*, Nov. 1939, p. 16.

14 Charles Champlin, *The Flicks, or Whatever Became of Andy Hardy*. Ward. Ritchie, Pasadena, CA, 1977, p. 4.

15 *Variety*, 21 April 1937, p. 14.

16 Margaret Farrand Thorpe, *America At the Movies*. Yale University Press, 1939, p. 131

17 Mickey Rooney, *i.e. An Autobiography*. G.P. Putnam and Sons, New York, 1965, p. 94.

18 *Ibid.*, p. 89.

19 *New York Times*, 22 July 1937, p. 10.

20 Charles C. Peters, *Motion Pictures and Standards of Morality*. Macmillan, New York, 1933, p. 128.

21 David M. Considine, "The Adolescent Within the Context of the Family in Films of the 1930's." Unpublished paper, University of Wisconsin, Madison, 1979.

22 Ruth Shonle Cavan and Katherine Howland Ranchk, *The Family and the Depression*. University of Chicago Press, 1938, p. 25.

23 Lawrence K. Frank, "Social Change and the Family." *Annals of the American Academy of Political and Social Science*, March 1932, pp. 95–99.

24 The White House Conference on Child Health and Protection, *The Adolescent in the Family: A Study of Personality in the Home Environment*. D. Appleton Century Co., New York, 1934, p. 3.

25 Sydney E. Goldstein, "The Family as a Dynamic Factor in American Society." *The Journal of Marriage and Family Living*, Winter, 1940, Vol. 2, No. 1, p. 9.

26 Lawrence K. Frank, "The Family as the Cultural Agent." *Journal of Marriage and Family Living*, Winter, 1940, Vol. 2, No. 1, p. 19.

27 Jean Waker MacFarlane, "Interpersonal Relations Within the Family." *Journal of Marriage and Family Living*, Feb. 1941, Vol. 3, No. 1, p. 28.

28 *Variety*, 21 September 1940, p. 12.

29 Review for the Library of Congress, *Miss Annie Rooney*, Department of War Information, 1942.

30 *Variety*, 13 June 1945, p. 17.

31 *New Yorker*, Briefly Noted Fiction. 21 August 1943, p. 58.

32 A.B. Hollingshead, *Elmstown's Youth*. John Wiley and Sons, New York, 1949, p. 149.

33 Rosen, *Popcorn Venus*, p. 253.

34 Hollingshead, *Elmstown's Youth*, p. 149.

35 *Variety*, 30 September 1942, p. 8.

Chapter 3

1 Gerold Frank, *Judy*. Dell Publishing, New York, 1976, p. 16.
2 *Commonweal*, 5 October 1945, p. 598.
3 *Ibid.*
4 Pam Cook, "Duplicity in Mildred Pierce," in *Women in Film Noir*. Edited by Ann Kaplan, British Film Institute, London, 1978, p. 68.
5 Edward A. Strecker, *Their Mother's Sons*. J.B. Lippincott Co., Philadelphia, 1946, p. 13.
6 Philip Wylie, *Generation of Vipers*. Holt, Rinehart, Winston, New York, 1942, p. 50.
7 David Dalton, *James Dean: The Mutant King*. Dell Books, New York, 1974, p. 18.
8 Reul Denney," American Youth Today: A Bigger Cast, A Wider Screen," in in *Challenge of Youth*. Edited by Erik Erikson, Doubleday, New York, 1963, p. 3.
9 Eve Merian, "The Matriarchal Myth." *Nation*, Nov. 8, 1958, p. 332.
10 Marjorie Rosen, *Popcorn Venus*. Avon, New York, 1973, p. 260.
11 Bob Thomas, *Joan Crawford*. Bantam Books, New York, 1978, p. 186.
12 "Are You an Everyday Neurotic?" *Cosmopolitan*, Aug. 1952, p. 39.
13 "Does Your Family Have Neurosis?" *Colliers*, Feb. 28, 1953.
14 Wylie, *Generation of Vipers*, p. 208.
15 Strecker, *Their Mother's Sons*, p. 71.
16 "Lady Are You the Man of the House?" *American Mercury*, Jan. 1961, p. 16.
17 Albert Ellis, "Counseling with Demasculizing Wives and Demasculized Husbands." *Journal of Marriage and Family Living*, Feb. 1960, p. 13.
18 *Time*, 5 January 1970, p. 10.
19 *Ibid.*
20 Urie Bronfenbrenner, "The American Family in Decline." *Current*, Jan. 1977, p. 43–44.

Chapter 4

1 "Eighteen Million Teenagers Can't Be Wrong." *Colliers*, Jan. 4, 1957, pp. 17–19.
2 David Dalton, *James Dean, the Mutant King*. Dell Books, New York, 1974, p. 184.
3 Joan Mellen, *Big Bad Wolves*. Pantheon, New York, 1977, p. 212.
4 Pauline Kael, *I Lost It at the Movies*. Little, Brown and Co., Boston, 1954, p. 56.
5 *Variety*, 20 October 1955, p. 6.
6 "The Decline and Fall of the American Father." *Cosmopolitan*, Apr. 1955, p. 21.
7 Joseph B. Duckworth and Peter K. Hoover, "Reel to Real: Teaching Adolescent Psychology Through Film." *Phi Delta Kapan*, May 1976, p. 7.
8 *Variety*, 2 October 1957, p. 6.

Chapter 5

1 "The Vanishing American Father." *Readers Digest*, July 1965, No. 87, pp. 116–117.

282   Notes — Chapters 5, 6

2 Henry Nouen, "Generation Without Fathers." *Commonweal*, June 1972, p. 288.
3 "The American Way of Mating; SI Children Only Maybe." *Psychology Today*, May 1975, p. 39.
4 Miles Beller, "Hollywood Kids Are Becoming Cherubs Again." *New York Times*, 14 October 1979, p. 19.
5 *Variety*, 3 November 1971, p. 1.
6 "The Fifties Americans Forgot." *New York Times*, 24 February 1980, p. 18.
7 *Variety*, 9 March 1977, p. 16.
8 *Variety*, 20 September 1978, p. 26.
9 *Ibid.*
10 Urie Bronfenbrenner, "The American Family in Decline." *Current*, Jan. 1977, p. 43.
11 "Conflict and Stress." *Films and Filming*, Dec. 1978, p. 12.
12 *Ibid.*, p. 14.
13 *Ibid.*, p. 14.

Chapter 6

1 Ralph Keyes, *Is There Life After High School?* Warner Communications, New York, 1977, p. 35.
2 *Ibid.*, p. 68.
3 *Ibid.*, p. 191.
4 *Ibid.*, p. 208.
5 Edna Lue Furness, "The Image of the High School Teacher in American Literature." *The Educational Forum*, May 1960, xxiv, 4, p. 462.
6 *Report on the Conference on Life Adjustment Education*. Sacramento, CA, Sept. 30 to Oct. 1, 1946, p. 4.
7 *Parents Magazine*, April 1955, p. 10.
8 "What High School Ought to Teach." *The Report of a Special Committee on the Secondary School Curriculum*, prepared for the American Youth Commission, American Council on Education, Washington, 1940, p. 16.
9 "Our Schools — Afraid to Teach?" *Colliers*, 19 March 1954, pp. 34–40.
10 "American Education in Crisis." *School and Society*, 22 January 1955.
11 Daryl F. Zanuck, letter to Dore Schary, 19 January 1956.
12 "German and Austrian Reaction to 'The Blackboard Jungle'." *School and Society*, 16 February 1957, p. 57.
13 *Parents Magazine*, April 1955, p. 10.
14 David Bernard, "How Progressive Education Failed Us." *Cosmopolitan*, April 1958, pp. 36–39.
15 Michael Connors, "Hoodlums in the High Schools." *Catholic World*, April 1959, p. 13.
16 "The Crisis in Teaching." Atlantic, September 1956, pp. 35–36.
17 Salomon Rettig and Benjamin Pasamick, "Status and Job Satisfaction of Public School Teachers." *School and Society*, 14 March 1959, p. 116.
18 James S. Coleman, "How Do the Young Become Adults?" *Review of Educational Reserach*, 1972, ilii, 4, 434.
19 *Life*, 7 July 1967, p. 11.
20 Norman S. Brandes, "Influence of the Emotionally Disturbed Teacher on School Children." *Mental Hygiene*, October 1969, liii, 4.
21 "Collision Course in the High Schools." *Life*, 16 May 1969, p. 24.

22 Douglas H. Heath, "Student Alienation and School." *School Review*, August 1970, p. 551.
23 "Collision Course in the High Schools." *Life*, 16 May 1969, p. 27.
24 "Retreat from Integration." *Time*, March 1970.
25 *Ibid.*
26 Judith Crist, quoted in *Film Facts*, 1971, xiv, No. 12, p. 12.
27 *Newsday* review, quoted in *Film Facts*, xv, No. 24, 1972, pp. 677–80.
28 E. Jack Neuman, correspondence and personal papers. Wisconsin State Historical Society, Madison, WI.

Chapter 7

1 Bruno Bettelheim, *Social Impact of Urban Design*. University of Chicago Press, Chicago, 1971.
2 E. Jack Neuman, correspondence and personal papers. Wisconsin State Historical Society, Madison, WI.
3 *Ibid.*
4 Edgar Z. Friedenberg, *The Vanishing Adolescent*. Beacon Press, Boston, 1959, p. 69.
5 Michael Connors, "Hoodlums in the High Schools." *Catholic World*, April 1959, p. 14.
6 Alan Peshkin, *Growing Up American*. University of Chicago Press, Chicago, 1978, p. 45.
7 Lester B. Ball, "The Free Jail: Another Look at the Senior High School." *The High School Journal*, April 1978, pp. 321–326.
8 Thomas E. Linton and Erwin Pollack, "Boredom Transcended: Adolescent Survival in the Suburban High School." *The High School Journal*, November 1978, pp. 69–72.
9 Philip A. Cusick, *Inside High School*. Holt, Rinehart and Winston, New York, 1973, p. 5.

Chapter 8

1 *Time*, 26 February 1979, p. 76.
2 Herbert Blumer, *Movies, Delinquency and Crime*. Macmillan, New York, 1933, p. 13.
3 David Marsland and Michael Perry, "Variations in Adolescent Societies." *Youth and Society*, September 1973.
4 *New York Times*, 14 November 1931, p. 15.
5 *New York Times*, 16 July 1933.
6 *American City*, March 1933, p. 70.
7 John Davis, "Notes on Warner Brothers' Foreign Policy." *Velvet Light Trap*, #4, p. 25.
8 Zelda F. Popkin, "Children of the Racketeer Age." *Harpers*, Feb. 1933, pp. 364–375.
9 "How Should We Deal With Delinquent Adolescents and Wandering Youth?" *American City*, March 1933, p. 70.
10 Gillian Klein, "Wellman's *Wild Boys of the Road*." *Velvet Light Trap*, #15, p. 6.

11 *Life*, 20 October 1942, p. 58.
12 *Variety*, 19 April 1942, p. 1.
13 *Variety*, 25 November 1942, p. 7.
14 *Junior Army*, review for Office of War Information, 1942.
15 *Time*, 25 September 1944.
16 "As the Youngsters See Juvenile Delinquency," *New York Times Magazine*, 6 August 1944, p. 32.
17 "Let the Children Speak," *Commonweal*, 31 May 1940, p. 117.
18 *American City*, February 1940, p. 5.
19 *New Yorker*, 14 April 1959, p. 83.

Chapter 9

1 "Teen-Age Punks: San Francisco Tries to Tame Them," *Colliers*, 29 April 1950, p. 19.
2 "Kid Vandals Rile All of Us," *Variety*, 11 November 1953, p. 5.
3 "Police Blast Crooked Cop Pix: Juve Crime Aid," *Variety*, 19 August 1954, p. 1.
4 "From 'Rock Around the Clock' to 'The Trip': The Truth About Teenage Movies," by Richard Staehling. In *Kings of the B's*, Todd McCarthy and Charles Flynn, editors, E.P. Dutton and Co., New York, 1975, p. 241.
5 "Are We Raising Another Lost Generation?" *Saturday Evening Post*, 29 April 1944, p. 28.
6 *Variety*, 23 December 1953, p. 6.
7 *Time*, 28 November 1955, p. 104.
8 *Nation*, 3 December 1955, p. 486.
9 Robin Bean, "*East of Eden.*" *Films and Filming*, May 1964, p. 39.
10 *Atlantic Monthly*, October 1956, p. 6.
11 "Teen-Age Punks ..." *Colliers*, 1950, p. 19.
12 "Teen-Age Terror in New York Streets," *Life*, 11 July 1955.
13 "Teen-Age Burst of Brutality, *Life*, 12 August 1957.
14 "Can Tough Cops Beat the Wild Kids?" *Look*, 16 September 1958.
15 "Teen-Age Trouble," *Look*, 2 September 1958.
16 "Let's Stop Maligning American Youth," *Readers Digest*, August 1956, pp. 133–136.
17 *Time*, 28 May 1956, p. 100.
18 *Variety*, 26 April 1961, p. 6.
19 Pauline Kael, *I Lost It at the Movies*. Little, Brown and Co., Boston, 1965, p. 144.
20 Dick Clark, *Rock, Roll and Remember*. Popular Library, New York, 1978, p. 107.
21 "Youth: The Cool Generation," *Saturday Evening Post*, 23/30 December (double issue) 1961, p. 64.
22 *Film Facts*.
23 *Variety*, 14 July 1971, p. 16.
24 *Variety*, 21 July 1971, p. 5.
25 "Hollywood's Sons of *Saturday Night Fever*," *After Dark*, March 1979, p. 68.
26 "The Low Riders of Whittier Boulevard," *American Film*, February 1979, p. 59.
27 Urie Bronfenbrenner, "The American Family in Decline." *Current*, January 1977, pp. 43–44.

Chapter 10

1 Vincent Canby, "Adrift in the Shallows of *The Blue Lagoon*." *New York Times*, 10 August 1980, p. 13D.
2 *New York Times*, 15 June 1980, p. 19.
3 Alexander Walker, *The Celluloid Sacrifice: Aspects of Sex in the Movies*. Joseph Publishing, London, 1966.
4 Murray Schumach, *The Face on the Cutting Room Floor*. William Morrow and Co., New York, 1964, p. 5.
5 Robert J. Havighurst, *Developmental Tasks and Education*. Longman and Co., New York, 1948, pp. 111-147.
6 Erik Erikson, as quoted in: Raymond L. Johnson, Herbert L. Friedman and Herbert S. Gross, "Four Masculine Styles in Television Programming: A Study of the Viewing Preferences of Adolescent Males," in *Television and Social Behavior*, Vol. 13. G.A. Comstock, E.A. Rubinstein Murray, et al. Government Printing Office, Washington, D.C.
7 Alice Miller Mitchell, *Children and the Movies*. Chicago University Press, Chicago, 1929.
8 Herbert Blumer, *Movies and Conduct*. Macmillan and Co., New York, 1933, p. 54.
9 W.D. Wall and W.A. Simson, "The Emotional Response of Adolescent Groups to Certain Films, Part I." *British Journal of Educational Psychology*, 20, 1950, p. 156.
10 *Rhythm and Blues*, Madison, WI, 1977.
11 A. Bandura and R.H. Walters, *Social Learning and Personality Development*. Holt Rinehart, Winston, New York, 1963, p. 65.
12 *Newsweek*, June 15th, 1981, p. 107.

Chapter 11

1 *Christian Century*, January 1930.
2 Erich Maria Remarque, *All Quiet on the Western Front*. Fawcett Publishers, Greenwich, CT, 1928, p. 93.
3 Charles C. Peters, *The Motion Pictures and Standards of Morality*. Macmillan, New York, 1933, p. 96.
4 Editorial in *America*, 28 October 1933.
5 Donald P. Cottrell, as quoted in Hollis L. Caswell, *American High School*. Harper Brothers, New York, 1946, p. 44.
6 Bosley Crowther, *Hollywood Rajah*. Henry Holt and Co., New York, 1960, p. 239.
7 *Ibid.*, p. 127.
8 Willard Waller, *War and the Family*. Dryden Press, New York, 1970, p. 34.
9 William Foote Whyte, "A Slum Sex Code." *American Journal of Sociology*, 1943, p. 25.
10 Donald McLean and Walter A. Helfrich, "Sex Guide in Wartime." *National Parent Teacher*, October 1943, pp. 5-6.

Chapter 12

1 Kingsley Davis, "The Sociology of Parent Youth Conflict." *American Sociological Review*, Vol. 5, No. 4, August 1940.
2 Joshua Logan, *Movie Stars, Real People and Me*. Delacorte Press, New York, 1978, p. 265.
3 Judd Marmor, "Psychological Trends in American Family Relationships." *Journal of Marriage and Family Living*, November 1951, p. 143.
4 H.R. Remmers and D.H. Radler, *The American Teenager*. Bob Merrill and Co., New York, 1957, p. 46.
5 *New York Times*, 13 October 1961.
6 *New Yorker*, 14 October 1961, p. 177.
7 Larry McMurtry, *Horsemen Pass By*. Harper Brothers, New York, 1961, p. 55.

Chapter 13

1 Murray Schumach, *The Face on the Cutting Room Floor*. William Morrow and Co., New York, 1964.
2 Thomas R. Atkins, *Sexuality in the Movies*. Indiana University Press, 1975, p. 159.
3 Letter from Geoffrey Shurlock to Samuel Briskin dated 8 November 1960. Wisconsin State Historical Society, Madison, WI.
4 Jack Curry, "Dadism: Movies Make Room for Fathers." *After Dark*, June 1980, p. 49.

Chapter 14

1 E.O. Smigel and R. Seiden, "The Decline and Fall of the Double Standard." *American Academy of Political and Social Science*, No. 36, 1968, pp. 6–17.
2 R.R. Bell and J.B. Chasker, "Premarital Sexual Experience Among Coeds, 1958–1968." *Journal of Marriage and Family Living*, 32, 1970, pp. 81–84.
3 Richard Randall, *Censorship at the Movies*. University of Wisconsin Press, 1970, p. 221.
4 *Ibid.*, p. 201.
5 Arthur Mayer, "How Much Can Movies Say?" *Saturday Review*, 3 November 1962, p. 18.
6 "How to Stop the Sickening Exploitation of Sex." *Readers Digest*, February 1961.
7 Pauline Kael, *Going Steady*. Little Brown and Co., Boston, 1971, p. 64.
8 *Film Facts*, XII (9), 1969, p. 193.
9 *Ibid.*, p. 195.
10 Erik Erikson, *Identity, Youth and Crisis*. W.W. Norton and Co., New York, 1968, p. 137.
11 George N. Boyd, "Movies and the Sexual Revolution: Should the Ratings be Revised?" *Christian Century*, 23 September 1970, p. 1125.
12 Hass, "Flaming Youth: A Hite Report on Teens." *Time*, 8 October 1979.
13 Robert C. Sorensen, *Adolescent Sexuality in Contemporary America*. World Publishing Co., New York, 1973, p. 71.

14 Michael Schofield, *The Sexual Behavior of Young People*. Longman Green and Co., London, 1965, p. 536.

15 *Film Facts*, XIIIV (13), 1971, p. 303.

16 Richard Hawley, "Television and the Adolescent: A Teacher's View." *American Film*, October 1978, p. 55.

17 *Time*, 21 August 1972, p. 29.

18 *Newsweek*, 1 September 1980, p. 49.

19 Interview given in *The Americans* with Desmond Wilcox, BBC, Time/Life Television Productions.

20 Margaret Mead, *Male and Female*, William Morrow and Co. New York, 1949, p. 290.

Chapter 15

1 *Variety*, 17 July 1968, p. 5.

2 Joseph Adelson, "Adolescence and the Generalization." *Psychology Today*, February 1979.

3 *Ibid.*

4 Edgar Friedenberg, *The Vanishing Adolescent*. Beacon Press, Boston, 1959, p. 114.

Index